Wisconsin With Kids

by Kristin Visser and Jerry Minnich

PRAIRIE OAK PRESS

Madison, Wisconsin

First edition, first printing, 1991
First edition, second printing, 1992
First edition, third printing, 1993
Second edition, first printing, 1994
Second edition, second printing, 1997
Copyright ©1991, 1994 by Prairie Oak Press, Inc.

Prairie Oak Press
821 Prospect Place
Madison, Wisconsin 53703

Typeset by KC Graphics, Inc., Madison, Wisconsin
Cover design: Moonlit Ink, Madison, Wisconsin
Printed in the United States of America
by BookCrafters, Chelsea, Michigan

Photo credits: Front cover, left: Robert Queen. Front cover, right: Christine Linder. Back cover, left: Dean Tvedt. Back cover, right: Christine Linder.

Library of Congress Cataloging-in-Publication Data

Visser, Kristin, 1949–
    Wisconsin with kids / by Kristin Visser and Jerry Minnich.—2nd ed.
        p.   cm.
    Includes bibliographical references and index.
    ISBN1-879483-19-X : $12.95
    1. Wisconsin—Description and travel—1991– —Guide-books.2. Family recreation—Wisconsin—Guide-books. 3. Children—Travel—Wisconsin—Guide-books.
I. Minnich, Jerry. II. Title.
F579.3.V57 1991
917.7504'43—dc20   91-7975
                                                                                            CIP

Wisconsin with Kids

Wisconsin's natural beauty has been attracting vacationers for more than a century. Our state is blessed with
thousands of sparkling lakes, verdant, rolling hills, and
lush, green forests. Many of the activities kids love best—
swimming, boating, bicycling, camping—take place in
these natural surroundings. In the winter, Wisconsin kids
don't dread the snow—they revel in it, with cross-country
and downhill skiing, sledding, and ice skating.

At the same time, the Badger State is home to major
attractions of a different kind. The Milwaukee County
Zoo is one of the nation's largest and finest. The Experimental Aircraft Association Museum, in Oshkosh, is
unique in the world, as is the Circus World Museum in
Baraboo. Wisconsin Dells is chock-full of water parks and
exciting children's activities. All across the state are outstanding attractions for children of all ages.

Our book is meant for visitors and vacationers to the
Badger State, certainly, but also for Wisconsin residents,
old and new, who might be looking for ideas for fun-
filled day, weekend, or longer trips with kids. We hope
that even long-time residents might unearth in these
pages some hidden treasures from their own backyards.
(Conversely, we hope that readers might take the time to
tell us of some treasures that we have missed!)

Our criteria for selecting attractions, lodging and
restaurants were few and, we think, logical. We sought
eating places that are informal (no jackets and ties
required), moderately-priced and family-oriented. We
favored locally-owned and family-run establishments
over national chains—not because chains are bad, but
because one of the best parts of traveling is experiencing
regional diversity. Certainly there are times when young
travelers are going to find comfort in a familiar burger
chain ("Just like at home!"), and fast food chains are easy

to find. But we prefer to tell you where to find an old-fashioned ice cream sundae, a good restaurant that's not on a major highway, or a small-town bakery that serves wonderful homemade pies. These are the experiences you'll remember.

We recommend hotels and motels that welcome children, that offer some recreational amenities—swimming pools, game rooms, cable TV, etc.—and are for the most part moderately priced. Those few resort and luxury hotels that we do recommend, and that are expensive by Wisconsin standards, are so indicated in the listings. We tried, insofar as possible, to choose lodgings that are close to major attractions. And in all cases, we tried to balance the needs and wants of both children and their adult companions.

We chose museums, amusement centers, parks, and other attractions by much the same criteria. The ones we include in this book are inexpensive, informal, and, we feel, offer good entertainment value for the dollar. Many are free. We have tried to concentrate, also, on attractions that allow children's active participation—go-kart tracks, water parks, animal farms and zoos that allow petting and feeding, and museums with hands-on exhibits—instead of attractions that require kids to sit down and "be entertained," or to "look but not touch." The listings in our "Things to Do" sections were chosen because kids can have fun there, don't have to worry about breaking things, and don't have to be perfectly behaved. Similarly, the fairs, festivals, and other events we recommend all offer child-centered activities such as rides, games, and entertainers. And, we point you to some good parks and playgrounds where kids can simply run off steam whenever the need arises.

We do not include prices in this book because prices change too frequently (we do, however, indicate whether fees are charged for admittance to attractions).

> We suggest that you call ahead before driving any distance to, or planning your day's activities around, any single attraction. Hours change, places close for repairs, and sometimes they just close, period. A few minutes calling ahead can save much disappointment.

Our "Shopping" listings include places where kids want to shop, or where adults can shop for children. And since every vacation should include some serious indulging, our "Treats" listings recommend outstanding ice cream and candy shops and bakeries.

Finally, the listings include emergency phone numbers, grocery and drug stores that are open early and late, and addresses and phone numbers for additional information.

To help while away vacation hours, both in the car and at your destination, we have included a selection of car games.

We're pleased that adults traveling without children have also used and appreciated the earlier editions of this book. For those traveling with children, we hope this book will make those trips more interesting, more fun, and less stressful for both adults and children, and that it provides a few educational tidbits now and then. These are the purposes we intended to serve as we researched and compiled this book. We hope we have succeeded.

Kristin Visser
Jerry Minnich
April, 1997

PLEASE NOTE: The 414 telephone area code will be split into two codes as of October 1997. Phones in southeast Wisconsin (Milwaukee, Racine, Kenosha, Lake Geneva, etc.) will keep the 414 code, but phones in Fond du Lac, Manitowoc, Sheboygan, the Fox Cities, Green Bay, Door County, and other parts of the old 414 code will have a new area code—920. That change is noted in the listings. The toll-free 800 phone numbers will not be affected by this change.

Contents

1

Wisconsin Dells and Vicinity

Including Baraboo, North Freedom, Merrimac, Sauk City, Prairie du Sac, and Poynette

If there's one place in Wisconsin that's Kid Central, it's the Dells area. Though famous for its water parks, boat tours, thrill shows, and fudge shops, the area also offers truly lovely scenery along the Wisconsin River, circus performers under the Big Top, and one world-class bunch of birds.

The scenery is a result of aeons of geologic forces changing and shaping the landscape. Millions of years ago, the area was on the bed of a great sea, which left huge deposits of sandstone. The land was uplifted by continental movement, creating mountains higher than today's Rockies. Subsequent glaciers, erosion, and the changing course of the Wisconsin River have produced the Wisconsin Dells, Devil's Lake, and the Baraboo Hills, all that remains of the once-mighty mountain range.

Most 19th-century visitors arrived by train. Two Amtrak trains still stop daily in Wisconsin Dells. Today, though, virtually all visitors travel to the area by car via I-90/94, or on Hwys 12 and 13.

Wisconsin Dells

Kilbourn City, a railroad and lumbering town, was founded in 1856. Residents changed the town's name to Wisconsin Dells in 1931, feeling that that moniker was more appealing to tourists. And the Dells is a one-industry town. This community of less than 4,000 permanent residents hosts some two million visitors annually.

Almost from the first, tourism was an important part of the area's economy, largely due to H.H. Bennett, a pioneering photographer whose photos of the area's rock formations and river scenery circulated nationwide and attracted visitors to the area.

The real boom, though, began after World War II when Herman Breitenbach bought a fleet of Army surplus amphibious vehicles colloquially known as "ducks." He began offering tours of the river and its sandstone formations. The fudge shops, haunted houses, water parks, and waterski shows soon followed.

The centerpiece of a Dells visit is still a tour of either the Upper or Lower Dells (or both, if tour boat operators can convince you). The Upper Dells are on the river upstream from the Wisconsin Dells dam, while the Lower Dells are, naturally, downstream from the dam.

As tourism has increased, Lake Delton, the community adjoining Wisconsin Dells, has become part of the Dells metropolis. Lake Delton itself was created in 1931 by damming Dell Creek, a tributary of the Wisconsin River that flows into the Lower Dells area. Resorts and vacation homes line its shore. Upstream on Dell Creek, another dam forms Mirror Lake, site of more vacation homes and a state park.

Spending a day or two in the Dells can be expensive—admissions, food, motels, souvenirs, a couple of pounds of fudge—so check out the discount coupons available from the Convention and Visitors Bureau (see below), or directly from the businesses themselves at booths in Lake Delton and downtown Wisconsin Dells, or contact the business beforehand and ask about discounts.

Things to Do

This listing includes some of the more popular attractions in and around the communities of Wisconsin Dells and Lake Delton. Many haunted houses, do-it-yourself recording studios, wax museums, and other activities, not listed here, also await you.

Dells Boat Tours. Several boat lines offer tours of the Upper and Lower Dells. The Upper Dells offer more spectacular scenery, with the boat sliding through narrow channels next to sheer rock walls. In the Lower Dells the

river is wider and the sandstone formations less spectacular. All tours are narrated, and Upper Dells tours offer
shore landings at the unique Stand Rock formation,
where a trained labrador retriever or German shepard
(whoever is on duty that day) jumps a six-foot gap
between rock formations, and at deep and narrow Cold
Water Canyon and Witches Gulch.

Three boat lines have similar tours of one to two-and-one-half
hours. Upper Dells tours leave from the upper docks, center of town on
W. Broadway. Lower Dells tours leave from lower docks, at the intersection of Hwys 12 and 13. Phone Dells Boat Company, 608-253-1561;
or Olson Boat Company, 608-254-8500; or Riverview Boat Line, 608-254-
8336. Frequent departures 8-6 daily, early April through October. $.

Boats are nice, but kids just love the **Dells Ducks.** These
amphibious vehicles offer a splash-filled tour of the
Lower Dells and Lake Delton. The hour-long ride
includes charging in and out of lake and river, quick shots
down steep hills and through narrow sandstone canyons,
and narration that's geared to kids—or at least to those
who like corny jokes. As with Dells boat tours, competing
companies offer very similar duck tours.

Duck tour operators are near each other on Hwy 12 one mile south
of Hwys 12-13 intersection. Phone Original Wisconsin Ducks, 608-
254-8751; or Dells Duck Tours, 608-254-6080. Frequent departures
9-6 daily, early May through mid-October. $.

Several giant full service water/amusement parks have
become major Dells draws. **Familyland** is guaranteed to
keep your kids occupied for an entire day. Within its 40
acres are bumper boats, wave pool, go-karts, inner
tube rides, and some amazing water slides, as well as
carnival rides and miniature golf. Familyland boasts the
steepest (and fastest) waterslide in the Dells as well
as tiny tots water slides and play areas. A picnic area,
snack bar, ice cream parlor, and gift shop round out the
park's offerings.

On Hwy 12 one mile south of intersection of Hwys 12-13. Phone
608-254-7766. Partially wheelchair accessible. Open daily, late May
through early September. $.

Noah's Ark claims to be America's largest waterpark.
With two wave pools, 24 waterslides, three inner tube
slides, bumper boats, four kiddie pools, go-karts, carnival
rides, miniature golf, and other attractions, it certainly
could be. Waterslides include the dreaded Black Thunder,

which is totally enclosed so you slide in darkness, emerging at full speed into the pool at the end. Thrilling. The park also has an arcade, gift shops, picnic areas, and snack bars. Plenty to keep everyone in the family occupied for hours.

On Hwy 12 one-and-one-half miles south of Hwys 12-13 intersection. Phone 608-254-6351. Partially wheelchair accessible. Open daily late May through early September. $.

Riverview Park and Waterworld has three "regular" waterslides, five inner tube slides, a couple of high speed waterslides for daredevils, bumper boats, kiddie boats and pools, wave pool and other water activities. Riverview has a larger dry land section than the competing parks, with carnival rides, Grand Prix car driving, go-karts, miniature golf, an arcade, picnic area, snack bar, and gift shops. Here too, the entire family can find enough to keep everyone occupied for hours.

On Hwy 12 one-fourth mile south of Hwys 12-13 intersection. Phone 608-254-2608. Partially wheelchair accessible. Open daily late May through early September. $.

For a quieter experience, tour **Lost Canyon** by horse-drawn wagon. The half-hour tours wind through the narrow mile-long canyon, the walls of which reach as high as 80 feet. A picnic area and swimming beach on Lake Delton are available to Lost Canyon guests, as is a refreshment stand.

Take Hwy 12 south three miles from Wisconsin Dells to Canyon Road, then one-half mile east. Phone 608-254-8757. Open 8:30-8 daily mid-May through September. $.

Younger children will enjoy **Storybook Gardens**, where they can wander among 30-plus life-size, moving fairy tale and nursery rhyme characters and hear the appropriate story or rhyme from each. Also on the beautifully landscaped 13-acre grounds are a minitrain, carousel, puppet show, petting zoo, and picnic area.

On Hwy 12 two miles south of Hwys 12-13 intersection. Phone 608-253-2391. Wheelchair accessible. Open 10-5 daily, late May through early September. $.

Tommy Bartlett's Robot World and Exploratory is always jammed on rainy days. The half-hour tour of a futuristic house is led by a robot guide. More than 90 hands-on displays let kids draw laser pictures, ride in a giant gyroscope, try their skill on computerized touch-screen games, and otherwise learn about the wonders of gravity, electricity, robotics, and other fun stuff. The newest exhibit is part of a Russian Mir space station along with a replica of the first Sputnik and a cosmonaut suit.

On Hwy 12 two miles south of Hwys 12-13 intersection. Phone 608-254-2525. Wheelchair accessible. Open 8 a.m.-10 p.m. daily late May through early September, reduced hours the rest of the year. $.

Animal lovers will enjoy a visit to **Wisconsin Deer Park**, which houses more than a hundred tame deer of several species in a 28-acre reserve. The park is also home to a variety of other more-or-less tame elk, buffalo, birds, and small furry critters. You may feed, pet, and photograph many of the animals. Gift shop.

On Hwy 12 one mile south of Hwys 12-13 intersection. Phone 608-253-2041. Wheelchair accessible. Open 9-8 daily, May 1 through Labor Day, 10-5 daily, day after Labor Day through mid-October. $.

Many Dells attractions include miniature golf courses, but for real world-class miniature golf, you'll have to visit one of the mega-miniature golf establishments. **Timber Falls Adventure Golf**, perched on a cliff overlooking the Wisconsin River, lets you play 90 holes (18 at a time) through some pretty spectacular obstacles, including waterfalls and lots of water hazards plus the Midwest's only "active volcano." A missed putt and your ball could end up in the river or swallowed by a volcano. The complex also has a log flume ride that ends with a steep plummet.

On Hwy 13 at the Wisconsin River bridge just across the river from downtown Wisconsin Dells. Phone 608-254-8414. Open daily early May through mid-October. $.

Pirate's Cove Adventure Golf claims to be the "best" miniature golf course in the U.S., with the longest miniature golf hole. Among its 90 holes are enough waterfalls, water traps, strategically placed rocks and other obstacles to challenge the most avid miniature golfer.

On Hwy 13 just west of downtown Wisconsin Dells. Phone 608-254-8336. Open daily 10 until the last customer goes home, early April through October. $.

As with miniature golf, if you want the biggest and most complex go-kart track, you won't find it among the attractions at a water park. You'll have to take the kids to one of the two **Big Chief Go-Kart Worlds**, the nation's largest go-kart complex. Each location has a variety of tracks for all ages and skill levels, including the slick track for those who like spinning out, and the four-level track, dubbed "more electrifying than the Los Angeles freeway." There are different track configurations at each location. Big Chief #2 also boasts the Cyclops and Pegasus rollercoasters (the Cyclops reachs 90 feet high) that go over and under the go-kart tracks.

Big Chief #2 on Hwy 12 one mile south of Hwys 12 and 13 intersection; Big Chief #1 on County Hwy A two blocks off Hwy 12. Phone 608-254-2490. Open daily Memorial Day weekend through Labor Day, weekends through October. $.

Crazy King Ludwig's Adventure Park is the latest entry in the all-in-one amusements sweepstakes. It features the world's only four-story go-kart track, plus four other shorter and smaller go-kart tracks for the younger or less intrepid. There's also boat tag (blast your opponent with harmless rubber balls from inside your armored floating tank), bumper boats, bungee jump, batting cages, and video arcade.

On Hwy 12 one mile south of the Hwys 12-13 intersection; phone 608-254-5464. Open daily mid-May through mid-October. $.

For real car racing action, take your kids to the **Dells Motor Speedway**. Stock car racing is noisy, fast, and exciting. Kids love it.

On Hwy 12 five miles north of Wisconsin Dells. Phone 608-254-7822. Races every Saturday night mid-May through Labor Day weekend. $.

If you and your kids would like to see those amazing miniature golf courses, go-kart tracks, water parks, and, of course, the Dells rock formations, from the air, either **Badger Helicopters** or **J.B. Helicopters** will gladly take you aloft.

Badger Helicopters takes off from Olde Kilbourn Amusements, on Hwy 12 a half mile south of the intersection with Hwy 13. Phone 608-254-4880. The J.B. Helicopter landing pad is on Hwy 13 behind Pirates Cove Adventure Golf just west of downtown. Phone 608-254-6381. Rides daily, late May through early September. $.

Horseback riding is a popular Dells pastime. **Canyon Creek Stables** takes riders on scenic trail rides near Lost Canyon. They also have a pony ring for the younger set. On Hillman Rd. off Hwy 12 in Lake Delton, phone

608-253-6942. **OK Corral Riding Stable**, one mile south of Wisconsin Dells on Hwy 16 (phone 608-254-2811), conducts guided trail rides along the Lower Dells. **The Ranch at Christmas Mountain** offers lessons, trail rides, and hay rides (S835 Lyndon Rd., off Hwy H; phone 608-254-3935).

Tommy Bartlett's Ski, Sky and Stage Show provides a little of everything to keep the kids on the edge of their seats, including high speed motorboats, water skiing daredevils, comedians, acrobats, and evening fireworks and lasers. There's a covered grandstand, so shows go on rain or shine.

On Hwy 12 two miles south of Hwys 12-13 intersection. Phone 608-254-2525. Wheelchair accessible. Shows at 1:00, 4:30, and 8:30 daily late May through early September. $.

The longest running Dells show, since 1929, is the **Stand Rock Indian Ceremonial**, a show that combines Indian lore, costumes, and dances. The kids can mingle with the costumed dancers during intermission. The Indians perform at the base of Stand Rock in a natural amphitheater on the bank of the Wisconsin River. You can take an evening Upper Dells boat tour that includes a stop at the ceremonial, or drive in by car.

Four miles north of downtown Wisconsin Dells on Stand Rock Road. Phone 608-253-7444. Performance 8:45 p.m. nightly mid-June through Labor Day. $.

Downtown Wisconsin Dells used to be THE place to go, but attractions on the Hwy 12 strip south of town have usurped much of the action. But downtown is still the spot for rainy day activities, souvenir shopping, and for fudge shops. You'll find some of the largest T-shirt shops in Wisconsin on Broadway, the main drag (it's also Hwy 13), not to mention wall-to-wall fudge emporiums, plus eating establishments. There are also a number of smaller attractions perfect for inclement weather or just for a change of pace from the waterparks and boat rides. One of the most popular downtown attractions is **Ripley's Believe It or Not Museum** (115 Broadway, phone 608-253-7556), which is chock full of oddities such as the two-headed calf, shrunken heads, and an exhibit about King Tut's curse. **Wax World of the Stars** (105 Broadway, phone 608-254-2184) has likenesses of all your favorites, living and dead. **The Skreemer** is a motion simulator that gives you the sights, sounds, and thrills of a bunch of different rides like rollercoasters and race cars. Just off Broadway downtown, phone 608-254-7777. The **Haunted Mansion** (on Broadway downtown) features dungeons, monsters, and ghouls.

For a quiet break from the bustle of water parks and souvenir shops, an interlude at either **Rocky Arbor State Park** or **Mirror Lake State Park** will calm your frayed nerves and give the kids a chance to hike, swim, canoe, or just run around. Rocky Arbor is a beautiful wooded park with lovely trails, picnic areas, and camping facilities. Mirror Lake is a larger park with many miles of hiking trails, winter cross-country ski trails, a swimming beach, picnic areas, canoe rentals and boat launch, camping, and a summer nature program with evening naturalist lectures.

Rocky Arbor is one and one-half miles north of Wisconsin Dells on Hwy 12. Phone 608-254-8001. Handicap accessible picnic and camping facilities. Open Memorial Day weekend through Labor Day. $.

Mirror Lake is one-half mile south of I-90/94 on Hwy 12, then west one and one-half miles on Ferndell Rd. Phone 608-254-2333. Handicap accessible picnic area, trails, fishing pier, camping. Open year-round. $.

Winter Fun

The Dells slows down in the winter, but some resorts, restaurants, parks, fudge shops, and souvenir stands are open. **Robot World and Exploratory** (see above) operates year-round, as do the **Canyon Creek Stable** and the **Ranch at Christmas Mountain** (see above—in winter, call for reservations; Canyon Creek winter phone 608-253-1371), which offer horseback riding and sleigh rides.

Christmas Mountain Resort grooms nearly 15 miles of cross-country ski trails and also offers ski rental, a warming shelter, and snack bar. The resort also has a downhill ski area with seven runs on a hill with a vertical drop of 250 feet. Downhill ski rentals and lessons are available. There's also an ice skating rink. Horsedrawn sleigh rides are also offered. At S944 Christmas Mountain Rd., Wisconsin Dells; phone 608-254-3971 for snow conditions.

Cascade Mountain is one of the most popular downhill ski areas in southern Wisconsin, with 25 runs and a vertical drop of 460 feet. The hill offers special instruction for kids ages four to ten. Rentals, adult lessons, chalet, snack bar, and ski shop are offered by the hill. Fifteen miles south of Wisconsin Dells near Portage. Take exit 106 off I-90/94 to Hwy 33, then west one-fourth mile to Cascade Mountain Rd. Phone 608-742-5588 or 800-992-2SKI.

Mirror Lake State Park has 17 miles of groomed ski trails for skiers of all skill levels. The Park also offers special candlelight ski outings throughout the winter. For information, contact the Park Superintendent (see Things to Do above).

Chula Vista Resort has a lighted ice skating rink and skate rentals. 4031 River Rd., north of Wisconsin Dells; phone 608-254-8366.

Events

JANUARY. The annual **Flake Out Festival** is the Dells' winter frolic. There are snow sculpting and ice carving competitions, sleigh rides, ice skating, snowmobile races, hot air balloons, food, and entertainment. Many motels have weekend family discount packages for this event. Most activities free. For information, call 800-223-3557.

JUNE. The **Great Wisconsin Dells Balloon Rally** brings together nearly 100 of North America's most skilled hot air balloonists for a rally and festival. There's a mass ascent Saturday evening and Sunday morning (weather permitting) and balloon races throughout the two days. Live entertainment, sky diving, and plenty of food vendors and concessions round out the weekend. Spectacular, colorful, and fun. Held the first weekend in June. Free. For more information, call the 800-223-3557.

Shopping

No visit to the Dells is complete without a trip to the fudge shops and souvenir purveyors. You won't have any trouble finding both. If you need to keep the kids

occupied in the car or motel room, stop in at **Book World**, 317 Broadway (phone 608-254-2425), for games and books for them and for that best seller you've been meaning to read.

Winnebago Indian Museum displays Indian artifacts, beadwork, feather head dresses, and other interesting items, with an adjoining gift shop that sells Native American crafts. You can buy a beautiful locally made Winnebago basket or beadwork, opt for moccasins or other deerskin items, or purchase a Navaho blanket or silver jewelry. Prices are reasonable, and the Little Eagle family, who owns the museum and gift shop, works hard to find high quality items. You can wander through the gift shop, or pay a small fee and visit the museum as well. On Hwy 13 four miles north of Wisconsin Dells; phone 608-254-2268.

The same family also operates the **Little Eagle Trading Company** on the Hwy 12 strip in Lake Delton. Baskets, beadwork, moccasins, jewelry, dolls, wall hangings, crafts, sculpture, blankets, greeting cards, tapes of Native American music, T-shirts, and Native American clothing are some of the offerings in the store in the Parkway Mall. Phone 608-254-4945.

Parsons Indian Trading Post has been in business for some 70 years. They offer an amazing variety of merchandise—everything from beautiful and authentic (and expensive) Native American-made jewelry, beadwork, and baskets, to fake Indian schlock imported from Taiwan. They've got casual clothing, toys, souvenirs, shoes, and pottery from the Southwest all jumbled together in cheerful profusion. There's not another place like this in the Dells (or anywhere else). On Hwy 12 in Lake Delton.

Rentals

Lake Delton Water Sports and Marina rents ski boats, pontoon boats, fishing boats, canoes, wave runners, and paddleboats on Lake Delton and Mirror Lake. In addition, they rent rafts and canoes for a lazy trip through the Lower Dells. The company has two locations, one off Hwy 12 at Port Vista in Lake Delton, and the other on

Ishnala Rd. on the shore of Mirror Lake (phone for both 608-254-8702). The Mirror Lake location rents canoes, rowboats, and mountain bikes (no motorboats because Mirror Lake has limits on motorboat use). The Lake Delton location offers para-sail rides.

Holiday Shores Water Sports Rentals rents motorboats, canoes, wave runners, and pontoon boats. They also offer para-sail rides. Located at 3900 River Rd. (on the Upper Dells) four miles north of downtown Wisconsin Dells; phone 608-254-2878 or 608-254-2717.

Where to Stay

The Dells area has thousands of guest rooms for rent. On any given summer weekend, virtually all of them are booked. Accommodations run the gamut from luxury resorts to small motels. Many require a minimum nights stay during the peak summer season.

Chula Vista Resort, 4031 North River Rd.,two miles north of Wisconsin Dells; phone 608-254-8366 or 800-388-4782. This 132-room resort with a Southwestern theme is situated on lovely riverside grounds along the Upper Dells. Choose a room or a suite. Indoor and outdoor pools, whirlpools, saunas, kiddie pools, and water play area with three waterslides, miniature golf, game room, cable TV, tennis courts, exercise room, playground, winter ice skating, refrigerators. Restaurant with children's menu. Golf course adjoining. An excellent choice for a family vacation away from the traffic and bustle.

Christmas Mountain Village, S-944 Christmas Mountain Rd. (off Hwy H two miles west of Wisconsin Dells); phone 608-254-3988 or 800-289-1066. A luxury resort with hotel, cabins, and plenty of activities—golf, tennis, horseback riding, indoor and outdoor pools, miniature golf, hiking, bicycling, cross-country and downhill skiing. On wooded grounds away from the traffic and congestion.

Holiday Inn, Hwy 13 just east of I-90/94, exit 87; phone 608-254-8306, or 800-54-DELLS. Standard Holiday Inn, with indoor and outdoor pools, game room, cable TV, coin laundry, restaurant. But this one has been upgraded with a mini-waterpark with waterslides, kiddie pools, and lots of other entertainment for the kids.

Copa Cabana, 611 Wisconsin Dells Parkway (Hwy 12); phone 608-253-1511 or 800-364-2672. In the heart of the Hwy 12 amusement strip within walking distance of many attractions. Indoor pool, whirlpool, game room, miniature water park, playground, cable TV, restaurant. Family suites available.

Mayflower Motel, 930 & 910 Wisconsin Dells Parkway (Hwy 12); phone 608-254-7878, 608-253-6471, 800-253-7666, or 800-345-7407. In the heart of the amusement strip, in walking distance of attractions and restaurants. Lofted family suites, two outdoor and two indoor pools, whirlpools and saunas, indoor kiddie pool, two game rooms, playground, cable TV and free movies, coin laundry.

Flamingo Motel, 1220 Wisconsin Dells Parkway (Hwy 12); phone 608-253-2911 or 800-24-DELLS. On the strip within walking distance of attractions and restaurants. Suites, indoor and outdoor pools, whirlpool, kiddie water playground, cable TV, coin laundry, cribs and rollaways available.

Shamrock Motel, 1321 Wisconsin Dells Parkway (Hwy 12); phone 608-254-8054 or 800-437-5825. In the heart of the strip within easy walk of attractions and restaurants. Two-bedroom family suites available. Indoor and outdoor pools and kiddie pools, whirlpool, playground, coin laundry, cable TV with free movies, picnic area with grills, cribs and rollaways available.

The Atlantis, 1570 Wisconsin Dells Parkway (Hwy 12); phone 608-253-6606 or 800-800-6179. On the amusement strip within walking distance of attractions. Modern motel with lots of amenities such as hot tubs in some rooms. Indoor and outdoor pools, whirlpool and sauna, outdoor mini-waterpark with waterslides, erupting "volcano," kiddie play area, cable TV.

Monte Carlo Resort and Motel, 350 E. Hiawatha Dr., Lake Delton; phone 608-254-8761. An older but quiet, well-maintained, and modestly priced resort with cabins and motel rooms on the lake just off the busy Hwy 12 strip. Eight-acre wooded grounds. Outdoor pool, beach, pier, tennis courts, playground, game room, cable TV and HBO, coin laundry. Rowboats, canoes, and paddleboats available. Open mid-April through early September.

Aloha Beach Resort and Suites, 1370 E. Hiawatha Dr., Lake Delton; phone 608-253-4741. On the shore of Lake Delton. Spacious, wooded grounds, indoor and outdoor pools and kiddie pool, indoor and outdoor whirlpools, sauna, large playground, beach, game room, free rowboats, canoes, and paddleboats, cable TV and HBO. On the lake and off the beaten path but only about a mile from all the entertainment on the Hwy 12 strip.

Indian Trail Motel, 1013 Broadway; phone 608-253-2641. An older but well-maintained motel on the far side of town, within walking distance of downtown Wisconsin Dells. Less hectic and noisy than the Hwy 12 strip. Indoor and outdoor pools, whirlpool, sauna, playground, game room, cable TV and free movies, some rooms with microwaves, cribs available, restaurant adjoining. Spacious wooded grounds with a picnic area (and plenty of space for kids to run off excess energy). One of the lowest priced motels in the Dells area.

A number of public and private campgrounds are near the Dells. Both **Mirror Lake State Park** and **Rocky Arbor State Park** offer more rustic sites with some electrical hookups.

Sherwood Forest Campground, S-352 Hwy 12 (one-half mile north of Hwys 12-13 intersection); phone 608-254-7080. Tent, trailer, and RV camping with full hookups, close to rides and attractions. Outdoor pool, wading pool, playground, game room, showers, dump station, laundromat, store. Wooded grounds.

Jellystone Park Camp-Resort, Ishanla Rd., Lake Delton; phone 608-254-2568 or 800-462-9644. A large, mostly wooded campground that fronts on I-90/94 (ask for a site away from the road). Sites for RVs, tents, trailers, plus camping cabins and trailer rentals. Full hook-ups, showers, laundry, store, restaurant. Amenities include three game rooms, miniature golf, outdoor pool and kiddie pool, ranger station with cocktail bar (for Mom and Dad), access to Mirror Lake,daily hayrides, cartoons, planned activities for kids, live entertainment and special weekend activities, boat rentals on Mirror Lake. A little of everything.

Holiday Shores Camp-Resort, 3900 River Rd.; phone 608-254-2717. On the Wisconsin River four miles north of Wisconsin Dells. Tent, trailer, and RV sites with full hookups. Swimming beach, game room, hiking trails, playground, outdoor pool, store, restaurant, showers, dump station, canoe and motorboat rental. Wooded grounds.

Where to Eat

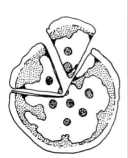

Pizza Pub offers thin or thick crust pizza with a variety of toppings ranging from pineapple to pepperoni. The menu also includes lasagna, subs, burgers, and salads. Best of all, they deliver, so you don't have to leave your motel room after a long day at the water park. Children's menu. 1455 Wisconsin Dells Parkway (Hwy 12); phone 608-254-7877. Open daily for lunch and dinner.

Ishnala, overlooking beautiful Mirror Lake, is a Dells tradition. Watch ducks (the birds, not the ride) and boaters as you dine on ribs, steaks, seafood, chicken dishes, or sandwiches. Children's menu. The restaurant also offers pontoon boat cruises on Mirror Lake. On Ishnala Road (take Gasser Road west from Hwy 12 near the exit off I-90/94). Phone 608-253-1771. Open daily for dinner Memorial Day through Labor Day.

The **Cheese Factory** serves a vegetarian menu, but don't let that scare you. They love butter, cream, eggs, and other delights. The menu is heavy on pancakes, eggs, and homemade sweetrolls for breakfast, and sandwiches, fries, pasta, stir-fry, soups, salads, and dynamite desserts for lunch and dinner. They also do amazing things with ice cream and make wonderful gourmet coffee and expresso. Children's menu. 521 Wisconsin Dells Parkway (Hwy 12); phone 608-253-6065. Open daily except Tuesday May through October, weekends in winter.

Jimmy's Del-Bar is popular with the locals when they want an evening out. They go for the steaks, fresh seafood, pasta, and homemade soups and desserts. Although the restaurant is a bit more formal than some others in the Dells, kids are definitely welcome. There's even a children's menu. 800 Wisconsin Dells Parkway (Hwy 12); phone 608-253-1861. Open daily for dinner (reduced hours in winter—call first).

Wally's House of Embers features wonderful dinner menus with items such as veal medallions sauteed in brandy, sauteed pork tenderloin, barbequed ribs, pastas, salmon, prime rib, and other perfectly prepared delights. Excellent. And as always in the Dells, kids are welcome. 935 Wisconsin Dells Parkway (Hwy 12); phone 608-253-6411. Open daily for dinner (call first in winter—they sometimes close for a vacation).

The **Dells Grill** has been a gathering place for local residents since 1949, and no wonder. The Grill offers good, inexpensive meals, including full breakfasts, plate lunches, and a complete dinner menu as well as sandwiches. The homemade soups, pies, and pastries are terrific. 318 Broadway; phone 608-254-2727. Open daily for breakfast, lunch and dinner in summer, closed Mondays in winter.

Thunder Valley Restaurant is worth the short drive for the outstanding breakfasts they serve up. Picture homemade cinnamon roles, potatoes, pancakes, eggs, toast made of homemade bread. It's all there, on a working farm where the kids can pet the goats and cows. W15344 Waubeek Road (off Hwy 13 north of Wisconsin Dells); phone 608-254-4145. Open daily for breakfast, Friday and Saturday for dinner during the summer season. Saturday night singalongs.

It's a short drive to **Jeanie's Deli & Coffee Shop**, but it's definitely worth the trip. Jeanie's is homey and friendly, with excellent food moderately priced. She puts her heart into her soup, desserts and pastries, she does extremely well with hamburgers and her entire sandwich menu, and her dinners are famous among local residents. Plus, Jeanie has an ice cream parlor. Four miles north of Wisconsin Dells on Hwy 12; phone 608-254-8106. Open daily for lunch and dinner. Closed Mondays after Labor Day.

Extended Hours Grocery Store

Zinke's Shop Rite
216 Washington Ave.
Wisconsin Dells
608-254-8313.

Emergency

For fire, police or ambulance, dial 911

Tourist Information

Wisconsin Dells Visitor & Convention Bureau
701 Superior St.
Wisconsin Dells, WI 53965
608-254-INFO
800-22-DELLS
or try their World Wide Web site at
http://www.dells.com

Baraboo

A French fur trader named Baribault set up shop here in the early 19th century and Baraboo was born. The community is most famous as the home of the Ringlings. From 1884 to 1918 Baraboo was headquarters of the Ringling Brothers Circus.

Baraboo is a lovely town, with its courthouse square and commercial district, historic homes and shaded parks. The town is a commercial center and county seat and has a two-year University of Wisconsin campus.

Most travelers arrive in Baraboo on Hwy 12 from either Wisconsin Dells 10 miles north, or from Madison 35 miles south.

Things to Do

The **International Crane Foundation**, a center for the study, propagation, and preservation of the world's crane species, is the only facility of its kind. The 90-minute tours explain the worldwide work of the foundation and allow visitors to view many of the majestic cranes living at the foundation. You can watch human "chick mamas" feed and exercise young cranes, and, depending on the time of year, see tiny newly-hatched chicks, or watch mating displays. There's also an excellent display that includes endangered whooping cranes.

E-11376 Shady Lane Rd., five miles north of Baraboo off Hwy 12; phone 608-356-9462. Wheelchair accessible. Open 9-5 daily May 1 through October. Guided tours daily Memorial Day through Labor Day and on weekends in May, September, and October, or you may stroll the grounds. $.

Circus World Museum is a must-see for children. A state historic site, the museum is partly housed in the former winter quarters of the Ringling Brothers Circus. The 50-acre museum offers circus performances in the big top, magic shows, clowns, acrobats, pony and elephant rides, circus animals, demonstrations of 19th century circus equipment such as steam calliopes, and exhibits showing the history and lore of circuses. Adults and children alike will be amazed by the display of antique circus wagons. Plan to spend the day.

426 Water St.; phone 608-356-8341, or 608-356-0800 for recorded information. Wheelchair accessible. Exhibit hall open daily year round with wagons, miniature circus, films, circus posters, memorabilia. Summer season has circus performances, demonstrations and other outdoor activities 9-6 daily early May through mid-September. Open until 9:30 p.m. in late July and August. $.

Devil's Lake State Park encompasses some of the most spectacular scenery in Wisconsin. At the heart of this 9000-acre park is spring-fed, 360-acre Devil's Lake, surrounded by 500-foot bluffs of the ancient Baraboo Range. Trails, picnic areas, beaches, boat and sailboard rental, naturalist programs and camping attract visitors.

S5975 Park Rd., three miles south of Baraboo off Hwy 123; phone 608-356-8301. Handicap accessible picnic and camping facilities. Open daily year-round. $.

The **Mid-Continent Railway Museum** in nearby North Freedom features a 50-minute ride on a turn-of-the-century steam train, a restored 1894 depot, and exhibits of

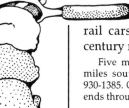

rail cars and locomotives from 19th and early 20th-century railroads. There's also a picnic area.

Five miles west of Baraboo on Hwy 136, then two and one-half miles southwest on County Hwy PF; phone 608-522-4261 or 800-930-1385. Open 9:30-5 daily mid-May through Labor Day, 9:30-5 weekends through mid-October. Four steam train trips daily. $.

Few things are free anymore, so the **Merrimac Ferry** would be worth a side trip for that reason alone. Of course, it's also fun. The ferry takes cars (and pedestrians and bicyclists) across the Wisconsin River because Hwy 113 has no bridge. The ten-minute ride is just long enough for the kids to explore the ferry and watch boat traffic on the river. Waiting lines in summer may be long, but there are ice cream parlors on both sides of the river.

On Hwy 113 ten miles south of Baraboo. No phone. Runs 24 hours a day from ice-out in mid-April through freeze-up in December. Free.

Shopping

Just Imagine is a unique store selling toys, puzzles, games, and other fun stuff. Go just to browse, but you'll probably find something for both you and the kids. At 120 4th Ave. (on the courthouse square downtown); phone 608-356-5507.

Treats

Venerable Bean coffeehouse does indeed have great gourmet coffee and teas. It's also a great place for wonderful bakery items and it has a whole big freezer full of ice cream for shakes, malts, sundaes, and cones. Plus they have homemade soups and sandwiches. Books and games are available for patrons to while away a rainy day or rest up between tourist attractions. 532 Oak St. (on the courthouse square downtown); phone 608-356-7272.

Winter Fun

For cross-country skiing, the place to go is **Devil's Lake State Park**, with 17 miles of groomed trails that wind through the woods and even take you to the top of the spectacular bluffs.

Devil's Head Resort has one of the largest downhill ski areas in southern Wisconsin, with 22 runs and a 500 foot vertical drop. The resort offers rentals, instruction, ski shop, restaurants, and such amenities as hot tubs and an indoor pool. There's a weekend ski school for beginning skiers ages five to eight. The hill also has a snowboarding area and snowboarding lessons, plus groomed cross-country ski trails. On County Hwy DL, five miles south of Baraboo (take Hwy 113 to DL). Phone 608-493-2251, or 800-472-6670 (WI), or 800-338-4579 (Illinois)

Where to Stay

Baraboo Inn, 725 W. Pine (Hwy 12); phone 608-356-1100 or 800-528-1234. A Best Western affiliate, this modern motel's amenities include an indoor pool, whirlpool, game room, cable TV, some rooms with refrigerators. Kids under 12 stay free with parents.

Pinehaven B&B, E13083 Hwy 33 (two miles east of Baraboo); phone 608-356-3489 welcomes children over 5 with their family to either the modern B&B rooms or the adjoining rental cabin. Situated on spacious grounds in the country, Pinehaven offers a small private lake with rowboat and paddleboats, plenty of room to roam, and perhaps a wagon ride or winter sleigh ride, pulled by the hosts' Belgian horses.

Campers should head for **Devil's Lake State Park**, with 406 campsites, over 100 of which have electrical hookups. The campground has showers, flush toilets, and a dump station.

Where to Eat

The **Alpine Cafe** has been serving up hearty meals to Baraboo folk since 1930. Their big breakfasts and home-made soups and pies will make you glad you stopped in. 117 4th St., one block east of the courthouse square; phone 608-356-4040. Open daily for breakfast and lunch.

The **Log Cabin Family Restaurant** features great breakfasts, including omelettes and homemade bakery items, daily homemade soups, and terrific sandwiches, plus a large dinner menu. Children's menu. And it really is in a log building. 1215 8th St. (Hwy 33) on the east edge

of Baraboo); phone 608-356-8245. Open daily for breakfast, lunch, and dinner.

Emergency

For fire, police or ambulance, dial 911.

Tourist Information

Baraboo Area Chamber of Commerce
124 Second St.
Baraboo, WI 53913
608-356-8333
800-BARABOO

Sauk City and Prairie du Sac

These twin cities along the north bank of the Wisconsin
River are best known for their feathered winter residents.
Get there on Hwy 12, twenty-five miles south from Wis-
consin Dells, or twenty miles north of Madison.

Things to Do

The **Lower Wisconsin State Riverway** begins below
the dam at Prairie du Sac. From here to its confluence
with the Mississippi River 92 miles downstream, the Wisconsin is free-flowing, the longest stretch of undammed
river east of the Mississippi. Forested bottomlands and
dramatic bluffs line the river. Sandbars and islands offer a
cool resting place for boaters. Wildlife abound, and the
fishing is pretty good, too. Canoeing, kayaking, motorboating, fishing, hunting, swimming, hiking, and camping draw visitors to the riverway.

For information, contact the Riverway Coordinator, Hwy 23, Rt. 1,
Dodgeville, WI 53533; phone 608-935-3368.

Events

JANUARY. **Eagle Watching Days**, Prairie du Sac. Every
winter, hundreds of bald eagles congregate in the area to
take advantage of the open water produced by the spill-
ways of the Prairie du Sac Dam. The Department of Natural Resources provides expert biologists, binoculars,

videos, and kids activities for ages five to ten. Held the second and third weekends in January along the river in Prairie du Sac. Phone 608-643-4168 for information. Free.

SEPTEMBER. **Wisconsin Cow Chip Throw**, Sauk City. The state's homage to the meadow muffin. Games, food, art show, and parade (don't miss the Trojan Cow), all culminating in the children's cow chip throw and the championship cow chip throw (winner gets a trip to Oklahoma to compete in the nationals). Great fun. Held the Friday and Saturday of Labor Day weekend at Marion Park in Sauk City. Phone 608-643-4168 for information.

Rentals

A number of outfitters offer canoe rentals and shuttle service on the Wisconsin River.

Sauk Prairie Canoe Rental, 932 Water Street, Sauk City; phone 608-643-6589.

Bender's Bluffview, 614 Spruce St., Sauk City; phone 608-643-8247.

Blackhawk River Runs, one mile south of Sauk City on Hwy 78, then two miles west on County Hwy Y; phone 608-643-6724 or 608-643-2273.

Where to Eat

Eagle Inn has everything you want in a small town cafe—homemade pastries, pie, hearty sandwiches and soups, salad bar, full dinners—plus you can watch eagles while you eat. Children's menu. On Water Street at the Hwy 60 bridge in Prairie du Sac; phone 608-643-4516. Open daily for breakfast, lunch, and dinner.

Green Acres Supper Club features seafood, pasta, chicken, and great steaks as well as daily specials and the traditional Wisconsin Friday night fish fry. They also serve sandwiches and have a salad bar. Where the locals go. Children's menu. At the intersection of Hwys 12 and 78 just south of Sauk City; phone 608-643-2305. Open daily for dinner.

Tourist Information

Sauk Prairie Area Chamber of Commerce
207 Water St., Suite D
Sauk City, WI 53583
608-643-4168
800-68-EAGLE

Poynette

Things to Do

MacKenzie Environmental Education Center has exhibits of native Wisconsin wildlife, including bison, deer, wolf, lynx, and eagles. The 280-acre facility also offers self-guiding nature trails, a conservation museum and two smaller museums, a fire tower, and picnic areas.

On County Hwy CS two miles east of Poynette. Take I-90/94 twenty-five miles south of Wisconsin Dells to County Hwy CS exit. Phone 608-635-4498. Partially wheelchair accessible. Grounds open dawn to dusk daily except closed during late November. Exhibits and museums open 8-4 daily early May through mid October, 8-4 Monday-Friday rest of the year. Free.

2

Madison and Vicinity

Including Mount Horeb, Blue Mounds, and Stoughton

Bike along a lake. Learn about stars, and about cows. Ride a camel. Enjoy a museum just for kids. Madison is Wisconsin's center of government and education—and yet it's tailor-made for kids.

With its lakes and parks and its cultural and social amenities, Madison offers dozens of easily accessible, and often free, family activities. The kids can choose between an open-air farmers market, museums, beaches, live theater, serious toy shopping, and even bicycling—all without leaving the Madison downtown area. A short trip out of town provides opportunities to tour a cave, learn how Norwegian immigrant families lived, or climb the highest hill in southern Wisconsin.

Madison came to be because land speculator James Doty convinced the Territorial Legislature to move the capital in 1836. In 1848 the first buildings of the University of Wisconsin campus were constructed on a hill a mile from the Capitol building.

Today, Madison is a city of 200,000 in a metropolitan area of nearly 400,000. Madison is home to the largest University of Wisconsin campus, with more than 40,000 students, as well as state government agencies and a variety of businesses including Oscar Mayer, Rayovac, insurance, banking and financial services, health care, and a growing high-tech sector. Though Madison was originally settled by Norwegians, Germans, and other northern Europeans, the city has attracted new residents from throughout the world. Citizens of Middle Eastern, Asian, southern European, and Latin American descent enliven the mix of restaurants, entertainment, and business in the city.

To the east and south lies rolling farmland dotted with lakes and small communities such as Cottage Grove and

23

Stoughton. Madison and the adjoining communities of Middleton, Fitchburg, and Monona, which surround the four Madison lakes, are the population and geographic center of the area. Ten miles west of Madison, the glaciers stopped on their last trip through, and the landscape here has the hilly and varied topography typical of the unglaciated southwestern part of the state. Farms, wooded ridges, and small communities such as Verona, Mount Horeb, and Blue Mounds are found just west of Madison.

Many travelers to the Madison area arrive via one of the many scheduled flights to the Dane County Regional Airport. Most, though, drive to the area on I-94 from the east, or on I-90 from the north or south. Other major area roads include Hwy 151, which runs from southwest to northeast; and Hwys 12 and 14, which run southeast to northwest.

Madison

Madison's historic central heart is located on a narrow isthmus between lakes Monona and Mendota. Lake Wingra, a smaller lake just west of Lake Monona, lies entirely within the city. Most attractions, specialty shops, and recreational activities are centered on the downtown, University of Wisconsin campus, and Lake Wingra areas.

Things to Do

A tour of the **State Capitol** is a good way to start your Madison visit. The Capitol is one of the most beautiful public buildings in America. Designed in Italian Renaissance style, the granite and marble Capitol is noted for its classical columns, formal layout, and granite dome. Kids love to lie on the floor in the center of the rotunda and look up at the huge mural suspended in the dome 200 feet overhead. Tours highlight the legislative, gubernatorial and Supreme Court wings of the building. During warm weather, visitors are allowed on the platform at the base of the dome for a magnificent view of Madison and the lakes.

On the Capitol Square in the center of Madison, most easily approached on either East Washington Ave. or West Washington Ave.

Phone 608-266-0382. Wheelchair accessible. Building open 6 a.m.-8 p.m. daily. One-hour tours daily year-round, except major holidays. Free.

Across the street from the Capitol is the **State Historical Museum**, with exhibits illustrating Indian life, fur trading, the exploration of the Great Lakes area, and life on the Wisconsin frontier. Films and slide shows are part of the exhibits. There's an excellent gift shop with books and toys for children and adults. Most Saturday mornings at 10:30, the museum presents free "Focus on History" programs for families. The programs include films, storytellers, folk singers, lectures, slide shows, and other presentations on a wide variety of Wisconsin subjects.

30 N. Carroll St. (corner N. Carroll and State); phone 608-264-6555. Wheelchair accessible. Open 10-5 Tuesday-Saturday, noon-5 Sunday. Closed Monday and major holidays. Free.

The **Madison Children's Museum** is part of the museum complex developing across from the Capitol. This facility features hands-on exhibits including "Leap into Lakes," about the Madison lakes, the Great Lakes, wetlands, and all things damp. There's another exhibit about the Brazilian rainforest, and one about farming. Everything is to be touched, tried, and played with. For kids from toddler to early teen.

100 State St.; phone 608-256-6445. Wheelchair accessible. Open 10-5 Tuesday-Sunday. Closed Monday and major holidays. $.

The **Wisconsin Veterans Museum**, within a half block of both the Children's Museum and the Historical Museum, honors the men and women of Wisconsin who served in America's conflicts from the Civil War to the Persian Gulf War. Dioramas depicting battles and other important events are the centerpiece of the museum. Equipment displayed includes everything from Civil War rifles to a Huey helicopter from the Vietnam War. There are also scale models of military ships. Visitors can look through a submarine periscope to get a unique view of the Capitol and other buildings near the museum. Preschool kids won't find much of interest here because there's little to push, pull, or punch.

30 W. Mifflin St.; phone 608-264-6086. Wheelchair accessible. Open 9:30-4:30 Tuesday-Saturday October through March; 9-5 Monday-Saturday and noon-5 Sunday April through September. Free.

The **Madison Farmers Market** is where everyone meets everyone on Saturday mornings. Vendors set up stalls around the entire Capitol Square and sell everything from turnips to gourmet chocolate. A favorite local pastime is a Saturday morning stroll around the market to buy produce and pick up breakfast from the bakery, candy, fruit juice and coffee stands, then picnic on the Capitol lawn and watch people. Dancers and musicians often entertain at various locations around the Capitol and on sidewalks around the Square. The first Saturday in June is Cows on the Concourse, when Dairy Month is celebrated by trucking in a half-dozen cows for kids to pet while chowing down the dairy products that are on sale all around the Square. Ice cream for breakfast? Sure.

Capitol Square. No phone. Wheelchair accessible. Public rest rooms available in the Capitol. Market 6 a.m.-1 p.m. Saturdays from late April through early November. Free.

The **Madison Civic Center** houses the **Children's Theater of Madison** as well as the **Madison Art Center**. Civic Center presentations include music, dance, and plays performed in three theaters by both resident companies and traveling performers. The Children's Theater of Madison is one of the resident companies, presenting plays throughout the fall-winter-spring theater season, including the annual holiday production of "A Christmas Carol." Also at the Civic Center are free performances in a commons area called the Crossroads. Saturday "Kids in the Crossroads" performers include clowns, jugglers, magicians, musicians, and storytellers.

211 State St. Box office phone 608-266-9055 for information about theater presentations and "Kids in the Crossroads." Art Center phone 608-257-0158. All Civic Center facilities are wheelchair accessible. Art Center open 11-5 Tuesday-Thursday, 11-9 Friday, 10-5 Saturday, 1-5 Sunday. $, except "Kids in the Crossroads" is free.

The University of Wisconsin campus is not just for students. Families can find a number of fun things to do. The **UW Geology Museum** houses wonderful rock and fossil exhibits, including several dinosaur and mastodon skeletons. The limestone cave exhibit and the explanation of fluorescence are great kid-grabbers. The museum has self-guided tours using loaned booklets that explain the exhibits. This little museum is a real hidden treasure.

Some days, you can even watch paleontologists putting together dinosaur skeletons.

In Weeks Hall, 1215 W. Dayton St.; use main entrance and follow the signs; phone 608-262-2399. Wheelchair accessible. Open 8:30-4:30 Monday-Friday, 9-1 Saturday. Closed for some university holidays. Free.

Glimpse the stars and planets through the 15-inch telescope at the UW's **Washburn Observatory** during the twice-monthly public viewing hours. Astronomers are on duty to explain what you're seeing. Remember to dress warmly on cold nights, since the telescope room is not heated.

1401 Observatory Dr., on UW campus; phone 608-262-9274. Viewing the first and third Wednesday of each month if the sky is clear. CALL FIRST. Viewing begins 9 p.m. April 30-October 31, and at 7:30 p.m. the remainder of the year. The building was built in the 1880s and is not handicap accessible. Free.

Space Place has hands-on displays about astronomy and space science plus lectures and workshops every second and fourth Tuesday and Saturday. Organized and operated by the UW Astronomy and Space Science Department.

1605 S. Park St.; phone 608-262-4779. Workshops 10 a.m. Saturday for kids ages 6-11 and their parents. Lectures Tuesday evenings for adults and older children. Also special events and programs. Free.

UW has its own cow herd right on campus. You can watch students and dairy experts milking and feeding the cows at the **Dairy Cattle Center**. There's always someone available to answer questions.

1815 Linden Dr.; phone 608-262-2271. Milking 4-7 p.m. weekdays. No advance notice needed, just show up. The cows are always there. Free.

The 800-plus residents of the **Henry Vilas Zoo** include Wisconsin natives such as otters and black bear, and exotics ranging from a Galapagos tortoise to lions and polar bears. There's a children's zoo with young goats, pigs, rabbits, and other animals to feed and pet. Kids can get a free camel ride most Sundays from 10:30 to noon in June, July, and August. The zoo is in **Vilas Park**, which has playgrounds, tennis courts, picnic areas, and a swimming beach with lifeguard and bath house on Lake Wingra.

702 S. Randall St.; phone 608-266-4732. Wheelchair accessible. Zoo open 9:30-8 daily June through Labor Day, 9:30-5 daily September through May. Children's zoo open Memorial Day weekend through Labor Day. Free.

Vilas Park open daily year-round. Beach open with lifeguard early June through late August. Free.

The zoo and Vilas Park adjoin the **UW Arboretum**, a 1,270-acre area used for university research and public recreation. The arboretum has miles of hiking trails through woods and restored prairies and along Lake Wingra. The road through the Arboretum is a local favorite for bicycling and jogging. The McKay Center has information about hiking, skiing, and nature study lectures that are conducted regularly throughout the year.

Enter off Seminole Hwy or off Wingra Dr.; phone 608-263-7888. Arboretum open daily dawn-dusk. McKay Center on Arboretum Dr. in center of arboretum, open 9:30-4 Monday-Friday, 12:30-4 Saturday & Sunday. Free.

Olbrich Botanical Gardens are a delight at any time. In season, there are fourteen acres of outdoor blooming plants of every description. The new Bolz Conservatory, open year-round, is a 50-foot-high glass pyramid enclosing a lush tropical paradise filled with exotic plantings, pools, a waterfall, and free-flying birds. Regular children's programs throughout the year.

2-1/2 mi. east of downtown Madison at 3330 Atwood Ave., across from Lake Monona. Phone 608-246-4550. Wheelchair accessible. Outdoor gardens open daily 9-5. Free. Conservatory open daily 10-4 except Christmas day. Gift shop. $

The national broadcast of Madison's own **Whad' Ya Know** radio show originates live most Saturday mornings from the Lecture Hall in the new Monona Terrace Convention Center on Lake Monona in downtown Madison. Host Michael Feldman jokes and talks with the audience, and chooses audience members to try a trivia quiz. He especially enjoys talking to kids.

Monona Terrace is on John Nolen Dr. along the north shore of Lake Monona. Also accessible from the Capitol Square. Phone 800-WHA-KNOW for ticket information. Tickets should be ordered in advance, as the show is very popular. 9 a.m. seating for 10 a.m. show. Free.

The **Mad City Ski Team** presents water ski shows from Memorial Day weekend through Labor Day. The show includes jumping, trick skiing, and clowns. Bring a lawn chair or blanket—seating is on the grass.

At Law Park on John Nolen Dr. on north shore of Lake Monona. Wheelchair accessible. Shows at 6 p.m. Sunday. Free.

University of Wisconsin athletic teams compete in more than two dozen sports ranging from football to rowing. Admission is charged for football, men's and women's basketball, and soccer, hockey, and women's volleyball. Big time college sports.

For information about athletic events and tickets, contact the UW Athletic Ticket Office, 1440 Monroe St.; phone 608-262-1440. The ticket office is open 8:30-4:30 Monday-Friday.

Madison has its own minor league baseball team, the **Madison Black Wolf**, which takes the field throughout the June-August season at Warner Park on the city's northeast side. A relaxing and fun way to spend an afternoon or early evening. There's a large picnic area where you can watch the action and eat dinner at the same time. Warner Park also has playgrounds, tennis courts, picnic areas, and lots of room for kids to run off excess energy.

The field is at Warner Park at the intersection of Sherman Avenue and Northport Drive, enter off Sherman Avenue. For schedules and ticket information phone 608-244-5666. Most games begin at 7 p.m. except Sunday, when games start at 1 p.m. $.

Madison lakes offer plenty of **swimming** opportunities. Popular beaches with lifeguards and bathhouses include **Vilas Park** on Lake Wingra (next to the zoo), **B.B. Clarke Beach** on the north shore of Lake Monona (835 Spaight St.) and the **Tenney Park Beach** on the south shore of Lake Mendota (1300 Sherman Ave.). Beaches are open and lifeguards on duty from early June through late August.

For more information, contact the Madison City Parks Division, 215 Martin Luther King, Jr. Blvd. Phone 608-266-4711 weekdays. Beaches are free.

Bicycling is extremely popular inthe Madison area. With more than 90 miles of signed bicycle routes, including bike lanes on city streets and separate bike paths, it's easy to get around town on two wheels. Three favorite routes are the 14-mile path-and-bike-lane route around Lake Monona, which passes through several parks with picnic areas, beaches and playgrounds; the three-mile (one way)

route along the Lake Mendota shore from the Memorial Union through the UW campus and out to Picnic Point, with its beach and picnic areas; and the six-mile ride around Lake Wingra, which includes a trip through the UW Arboretum and a pass through Vilas Park.

For information about Madison and Dane County bike routes, contact the Madison Department of Transportation, 215 Martin Luther King, Jr. Blvd, Madison 53703. Phone 608-266-4761 weekdays.

Just east of Madison in the community of Cottage Grove, the **Glacial Drumlin State Trail** follows an old railroad grade east for 51 miles to Waukesha.

For information, contact the trail manager, 1213 S. Main St., Lake Mills, WI 53551; phone 414-648-8774. Open year-round for bicycling and hiking in summer, snowmobiling and skiing in winter. $ for bicycling.

Beginning five miles west of Madison, the **Military Ridge State Trail** runs 40 miles from Verona to Dodgeville along an abandoned railroad grade. Great scenery from the ridge tops between Mount Horeb and Dodgeville.

For information, contact the trail manager, Route 1, Box 42, Dodgeville, WI 53533; phone 608-935-5119. Open year-round for bicycling and hiking in summer and snowmobiling and cross-country skiing in winter. $ for bicycling.

Governor Nelson State Park, on the north shore of Lake Mendota, provides hiking, swimming, boat launching and cross-country skiing as well as magnificent views of the Madison skyline. The park has a restored prairie as well as an oak forest and Indian mounds.

Five miles east of Middleton on County Hwy M; mailing address 5140 Hwy M, Waunakee, WI 53597; phone 608-831-3005. Open year round. $.

Winter Fun

Madison goes full steam through the winter, with cultural events, museums, and sporting events—a full range of indoor activities from bowling to ballet. The city also plunges into winter outdoors, with skating rinks, cross-country skiing and snowmobile trails, and the hardy band of souls who put up shanties and ice fish all winter.

Family cross-country skiing is especially enjoyable at **Odana Golf Course**, which in winter sprouts nearly 6 miles of groomed ski trails. The golf clubhouse becomes a

warming house with a snack bar, ski rentals, and weekend ski lessons. Trails are easy to moderate in difficulty.
Odana is at 4635 Odana Rd., phone 608-266-4724. Open
during daylight hours. Trail use free, $ for rental
and lessons.

The groomed ski trails at **Governor Nelson State Park**
wind through woods and prairie, have great views of the
Madison skyline and surrounding countryside, and are
for beginning to intermediate skiers. Restrooms but no
warming shelter. $.

Informal ski trails and some groomed trails at the **UW
Arboretum** follow hiking paths through woods and
prairie. Skiers of all abilities can find a trail to suit them.
No warming shelter. Free.

Elver Park on Madison's far west side has five miles of
groomed ski trails for all skill levels. The park even has
several miles of lighted trails for night skiing. There's a
warming shelter, snack bar, and a sledding hill for thrill-
seekers. At 1301 Gammon Rd. For information, contact
the Madison Parks Division, 608-266-4711. Free.

Ice skaters will enjoy the outdoor rinks at **Vilas Park** and
Tenney Park. Both have warming houses with snack
bars and skate rentals and both rinks offer plenty of room
to skate. For information, contact the Madison Parks Division, 608-266-4711. Free.

Indoor ice skating and skate rentals are offered at **Hart-
meyer Ice Arena**, 1834 Commercial Avenue, on the east
side of town; phone 608-246-4512.

Events

JULY. The annual **Art Fair on the Square** brings hundreds of artists, musicians, and other entertainers plus
dozens of food vendors to celebrate art, fun and summer.
One of the largest art fairs in Wisconsin. Held second
weekend in July on the Capitol Square and spilling off
down adjoining streets. Phone Madison Art Center,
608-257-0158, for information. Free.

Shopping

The three major shopping malls are East Towne, on the far east side near the intersection of East Washington Ave. and I-90/94; West Towne, at the intersection of Mineral Point Rd. and Gammon Rd. on the far west side; and Hilldale, five miles west of downtown at the intersection of Midvale Blvd. and University Ave. Those malls contain major department stores, bookstores, boutiques, jewelry stores and other typical mall stores.

Madison is home to some wonderfully interesting stores not found in the malls. State Street from the Capitol Square to the UW campus, and Monroe Street, on the city's near west side, both have an array of diverse and interesting shops that you and your kids will love.

Puzzlebox sells a variety of imported, handmade and otherwise unusual toys, books and games for kids from infant to teen. Stop in just to see their ever-changing and always imaginative store windows. 230 State St.; phone 608-251-0701. Open 10-8 Monday-Saturday, noon-5 Sunday.

For that only-from-Wisconsin souvenir, stop in at **Cheddarheads** for a foam cheesehead (made famous by the fans of the Green Bay Packers), Cheddarhead T-shirts, Green Bay Packer clothing, plus mugs, cards, and other souvenirs that say "Wisconsin." 122 State St.; phone 608-255-4007. Open daily.

Canterbury Booksellers Coffeehouse offers both books and light meals in a cozy setting a half block off State Street. The store has a large children's book section, and every Sunday afternoon there's a storyteller or other children's activity. The coffeehouse serves soups, salads, sandwiches, desserts, and non-alcoholic drinks. The bakery is outstanding. 315 W. Gorham St.; phone 608-258-9911. Open daily.

The **University Book Store's** children's book section is outstanding, and you can get just about any other book you've been wanting as well as UW clothing, mugs, lamps, and other souvenirs. 711 State St.; phone

608-257-3784. Open 9-5 Monday-Saturday. Also check out **UBS For Kids**, in the Hilldale Mall; phone 608-238-3332. Open 9:30-9 Monday-Friday, 9:30-5:30 Saturday, 11-5 Sunday.

Borders Book Shop has a huge selection of books, including a large children's section. The store schedules storytelling, reading, and other activities for kids. There's also a small coffee shop. 3416 University Avenue near Hilldale Mall; phone 608-232-2600.

Orange Tree Imports offers a potpourri of adult items such as cooking utensils, jewelry, and greeting cards plus kid stuff such as holiday decorations and toys. 1721 Monroe St.; phone 608-256-4040. Open 10-5:30 Monday-Saturday (Monday and Thursday til 8), 11-4 Sunday.

Wild Child is the place for all-natural cotton clothes for active kids. 1813 Monroe St.; phone 608-251-6445. Open 10-5:30 Monday-Friday, 10-5 Saturday, noon-4 Sunday.

Treats

The **Badger Candy Kitchen** makes hand-dipped chocolates as well as hard candies. Try the Badger Backs, which are caramel, pecans, and milk chocolate. Or try a hot caramel pecan sundae if ice cream is more to your liking. 7 West Main St. on the Capitol Square; phone 608-255-3538. Open daily except Sunday.

Deadman's Chocolate Shoppe Ice Cream does indeed serve killer malts, shakes, sundaes, and cones. Rich and creamy. Locally made ice cream. 468 State St.; phone 608-255-5454. Open daily.

James J. Chocolate Shoppe produces amazing chocolates, hard candies, and seasonal specialties. 2510 University Ave.; phone 608-238-4243. Open daily except Sunday.

Michael's Frozen Custard. Rich, creamy, incredibly delicious. Malts, shakes, sundaes, cones. They also serve decent burgers. Do not leave Madison without going to Michael's. Three locations: 3826 Atwood Ave., phone 608-222-4110; 2531 Monroe St., phone 608-231-3500; 5602

Schroeder Rd., phone 608-276-8100. There's also a Michael's in neighboring Verona, 407 W. Verona Rd., phone 608-845-8887, near the Military Ridge Bike Trail. All four Michael's are open daily 11-11 (midnight Friday and Saturday).

Before Michael's took the town by storm, **Babcock Ice Cream** from the UW Food Science Department (yes, your cone might be somebody's final exam) was in a race with the Chocolate Shoppes for the title of the town's primo dairy dessert. It's still terrific stuff. You can get it three places on the UW campus: Memorial Union, 800 Langdon St.; Union South, 227 N. Randall Ave.; and the UW Dairy Store in Babcock Hall, where it's made, 1605 Linden Dr.

Rentals

Bicycle rental is available from **Budget Bicycle**, 1230 Regent St., phone 608-251-8413; from **Yellow Jersey**, 419 State St., phone 608-257-4737; and from **Williamson Bicycle Works**, 601 Williamson St., phone 608-255-5292. All three are near bike paths and within an easy ride of lakes, the Capitol Square, and the UW campus.

Wingra Canoe & Sailing Center offers canoe, sailboat, and water bike rentals on placid Lake Wingra. 824 Knickerbocker St. (off Monroe St.); phone 608-233-5332.

The **Nau-ti-gal Restaurant** rents canoes and paddleboats on the Yahara River where it flows into the northeastern corner of Lake Mendota. You don't have to eat in order to rent boats, but the food's pretty good. 5360 Westport Dr. (off County Hwy M); phone 608-246-3130.

Cross-country ski rental is provided by **Sepp Sport**, 1805 Monroe St., phone 608-257-7956; at **Odana Golf Course**, 4635 Odana Rd., phone 608-266-4724; and at **Williamson Bicycle Works**, 601 Williamson St., phone 608-255-5292.

Where to Stay

Most attractions of interest to visitors are in the downtown-UW campus area. While there are many motels on the far east and west sides of town, this listing concentrates on accommodations that are close to the attractions you'll want to see.

Best Western Inn on the Park, 22 S. Carroll St., phone 608-257-8811 or 800-279-8811. On the Capitol Square near museums, State Street shopping, Civic Center. Hotel offers an indoor pool, whirlpool, exercise room, cable TV. Many rooms have refrigerators, some suites available, two restaurants in the hotel. Kids can play on the Capitol lawn across the street. Handicap-accessible rooms available. Children stay free with parents.

Concourse Hotel, 1 W. Dayton St.; phone 608-257-6000. One block from the Capitol Square, near State Street shopping, Civic Center, and museums. Hotel has an indoor pool, exercise room, and cable TV. Suites available, two restaurants, handicap-accessible rooms. Kids stay free with parents.

Howard Johnson Plaza Hotel, 525 W. Johnson St.; phone 608-251-5511 or 800-I-GO-HOJO. Next to UW campus, near State Street, six blocks from museums, Civic Center, Capitol Square. Hotel offers indoor pool, whirlpool, cable TV, restaurant, handicap-accessible rooms. Kids stay free with parents.

Best Western InnTowner, 2424 University Ave.; phone 608-233-8778 or 800-258-8321. At west end of UW campus, near stadium and fieldhouse. Two miles to Capitol Square, Civic Center, museums. Indoor pool, whirlpool, exercise room, cable TV, restaurant, handicap-accessible rooms. Kids stay free with parents.

The **Arbor House Bed & Breakfast**, 3402 Monroe St.; phone 608-238-2981. This B&B welcomes families with kids of any age. The beautifully restored and furnished former stagecoach inn is near Monroe Street shopping and restaurants, the UW campus and athletic venues, the UW Arboretum, and Lake Wingra, and is about three miles from the Capitol Square.

Sheraton Inn & Conference Center, 706 John Nolen Dr.; phone 608-251-2300 or 800-325-3535. Across from Dane County Coliseum; short drive to downtown, UW campus; adjoins city park with hiking trails, beach, boat launch, bike path. Indoor pool, exercise room, restaurant; suites available, refrigerators available. Kids stay free with parents.

Campers should head for **Mendota County Park**, on the northwest shore of Lake Mendota. This park has picnic areas, a boat launch ramp, and campsites with electrical hookups. The park is on County Hwy M one mile east of Middleton. For information and camping reservations, contact the Dane County Park Office, 4318 Robertson Rd, Madison 53714; phone 608-246-3896 or 608-242-4576.

Where to Eat

Dotty Dumpling's Dowry has the best burgers, fries, and milk shakes in town. Indeed, Dotty's burgers have been rated among the best in the U.S. Everything on the menu is excellent, from the sandwiches to the homemade soups and chili to the outstanding (and homemade) pies, cookies and brownies. Your kids will find happiness, and you can get a beer to go with the burger. 116 N. Fairchild St., near Capitol Square, museums, State Street; phone 608-255-3175. Open daily for lunch and dinner.

Lane's Bakery is a Madison institution. This traditional bakery produces doughnuts, sweet rolls, pies, cakes, cookies and breads and also has a restaurant, where you can have coffee and fresh bakery products or soup and sandwich. 448 S. Park St.; phone 608-256-6645. Wheelchair accessible. Open daily for breakfast and lunch.

Bluephies has a wonderful eclectic menu of breakfast entrees such as eggs, pancakes, and great pastries, plus amazing sandwiches, excellent homemade soups, and terrific salads. Nightly specials. Weekend brunch. Great for families. 2701 Monroe St.; phone 608-231-FOOD. Open daily for breakfast, lunch, and dinner.

Michael's Frozen Custard (see Treats above) also sells hot dogs, hamburgers, sandwiches, soups, and chili. Go easy on the sandwich so you can have a big dessert.

Madisonians go to **Pasqual's** for burritos, tacos, and other Mexican specialties, plus salads, soups, and desserts. Food will be spiced to your specifications. Three locations: 2534 Monroe St. (directly across from Michael's Frozen Custard), phone 608-238-4419; at 2049 Atwood Ave., phone 608-244-3142; and at 6913 University Ave., phone 608-836-6700. All three are open daily for lunch and dinner.

Monty's **Blue Plate Diner** has wonderful food. The menu is traditional diner (burgers and fries, bacon and eggs) with a few extras such as daily vegetarian specials, broiled chicken breast, and gourmet coffees. Even if you don't eat a meal there, stop in and pick up cookies, cinnamon rolls, or a piece of pie. 2089 Atwood Ave.; phone 608-244-8505. Wheelchair accessible. Open daily for breakfast, lunch, and dinner.

Ella's Deli and Ice Cream Parlor is amazing. Take an authentic Jewish deli with a 20-page menu featuring everything from lox to kosher hot dogs (plus burgers, fries, soups, and omelets) and add a 10-page dessert menu featuring dozens of homemade ice cream creations. Mix in circus decor with lots of movement (a mechanical tightrope walker rolls on a high wire above the patrons), and you've got the most popular family restaurant in Madison. Good food. Great desserts, and kids can ride the restored antique carousel during warm weather. 2902 E. Washington Ave.; phone 608-241-5291. Wheelchair accessible. Open daily for breakfast, lunch, and dinner.

Ella's Deli on State Street is the first of the two Ella's, a spot where '60s campus intellectuals used to hang out into the wee hours. The menu is the same, and the food just as good as the East Washington location, but without the circus decor. A good place to eat while roaming downtown Madison. 425 State St.; phone 608-257-8611. Open daily for breakfast, lunch, and dinner.

Everyone who visits the UW campus during warm weather eventually finds the **Memorial Union Terrace**. Choose from two cafeteria lines and take your food to the shaded lakeside terrace for duck and people watching. The food is good and the setting is wonderful. Kids can dangle their toes in the lake and feed leftover bread to the ducks. For dessert, get a cone of Babcock Ice Cream, sold at a counter in the Union lobby. 800 Langdon St.; phone 608-265-3000. Wheelchair accessible. Open daily (except during some school vacations) for breakfast, lunch, and dinner.

Another popular campus-area eatery is **Paisan's**, an excellent Italian restaurant with an extensive menu that includes salads, sandwiches, lasagna, spaghetti, and great pizza. 80 University Square; phone 608-257-3832. Wheelchair accessible. Open daily for lunch and dinner.

Antonio's is a popular Italian restaurant run by a friendly Italian family. Excellent pasta dishes of all kinds, great salads, lots of chicken, veal, and seafood dishes. 1109 S. Park St.; phone 608-251-1412. Open Tuesday-Saturday for dinner.

Essen Haus is an authentic German restaurant featuring everything you'd expect—250 brands of beer, sauerbraten, pork roast, sausages, sauerkraut, as well as salads, soups, and sandwiches. There's often an oompah band and a chance to polka. Talk your kids into trying something different. 514 E. Wilson St. (five blocks east of the Capitol Square); phone 608-255-4674. Wheelchair accessible. Open Tuesday-Saturday for lunch and dinner.

Extended Hours
Drug and Grocery Stores

Walgreens 24 hour pharmacy
2829 E. Washington Ave.
608-244-6141

Woodman's Food Market West
711 S. Gammon Rd.
608-274-8944

Woodman's Food Market East
3817 Milwaukee St.
608-244-6630

Emergency

For fire, police or ambulance, dial 911.

Tourist Information

Greater Madison Convention and Visitors Bureau
615 E. Washington Ave.
Madison, WI 53703
608-255-2537
800-373-6376
Web site http://www.visitmadison.com

Stoughton

This farm and manufacturing community 15 miles
south of Madison on Hwy 51 was settled by Norwegian
immigrants.

Things to Do

Lake Kegonsa State Park has a beach and bath house,
hiking and cross-country ski trails, boat launch ramp,
picnic area, and·campsites. A naturalist gives lectures and
leads nature walks during the summer.

2405 Door Creek Rd., (five miles north of Stoughton on County
Hwy N); phone 608-873-9695. Wheelchair accessible picnic and camping facilities. Open daily year-round. $.

Eugster's Farm Market & Petting Farm sells locally
grown seasonal produce—sweet corn, tomatoes, melons,
squash, Christmas trees, etc., plus jams, cheeses, eggs,
honey, maple syrup, and other goodies, many grown or
produced on their 314-acre farm. While you're shopping
for wholesome food, the kids can pet and feed deer,
goats, pigs, rabbits, peacocks, kittens, llamas, and other
animals. In spring, there are lots of baby animals to feed.
In October fall events include pumpkin picking, wagon
rides, and pony rides. Eugster's also has farm tours, a
picnic area, and play area.

3865 Hwy 138 (just west of Stoughton); phone 608-873-3822.
Wheelchair accessible. Open daily 10-6. $ for zoo, rides.

Events

MAY. **Syttende Mai**, May 17, is the Norwegian national
holiday, and the citizens of Stoughton go all out to
remember the old country. The festivities begin with a

20-mile foot race from Madison to Stoughton, then settle down for some serious partying with food and crafts vendors, two parades, a Norwegian costume show, performances by Norwegian dancers, and other special events. Held in downtown Stoughton the weekend closest to May 17. Call 608-873-7912 for information.

Treats

Fosdal's Home Bakery makes Norwegian delights plus terrific chocolate doughnuts and other goodies. 243 E. Main St.; phone 608-873-3073. Open 5a.m-5:30p.m. Monday-Saturday, 7-noon Sunday.

Tourist Information

Stoughton Tomorrow
532 E. Main St.
Stoughton, WI 53589
608-873-7912

Mount Horeb and Blue Mounds

These villages west of Madison off Hwy 18/151 offer many attractions and outdoor activities. Mount Horeb is known for its antique shops and Scandinavian import stores.

Things to Do

The **Military Ridge State Trail** (see Things to Do–Madison) passes through both communities.

Little Norway is a restored pioneer homestead complete with sod-roofed home, outbuildings, and chapel as well as a replica of a 12th-century Norwegian stave church that was exhibited at the 1893 World's Fair. Costumed guides explain Norwegian pioneer life. The grounds and setting are lovely, and the buildings and furnishings are well-maintained. There's a shaded picnic area and snack bar.

On County Hwy JG off Hwy 18/151 east of Blue Mounds; phone 608-437-8211. Grounds are wheelchair accessible. Open daily early May through late October. $.

Blue Mound State Park sits atop the westernmost, and highest, of two large hills known together as Blue Mounds. The park offers spectacular views of the surrounding countryside from two observation towers. On a clear day, you can see the Capitol dome in Madison. The park also has picnic areas, hiking and ski trails, naturalist hikes in summer, a swimming pool, and a campground. The Military Ridge State Trail runs along the base of Blue Mound.

One mile northwest of village of Blue Mounds on Blue Mound Rd.; phone 608-437-5711. Handicap-accessible swimming pool, picnic, and camping facilities. Open daily year-round. $.

Cave of the Mounds was discovered in 1939, when local farmers blasting for limestone revealed the cave. Hour-long tours show limestone formations created by aeons of flowing and dripping water. The cave grounds have picnic areas, snack bar, and gift shop. The Military Ridge State Trail runs just below the entrance to the grounds.

Off Hwy 18/151 just east of Blue Mounds; phone 608-437-3038. Open daily 9-7 Memorial Day weekend through Labor Day, daily 9-5 mid-March until Memorial Day weekend and Labor Day through mid-November, 9-4 weekends the rest of the year. $.

Winter Fun

Cross-country ski trails at **Blue Mound State Park** take you around the mound on groomed trails through the woods.

Tyrol Basin provides downhill skiing on 11 runs with a vertical drop of 300 feet. A small family-oriented facility, Tyrol has rentals, ski lessons, and a chalet and snack bar. Special weekend and holiday lessons for kids ages four to ten. The hill also has a popular snowboarding area. It's on County Hwy JG, off Hwy 18/151 west of Mount Horeb; mailing address 3487 Bohn Rd., Mt. Horeb 53572; phone 608-437-4135.

Where to Stay

Best Western Karakahl Inn, 1405 Business 18/151, Mt. Horeb; phone 608-437-5545. The largest and finest motel in the area, with an indoor pool, sauna, cable TV, adjacent golf course, restaurant, and spacious grounds.

Where to Eat

Schubert's Old Fashioned Cafe and Bakery really is old fashioned, with high-backed oak booths, a pressed tin ceiling and a real soda fountain. The food is old fashioned, too—good and plentiful, with wonderful doughnuts, sweet rolls, brownies and other baked goods, malts and ice cream, hamburgers and plate lunches, hearty breakfasts. 128 E. Main St., phone 608-437-3393. Open daily for breakfast, lunch, and dinner.

Mt. Horeb is blessed with a truly authentic Italian restaurant, run by a friendly family from Sicily. **Pronto Pizza/Sole e Sapori** (Sole e Sapori means "Sun and Flavor" in Italian) offers homemade pizzas, lasagna, spaghetti, and other Italian food, including terrific desserts. Something for everyone in the family, and it's all excellent. 209 E. Main St.; phone 608-437-4987. Open Tuesday-Sunday for lunch and dinner.

Tourist Information

Mount Horeb Chamber of Commerce
Box 84
Mount Horeb, WI 53572
608-437-5914

3

Southeastern Gateway

Including Beloit, Janesville, Delavan, Lake Geneva, Fontana, Williams Bay, Waterford, East Troy, Burlington, Racine, and Kenosha

Many travelers rush through this area on the extensive Interstate system on their way to somewhere else. Indeed, I-94, I-90, and I-43 make travel through the region a snap. But those who hurry through miss the many family activities the area has to offer. Here you can see medieval sword play, watch a truck assembly line, fish for lunker salmon, enjoy the antics of the national champion water ski team, or stay in a luxury lakeside resort where the whole family is pampered and entertained.

Janesville and Beloit

These historic Rock River industrial cities, which together have a population of 88,000, are easily accessible via I-90, which touches the eastern edge of each.

Things to Do

As befits cities best known for factories, the **General Motors Assembly Plant** tour is one of the featured attractions in the area. And it is definitely worth going out of your way for. The plant makes light and medium duty trucks. The giant machines that move the truck bodies, the robots, and the noise and activity of the assembly line keep kids engrossed through the entire one-hour tour.

1000 Industrial Ave., Janesville; phone 608-756-7681. Tours at 9:30 and 1 Monday-Thursday when the plant is in operation. Because there are irregular shutdowns for holidays and to retool for model changes, be sure to call in advance. Free.

Kids who tour the **Wisconsin Wagon Company** can watch coaster wagons, scooters, sleds, and other wooden toys being made. There's no crashing machinery here, and no robots, but you can buy the kids toys to take home.

507 Laurel Ave., Janesville; phone 608-754-0026. Tours 8-4 Monday-Friday. Free.

The **Rock Aqua-Jays** are a ten-time national champion water ski team. They're good. They perform acrobatics, pyramids, barefoot skiing, jumping, trick skiing, and other exciting acts. Don't miss the show if you're in the area.

Shows at Traxler Park, on N. Parker Dr. (Hwy 51) in Janesville; phone 800-48-PARKS. Shows at 7 p.m. every Wednesday and Sunday Memorial Day through July, and 6:30 p.m. in July and August. Free.

Janesville has an extensive park system. One of the best and largest city parks is **Rockport Park**, which has picnic areas, playgrounds, a large swimming pool, wading pool, hiking and ski trails, and soccer fields.

2801 Rockport Rd. west of downtown; phone 608-755-3035. Open daily year-round. $ for swimming.

Beloit's **Riverside Park** winds along the Rock River downtown. In addition to walking paths, tennis courts, and picnic areas, there's a major playground called Turtle Island which has a shipwreck theme, and features a tree house and a lookout tower.

Along Hwy 51 downtown; phone 608-364-2890. Open daily year-round, Turtle Island open April through November. Free.

The **Beloit Snappers**, a farm club of the Milwaukee Brewers, play Class A professional baseball from April through August at Pohlman Field in Telfer Park, 2301 Skyline Dr. For schedule and ticket information, contact the Snappers at Box 855, Beloit; phone 608-362-2272.

Winter Fun

The **Janesville Ice Arena** offers public indoor ice skating. Skate rentals, a pro shop and a changing area are available. 821 Beloit Ave., Janesville; phone 608-755-3015. If you prefer outdoor ice skating, try the **Traxler Park Lagoon**, on N. Main St., Janesville. Rink hours are 4:30–9 weekdays and noon-9 weekends. The park has a warming house, skate rentals, and a concession stand.

In Beloit, ice skating is offered outdoors on the **Riverside Park Lagoon** and indoors at **Edwards Ice Arena** located at 2101 Cranston Rd. Call the city parks department, phone 608-364-2890, for information about both.

More than 25 miles of groomed cross-country ski trails are provided in Janesville city parks. **Rockport Park** (2801 Rockport Dr.) has good beginner-intermediate trails.

In Beloit, **Big Hill Park**, off Hwy D north of downtown, has groomed trails for both beginner and experienced cross-country skiers. Maps available from the parks department, 608-364-2890.

Events

JULY. During **Riverfest**, Beloit pulls out all the stops to celebrate life along the Rock River. There's continuous live music, a large carnival, a children's stage, a farmers market, games and sporting events, and plenty of food booths. Four days during the middle of July in Riverside Park downtown. For information, contact the Beloit Convention and Visitors Bureau (see Tourist Information below).

Where to Stay

Best Western Janesville Motor Lodge, 3900 Milton Ave. (Hwy 26 and I-90); phone 608-756-4511 or 800-334-4271. Comfortable rooms, indoor pool and whirlpool, games area, cable TV, refrigerators available, restaurant.

Ramada Inn, 3431 Milton Ave. (Hwy 26), Janesville; phone 608-756-2341 or 800-433-7787. Standard Ramada with indoor pool, whirlpool, exercise room, game room, cable TV, restaurant.

Emergency

In Janesville and Beloit, for fire, police, or ambulance, dial 911.

Tourist Information

Beloit Convention and Visitors Bureau
1003 Pleasant St.
Beloit, WI 53511
608-365-4838
800-423-5648

Forward Janesville Visitor Information Center
51 S. Jackson St.
Janesville, WI 53545
Open 8-5 Monday through Friday
608-757-3160
800-48-PARKS

Delavan

This historic city of 6,000 was, in the last half of the 19th century, the headquarters and winter quarters of a number of traveling circuses. You'll see reminders of the circus as you drive through town on Hwy 11.

Things to Do

Fantasy Hills Ranch offers horseback riding through 65 acres of rolling hills and woodlands as well as pony rides for younger children and horse-drawn wagon and sleigh rides. They also have a free petting zoo.

4978 Town Hall Rd. (at intersection with Hwy 67), Delavan; phone 414-728-1773. Open daily, call for reservations. $.

For a summer play break, head for **Horton Park**, on Hwy 11 on the east edge of Delavan. There's a beach with lifeguard and bath house, plus a playground and picnic area. Open daily. Free.

Rentals

Lake Lawn Lodge Marina rents fishing boats, ski boats, paddle boats, canoes, sailboats, wave-runners, and pontoons, and they offer charter cruises on Delavan Lake. In Lake Lawn Lodge, on Hwy 50 east of Delavan. You need not be a Lake Lawn guest to rent boats. Phone 414-728-7950 or 800-338-5253, ext. 2935.

Where to Stay

Lake Lawn Lodge, Hwy 50 East, Delavan; phone 414-728-7950 or 800-338-5253. A complete luxury resort with more than two miles of shoreline on Lake Delavan. Lake Lawn has everything: tennis, swimming in the lake or indoor or outdoor pools, health club, game room, cross-country skiing, ice skating, golf, boat rental, horseback riding, a petting zoo, miniature golf, cable TV, VCR and movie rentals, restaurants, shops, a beauty salon, an airstrip, and lots of pampering. A special plus for families is the children's activity program. This program for kids 4-12 has organized activities such as games, hikes, and crafts Monday-Saturday in summer and on winter weekends. An outstanding resort on beautiful grounds.

Where to Eat

Traveler Restaurant has wonderful homemade cinnamon rolls and other bakery items, plus a large sandwich menu and full dinners. Good food, circus decor. 319 Walworth Ave. (Hwy 11); phone 414-728-6919. Open daily for breakfast, lunch and dinner.

Millie's Pancake Haus is famous for crepes, potato pancakes, Swedish pancakes, and many other breakfast treats as well as her wonderful, hearty Pennsylvania Dutch meals. Children's menu. N2484 County Hwy O at South Shore Dr., south of Delavan; phone 414-728-2434. Open for breakfast and lunch: daily in July and August; Tuesday-Sunday rest of the year, except open Saturdays and Sundays only in January and February.

Tourist Information

Delavan-Delavan Lake Chamber of Commerce
52 E. Walworth Ave.
Delavan, WI 53115
414-728-5095
800-624-0052

Lake Geneva, Fontana, and Williams Bay

These three historic resort communities are strung around 5,300-acre Lake Geneva, which for more than a century has drawn vacationers with its lovely shoreline and deep, cool waters. Though the permanent population of the Lake Geneva communities is less than 10,000, hundreds of thousands of visitors come to vacation for a few hours or a few weeks every summer. Hwy 12 brings most visitors to the area.

Things to Do

Enjoy the lake. Though most of the lakeshore is privately owned, there are several excellent local parks. The **Lake Geneva Municipal Beach** at the foot of Broad Street has a lifeguard but no bath house. The park also has picnic areas and lots of room to romp. There are plenty of restaurants nearby. There's a park with playgrounds and tennis courts just two blocks from the beach at the corner of Cook and Geneva streets. At the other end of the lake, the **Fontana Municipal Beach** has a beautiful sand beach with lifeguards, rest rooms, and changing facilities. Restaurants and a picnic area are adjacent to the beach, and there's a playground one block north. The **Williams Bay Municipal Beach** stretches along the lake next to Geneva Street. The beach has lifeguards, bath houses, picnic areas, and playgrounds, and there are restaurants close by. The municipal beaches all charge a fee for swimming. Playground and picnic areas are free.

Geneva Lake Cruise Lines offers sightseeing tours on the lake on restored or recreated turn-of-the-century paddlewheeler, lake steamers and yachts. Tours range from one to two and one-half hours, and some include lunch, brunch, or dinner. Kids may prefer the ice cream social cruise, or the mailboat cruise, during which the mail is actually delivered to lakeside homes by an agile mail carrier who jumps on and off the boat as it slowly makes its way around the lake.

All cruises depart the Riviera Docks at the foot of Broad St. in Lake Geneva; mailing address Box 68, Lake Geneva; phone 414-248-6206 or

800-558-5911. Cruises daily May 1 through October. Reservations recommended for meal cruises and for the mailboat. $.

Yerkes Observatory contains the largest refracting telescope in the world. (A refracting telescope uses a lens to gather light, while a reflecting telescope uses mirrors.) The 40-inch lens in the Yerkes telescope is the largest ever used for astronomical observations. Tours of this wonderful building, built in the 1890s for the University of Chicago, are offered weekly throughout the year. While you cannot look through the telescope, the 45-minute tour includes a walk through the unheated dome in which it is housed, an explanation of what the telescope is used for, and easy to understand information about astronomical research.

373 W. Geneva St.(Hwy 67) in Williams Bay; mailing address Box 258, Williams Bay, WI 53191; phone 414-245-5555. Tours 10, 11, and noon Saturdays year-round. Free, donation appreciated.

The **Lake Geneva Raceway** features regional stock car, mini-Indy car, 4X4 truck racing, and motocross racing throughout the summer. It's noisy, exciting and fast. Kids love it.

On Bloomfield Rd. off County Hwy H south of Lake Geneva; phone 414-248-8566. Auto racing Saturday nights mid-April through September, motocross racing Friday nights early May through August. $.

Shopping

Lake Geneva is full of galleries, antique shops, and boutiques. Not the sort of thing to get the kids interested in a shopping excursion. They might be willing to stop at **Allison Wonderland**, which is chock full of imported toys and games and stuffed animals and other wonderful things. Allison is at 720 Main St. in Lake Geneva; phone 414-248-6500. Open 10-5 Monday-Friday, 11-5 Saturday and Sunday.

The Book Buffet has an excellent selection of children's books plus puppets, audio tapes, and other gifts. The place to find beach reading for the kids. 152 Center St., just off Main St. in Lake Geneva; phone 414-248-8994. Open 9:30-6 Monday-Friday, 9:30-4:30 Saturday, noon-4 Sunday.

Treats

The entire shore of Lake Geneva is ringed with bakeries, candy stores, and ice cream parlors, so you can be sure you're never far from sugar. The best homemade candies come from **Kilwin's Chocolates**, 772 Main St., at the corner of Main and Broad streets in Lake Geneva; phone 414-248-4400. Kilwin's also makes their own ice cream. Delicious.

Rentals

Marina Bay Boat Rentals will rent you a motorboat, jet ski, or pontoon boat. At the dock at the Harbor Cove Resort and Wrigley Dr., Lake Geneva; phone 414-248-4477.

Gordy's Lakefront Marine rents ski boats and sailboats, and gives water ski lessons. On Lake Ave., Fontana; phone 414-275-2163.

Where to Stay

Harbor Cove Resort Hotel, 300 Wrigley Dr., Lake Geneva; phone 414-248-9181. Across the street from the lake, very nice rooms, amenities include an indoor pool, whirlpool and sauna, outdoor pool, exercise room, video game room, cable TV, restaurant with great lake view. Easy walk to cruise line, parks, restaurants, downtown Lake Geneva.

The Cove, 111 Center St., Lake Geneval phone 414-249-9460 or 800-547-2683). Across the street from the lake, this all-suite luxury hotel offers fireplaces, whirlpools, TV and VCR in all suites, plus cooking facilities. The hotel features indoor and outdoor pools and whirlpools, a fitness center, tennis and basketball courts, and an adjoining restaurant. Short walk to the cruise lines, parks, restaurants, and downtown Lake Geneva.

Interlaken Resort & Country Spa, W4240 Hwy 50, Lake Geneva; phone 414-248-9121. A luxury resort on Lake Como, a small lake just north of Lake Geneva. Lodging choices range from villas with fully equipped kitchens to single rooms in the main lodge. Indoor and outdoor pools, exercise room, video game room, tennis courts, rental boats and bicycles, cross-country ski trails, cable TV, restaurant.

The Abbey, on Hwy 67, Fontana; mailing address Box 60, Fontana, WI 53125; phone 414-275-6811. A luxury resort with excellent rooms and townhouses. Indoor and outdoor pools, marina with rental boats, tennis courts, rental bicycles, exercise room, cable TV, VCR and movie rentals, restaurants, close to the municipal beach and playground. Special activities for children offered throughout the year. Special kids movies on weekends.

Chippewa Resort, 55 N. Walworth Ave., Williams Bay, WI 53191; phone 414-245-9566. One- and two-bedroom log housekeeping cottages on Lake Geneva. Beach, rowboats, boat dock, TV, air conditioning. Short walk to restaurants, municipal beach, playground.

The **Grand Geneva Resort & Spa**, 7036 Grand Geneva Way (off Hwys 12 and 50 east of Lake Geneva); phone 414-248-8811 or 800-558-3417. A resort with everything, set on 1300 rolling and wooded acres east of the hustle and bustle of Lake Geneva. Private lake, ski hill, riding stables, two golf courses, indoor and outdoor pools, biking and hiking trails, and a big sports center with indoor and outdoor tennis courts, exercise rooms, and other activities. There's even a private airstrip serving this 355-room resort. (And they're really well-appointed rooms.) Plus there's a full schedule of children's activities such as hikes, movies, swimming, arts and crafts, and hayrides. The kids can enjoy themselves all day while you enjoy yourself.

Where to Eat

Annie's Ice Cream Parlor & Restaurant serves up 40 flavors of ice cream, plus sandwiches, salads, and plenty of other choices from her extensive menu. Children's menu. 712 Main St., Lake Geneva; phone 414-248-1933. Open daily for lunch and dinner.

Olympic Restaurant serves Italian and Greek specialties as well as traditional American food. Homemade pizza, a large sandwich menu and many kid staples such as burgers, spaghetti and chicken. This modestly priced, family-owned restaurant is hardly ever crowded. 748 Main St., Lake Geneva; phone 414-248-6541. Open daily for breakfast, lunch and dinner.

Lake Aire Restaurant caters to families, with a large menu of all the standards—eggs, pancakes, burgers, chicken, beef, soups and sandwiches. Modest prices. Corner of Main and Broad streets, Lake Geneva; phone 414-248-9913. Open daily for breakfast, lunch and dinner.

Emergency

For fire, police or ambulance, dial 911.

Tourist Information

Geneva Lake Area Chamber of Commerce
201 Wrigley Dr.
Lake Geneva, WI 53147
414-248-4416

Burlington, East Troy, and Waterford

I-43 takes you to East Troy, Hwy 11 runs through Burlington, and Hwys 20 and 36 meet in Waterford.

Things to Do

East Troy has been a commuter suburb of Milwaukee for a long time. In the early 1900s, it was the last stop on the inter-urban electric rail line. The **East Troy Electric Railroad** has restored a number of the cars that used to run between East Troy and Milwaukee and operates them over a six-mile stretch of track. Trains run to the Elegant Farmer, a large farm market with pick-your-own fields. Take the train, have a picnic, then catch another train back. The museum also has displays of trolley history, and you may go to the trolley barn and watch restoration work in progress.

2002 Church St. off the town square; phone 414-642-3263, or 414-542-5573. Museum open 11-5 Saturdays and Sundays from Memorial Day weekend through third week of October. Also open Wednesday, Thursday, and Friday mid-June through mid-August. Call for train ride schedules. $.

The **Hoppe Homestead Farm** has been in the Hoppe family since 1866. This 400-acre working farm offers visitors a glimpse of real farm life, with a tour and explanation of farm operations, a chance to pet and feed farm animals, and a cow milking demonstration (you can try too). A pony ride and horse-drawn wagon ride completes the day. The farm offers wonderful homemade breakfasts on Sundays from April through December.

33701 Hill Valley Drive, Waterford; phone 414-534-6480. Tours daily April through October (except closed Mondays July through September). $.

Rausch's Bear Den is a small but very well run game farm and petting zoo. The lions and tigers and bears are family pets, as are the goats, rabbits, monkeys, deer, and other animals, many of which kids can feed and pet. Spring is an especially good time to visit; there are lots of baby animals then.

6831 Big Bend Rd. (Hwy 164), Waterford, WI 53185; phone 414-895-6430. Open 11-5 weekends early May through October, weekdays by appointment. $.

Green Meadows Farm lets kids learn about farm animals and how farmers care for them. Visitors get a two-hour guided tour of the 80-acre farm, including milking demonstrations, a pony ride, and a chance to pet pigs, goats, sheep, and the other animals. A hayride rounds out the experience. The farm has a snack bar and large shaded picnic area.

On Hwy 20 between Waterford and East Troy; mailing address Box 182, Waterford, WI 53185; phone 414-534-2891. Wheelchair accessible. Open early May through October with a few periods when the farm is closed. Call for hours and tour times. $.

The **Aquaducks** put on a terrific water ski show complete with all the standards—jumping, pyramids, barefooting, and tricks. On Brown's Lake at Fischer Park off Hwy 11 in Burlington. Phone 414-763-9094. Shows every Saturday and holidays Memorial Day weekend through Labor Day. Free.

Winter Fun

Alpine Valley downhill ski area has a dozen runs on its 388-foot hill. The hill has rentals, lessons, a ski shop, game room, restaurant, cafeterias and pizza parlor, plus lodging. Special KinderKIDS ski lessons daily for kids under eight, and weekend ski schools for kids seven to twelve. At County Hwy D and Townline Rd. (take Hwy 120 south from East Troy to D, then west); mailing address Box 615, East Troy, WI 53120; phone 414-642-7374, or 800-227-9395.

Treats

J. Lauber's Old Fashioned Ice Cream Parlor is just what it says. An authentic 1920s ice cream parlor that features 20 flavors of malts, a giant ice cream menu, and a huge candy selection in case you don't get enough sugar in the sundae you just ordered. In East Troy on Church Street next to the East Troy Electric Railroad Museum; phone 414-642-3679. Open daily except Monday in warm weather.

Events

MAY. Burlington is the home of a Nestle chocolate factory, so it's only fitting that the city should honor that dark confection. The annual **Chocolate City Festival** includes a chocolate tasting tent, entertainment, carnival, children's activities, a parade, bike rides, arts and crafts, and other fun. Held the third weekend in May throughout Burlington. For information, contact the Burlington Chamber of Commerce (see Tourist Information below).

Tourist Information

Burlington Chamber of Commerce
112 E. Chestnut St.
Burlington, WI 53105
414-763-6044.

East Troy Chamber of Commerce
Welcome center on the square downtown
414-642-3770

Racine

An industrial and commercial city of 83,000 on the shore of Lake Michigan, Racine has excellent beaches and parks.

Things to Do

The heart of Racine is the city's downtown **lakefront marina and festival park** development. The area has playgrounds and playing fields, a festival center for concerts and special events, a marina and boat launch ramp, and restaurants.

Festival park on the lake at the foot of Lake Ave., marina at the end of the Fourth Street Causeway. Festival Park open year-round. Call the Convention & Visitors Bureau (see below) for calendar of events at the festival park.

North Beach city park has one of the finest public beaches on Lake Michigan. The mile-long white sand beach has lifeguards, a bath house and concession stand, and the park has picnic areas and playgrounds.

100 Kewaunee St., off Michigan Blvd. just north of downtown; phone 414-636-9233. Park open year-round, lifeguards mid-June through late August. Free.

A few blocks north of the beach is the **Racine Zoo**. Though small, the zoo is well-maintained and landscaped, with picnic areas and playgrounds as well as ducks and geese to feed.

2131 Main St.; phone 414-636-9189. Wheelchair accessible. Open daily 9-8 Memorial Day through Labor Day, 9-4:30 rest of year. Free.

Racine is the home of many **Lake Michigan charter fishing boats**. The captains will take you out for a full or half day of fishing for trout and salmon. They provide all the equipment and know-how, and they'll even clean your catch. For information, contact Fishing Charters of Racine, Box 1393, Racine; phone 414-633-6113 or 800-475-6113.

The **Golden Rondelle Theater** was originally built for the S.C. Johnson Company for the 1964 World's Fair. After the Fair it was moved to Racine and is now used to show a number of breath-taking documentary films such as the award-winning "On the Wing," about the beauty of flight. Visitors ages 14 and older can also tour the adjoining Johnson Wax Administration Building, designed by Frank Lloyd Wright.

1525 Howe St.; phone 414-631-2154. Films and building tours 10-3 Tuesday-Friday. All ages welcome for the films. Free.

See top-notch drag racing at **Great Lakes Dragaway**, on County Hwy KR in Union Grove, just west of Racine. Kids love the noise and speed.

Drag races Tuesday, Wednesday, Thursday, Friday, Saturday, Sunday, and holidays from mid-April through October. Phone 414-878-3783. $.

Winter Fun

The lakeside **festival park** has an outdoor ice skating rink, a warming shelter and snack bar. Downtown at the end of Lake St.; phone 414-636-9229.

River Bend Nature Center has four miles of groomed cross-country ski trails for beginner and intermediate skiers. The center has a main lodge, ski rental and lessons with pre-registration. 3600 N. Green Bay Rd. (off Hwy 38 north of downtown); phone 414-639-0930.

Events

JUNE. The **Racine Air Show** is one of the largest in the Midwest. Military, vintage, and aerobatic aircraft meet at the Racine airport for two days of displays, demonstrations, aerobatics, and family activities. This is the place to see wing walkers, stunt pilots, and skydivers, or take the kids through the space shuttle. At Batten Field in Racine. Call the Convention and Visitors Bureau (see below) for details.

JULY. Racine hosts one of the state's largest **Fourth of July festivals**, featuring a huge parade with over 140 floats, bands, clowns, and various other participants celebrating the day. Following the parade there are other activities throughout the day, culminating in lakeside fireworks in the evening. Crowded but fun. The parade is on Main Street, the fireworks are set off near the festival park a few blocks away. For information, contact the Convention & Visitors Bureau (see below).

Treats

Racine was settled by Danes, who brought with them their love of pastry. The city is the midwestern (and perhaps national) center for kringle making. Kringle is a flaky, oval pastry that comes with a variety of fillings and toppings. Delicious. Some of the best Racine kringlemakers are:

Lehmann's Bakery, 2210 Sixteenth St.; phone 414-632-2359

Larsen Bakery, 3311 Washington Ave. (Hwy 20); phone 414-633-4298

Bendtsen Bakery, 3200 Washington Ave. (Hwy 20); phone 414-633-0365

Where to Stay

Racine Marriott Hotel, 7111 Washington Ave. (Hwy 20); phone 414-886-6100 or 800-228-9290. Just off I-90 several miles west of downtown. Excellent rooms, indoor pool, game room, exercise room, cable TV, restaurant and lounge.

Radisson Harborwalk Racine, 223 Gaslight Circle (downtown at the harbor); phone 414-632-7777 or 800-333-3333. The newest and most luxurious motel in Racine, this lakeside motel features an indoor pool, whirlpool, cable TV and free movies, free continental breakfast, and a restaurant. Whirlpool suites available.

Holiday Inn, 3700 Northwestern Ave. (Hwy 38); phone 414-637-9311, or 800-HOLIDAY. Northwest of downtown on the Root River. Outdoor pool, video game room, guest passes to nearby YMCA for use of indoor pool and exercise facilities, coin laundry, cable TV, picnic area along the river, restaurant.

Where to Eat

The **Chartroom** has a traditional menu that's heavy on sandwiches, chicken, and steaks. It has a children's menu, and it's on the Root River at the harbor, so kids can watch the boats going past while waiting for their food. 209 Dodge St.; phone 414-632-9901. Open daily for lunch and dinner.

Apple Holler Restaurant is best known for their giant country-style breakfasts, but their sandwiches and full dinners are good, too. Hearty food, and plenty of it. 5006 S. Sylvannia Ave. (the west frontage road for I-94), near the County Hwy KR exit; phone 414-886-8500. Open daily for breakfast, lunch, and dinner.

Emergency

For fire, police, or ambulance, dial 911.

Tourist Information

Racine County Convention & Visitors Bureau
345 Main St.
Racine, WI 53403
414-634-3293
800-C-RACINE

Kenosha

This industrial and port city of 77,000 is most easily reached via I-94.

Things to Do

The Kenosha lakefront is dotted with a series of parks along the shore. **Simmons Island Park** has picnic and playground areas, bike paths, and a beach with lifeguards on duty from mid-June through mid-August. Downtown at the foot of 50th Street. Free.

Kenosha's **Lake Michigan charter boats** will take you for a half or full day of fishing for trout and salmon on the big lake. The captains supply all the equipment and they'll clean your catch. For a list of captains, contact the Kenosha Area Convention & Visitors Bureau (see Tourist Information below), or call the Kenosha Charter Boat Association at 800-522-6699.

Bong Recreation Area is a 4,500-acre oasis of green in the most heavily populated corner of the state. The area has facilities for just about every imaginable activity, including flying model airplanes, hang gliding, ATV and motocross trails, and horseback riding, as well as swimming, hiking and ski trails, picnic areas, campgrounds, and a nature program that's offered year-round.

Fifteen miles west of Kenosha on Hwy 142; mailing address 26313 Burlington Rd., Kansasville, WI 53139; phone 414-652-0377 or 414-878-5600. Handicap-accessible picnic facilities. Open daily year-round. $.

Dairyland Greyhound Park is the largest greyhound race park in the U.S. Kids can watch the dogs preparing for the next race and can get close to the track as the dogs speed along. (But they can't bet on the dogs until they're 18.) The track has snack bars and restaurants, gift shop, and indoor and outdoor seating. Kids under 12 are not allowed at the evening races but can accompany their parents to the afternoon races.

At I-94 and Hwy 158; phone 414-657-8200 or 800-233-3357. Wheelchair accessible. Racing year-round. Call for schedule. $.

Congo River Adventure Golf has 18 holes of challenging miniature golf. You'll face waterfalls, ponds, rocks, and vicious animals. If you tire of the outdoors, there's a video games arcade for after your golf game. On 120th Ave. at the intersection of I-94 and Hwy 50; phone 414-857-7888. Open daily May through October. $.

Action Territory features miniature golf, a video games arcade, go-karts, batting cages, a ferris wheel, a miniature train, and other fun stuff. On 120th Ave. at the intersection of I-94 and Hwy 50; phone 414-857-7000. Open daily May through October. $.

Winter Fun

Bong Recreation Area provides 13 miles of groomed cross-country ski trails, most of which are for novice or intermediate skiers. Bong also has 10 miles of snowmobile trails that connect to a larger county system.

Wilmot Mountain downhill ski area has 25 runs on its 230-foot-high hill. The mountain has rentals, lessons, a ski shop, restaurant and pizza parlor. Twenty miles west of Kenosha on County Hwy W; mailing address Box 177, Wilmot, WI 53192; phone 414-862-2301.

The **Kenosha County Ice Arena** is an outstanding indoor ice skating facility. Skate rental and concessions. 7727 60th Ave., Kenosha; phone 414-694-8010.

Events

JUNE-AUGUST. The **Bristol Renaissance Faire** recreates an English country fair of the 1500s, with authentically costumed townspeople, entertainers, knights, knaves and royalty. There's jousting, storytelling, puppets, jugglers, minstrels, sword fights, and much more, including a special kids area. Food, arts, and crafts are also in abundance. One of the best events in Wisconsin. Held 10-7 every weekend from late June through mid-August on the Faire grounds at I-94 and Hwy Q near the Wisconsin-Illinois line; phone 414-396-4320 or 847-395-7773. $.

Shopping

Kenosha is home to two large outlet malls that attract shoppers by the busload from throughout the region. **Lakeside Marketplace** features more than 50 stores with designer clothing, toys, glassware and crystal, cookware and leather goods. Stores include Oshkosh B'Gosh, Genuine Kids, Hanes Kids, and such designers as Liz Claiborne, Harve Benard, and Anne Klein. At I-94 and County Hwy Q (exit 347); phone 414-857-2101; open daily. The **Factory Outlet Center** has 110 stores featuring clothing, shoes, food, home furnishings, toys, books, and jewelry. Stores include Carter's Childrenswear, Toy Liquidators, Kids Express, and adult stores including American Tourister, Van Heusen, Eddie Bauer, and the Company Store. The Factory Outlet Center adjoins Congo River Golf and Action Territory. You can shop while the kids play. At I-94 and Hwy 50 (exit 344); phone 414-857-7961. Open daily.

Treats

Many Kenoshans are of Italian heritage, and **Tenuta's** provides everything they need to carry on their traditions. This wonderful Old World deli, grocery store, and carry-out features an outdoor cafe serving Italian sausage and brats. Inside, there are aisles of cheese, breads, pastries, pasta, salads, and wine and beer. This is the place to buy your picnic supplies. Then drive a couple miles east to the lakeside parks for a fun afternoon. 3203 52nd St., Kenosha; phone 414-657-9001. Open daily.

Where to Stay

Holiday Inn, 5125 Sixth Ave.; phone 414-658-3281 or 800-465-4329. Downtown on the harbor, near lakeside parks. Facilities in the 110-room motel include an indoor pool, whirlpool and sauna, game room, exercise room, cable TV, and a restaurant.

Emergency

For fire, police or ambulance, dial 911.

Tourist Information

Kenosha Area Convention & Visitors Bureau
800 55th St.
Kenosha, WI 53140
414-654-7307
800-654-7309

4

Milwaukee and Vicinity

Including Eagle, Waukesha, Oconomowoc, Hartland, Hartford, and Cedarburg

Milwaukee, with a population of 600,000, is by far Wisconsin's largest city. And this metropolitan area of more than 1.5 million offers all the attractions and excitement of the big city—culture, museums, dining, and shopping. Milwaukee is also one of the most beautiful cities in America, with thousands of acres of parklands, carefully tended municipal gardens, and the beautiful, and largely public, Lake Michigan shoreline.

Family activities in the Milwaukee area are virtually endless, and of high quality. The zoo, the Public Museum, the symphony, and the park system are considered among the finest in the U.S. The city is on the move year-round, so there's always plenty to do: spectator sports ranging from bocce to professional hockey; boating, biking, ice skating, skiing; spectacular toy stores; top professional theater; cow judging and carnival rides at the state fair; circus wagons on parade; and much more.

Milwaukee is easily accessible to travelers via I-94 from the south and west, I-43 from the southwest and north, and U.S. Hwys 41 and 45, which run north-south through the city. Many visitors arrive by scheduled airline at General Mitchell Field, the largest airport in Wisconsin, with dozens of flights daily. Amtrak also provides daily rail passenger service to downtown Milwaukee.

Things to Do

This listing is arranged geographically, with attractions and activities in Milwaukee and adjacent communities first, then a listing of attractions in outlying areas.

Whatever else you do while in Milwaukee, be sure to take time to visit the **Milwaukee Public Museum**, one of the largest and finest natural history museums in the U.S. Kids love the exhibits, many of which are enlivened with sound tracks and movement. Favorites with kids are the dinosaur and early mammal exhibits, including full size replicas and the largest dinosaur skull yet found, and the rain forest exhibit, which faithfully recreates a Costa Rican rain forest, right down to the bugs. Other exhibits are about Wisconsin woodlands, the Streets of Old Milwaukee, the oceans, and human cultures around the world. The Curiosity Zone and Exploration Station are special sections with hands-on exhibits and interactive exhibits for kids. The museum has great gift shops, including one just for kids, plus a restaurant (lunch only).

800 W. Wells St., downtown; phone 414-278-2702. Wheelchair accessible; wheelchairs and strollers available; braille tours available. Open daily 9-5 (closed July 4, Thanksgiving, Christmas). $.

Also in the Public Museum complex is **Discovery World**, a hands-on museum of science and technology just for kids. Exhibits teach kids about electricity, lasers, artificial hearts, gears and levers, computers, gyroscopes, mirrors and lenses, and dozens of other subjects. And they love learning, because they get to move, bend, push and play with everything. There are also special shows about electricity and lasers. Kids of all ages can find something to enjoy here, but most exhibits are geared to kids 6 and over.

800 W. Wells St.; phone 414-765-0777. Wheelchair accessible. Open 9-5 Monday-Saturday, 11-5 Sunday. $ for ages 6 and up.

The third attraction in the Public Museum complex is the **Humphrey IMAX Theater**, with its 7,500-square-foot screen and a six-channel surround-sound audio system. The changing 45-minute features include trips to Mars, a dive beneath the ocean, a helicopter flight over Milwaukee, and many other you-are-there sorts of films. And you really do feel that you're part of the action.

800 W. Wells St.; phone 414-278-2700 (information) and 414-319-4629 (reservations). Shows every hour on the half hour, 11:30-4:30 Sunday-Wednesday, 11:30-8:30 Thursday-Saturday. $.

The **Betty Brinn Children's Museum** offers lots of hands-on exnibits and activities for kids ages 1-10. Kids can crawl through a giant human ear, captain a sailing ship, play doctor, or spend some time in the arts and crafts area. In summer, special weekend programs and a summer camp are offered.

929 E. Wisconsin Ave., at the lakefront downtown; phone 414-291-0888. Open 9-5 Tuesday-Saturday, noon-5 Sunday. Children must be accompanied by an adult. $.

The **International Clown Hall of Fame**, recently relocated from Delavan to Milwaukee, is a tribute to circuses and to clowning. Exhibits include clown costumes, clown and circus posters and paintings, a Red Skelton exhibit, and the Hall of Fame, honoring 29 world-famous clowns. In addition to the exhibits, there's a 45-minute clown show featuring juggling, magic tricks, and, of course, balloon animals. Guided tours are offered for groups and you can call and join an already-scheduled group.

161 W. Wisconsin Ave., in the Plankington Arcade of the Grand Avenue Mall; phone 414-319-0848. Open 10-4 Monday-Saturday, noon-4 Sunday. Call for information about group tours and for clown show schedule. $.

In addition to the Public Museum, the other Milwaukee must-see is the **Milwaukee County Zoo**, which is one of the top zoos in the world. Exhibits are designed to present animals in a natural setting, without bars, with room to move comfortably, and with animals from the same area of the world. The zoo is spread around the 184-acre grounds, with lots of trees and open spaces between the animal exhibits, allowing plenty of room for picnic areas and open space. In addition to the thousands of animals ranging from lions and tigers and bears to tiny lizards, the  zoo has a farm area where kids can learn about farm animals and watch cows being milked. The zoo offers pony and camel rides, a miniature train that travels around the grounds, and a zoomobile, which provides 20-minute narrated tours of the grounds. There's a sea lion show and special summer animal events and lectures. The zoo has a restaurant, plus snack bars located throughout the grounds, and two gift shops. The zoo offers many special family events throughout the year—a Halloween costume party, breakfast with Santa, Father's Day, and others. The zoo also has three miles of groomed cross-country ski trails and ski rental for winter visitors. Where else can you ski with camels?

10001 W. Bluemound Rd. (take I-94 west from downtown to Hwy 100, then north); phone 414-771-3040 or 414-256-5412. Wheelchair accessible; child and adult stroller rental available. Open 9-5 Monday-Saturday and 9-6 Sundays and holidays May 1 through September, 9-4:30 daily the rest of the year. $.

Mitchell Park Conservatory, called "**The Domes**" by local residents, consists of three huge climate-controlled glass and steel domes 140 feet wide and 85 feet high. Each dome has a horticultural theme. The tropical dome houses a mini-rain forest of orchids, ferns, bamboo, and hundreds of other tropical species. The arid dome contains the palms, cacti, and other species found in deserts throughout the world. The third dome is used for the five major horticulture shows held annually. The domes are fun and educational. Mitchell Park also has beautiful outdoor gardens and plenty of room to play.

524 S. Layton Blvd.; phone 414-649-9830. Open 9-5 daily. $.

The **Milwaukee Art Museum** has a very good collection of painting, sculpture, and decorative arts with emphasis on American and European works. It's a bit static, though, and the average kid won't be excited by a trip to simply view the art. However, the museum has regular special events for kids and families, especially on Sundays, and there are also art classes, films, lectures, and other events geared to kids. So call the museum find out what's coming up for the younger set, and plan your art museum trip around that activity. The museum has a good gift shop and a wonderful restaurant that serves lunch.

750 N. Lincoln Memorial Dr., downtown at the lakefront; phone 414-224-3825. Wheelchair accessible. Open 10-5 Tuesday, Wednesday, Friday, Saturday; noon-9 Thursday; noon-5 Sunday. $.

The **Milwaukee lakefront** is one of the best public park areas in the U.S. The parks encompass the lakefront and adjoining bluffs, allowing lots of room for hiking, swimming, boating, biking, duck feeding, kite flying, frisbee playing, roller skating, and relaxing. North from the Milwaukee Art Museum are **Juneau Park** and **Veterans Park**, then **McKinley Park and Marina**, then **Bradford Beach**, with lifeguards watching over a terrific sand beach, then Lake Park. A paved bike path runs through the parks along the lake. Veterans Park offers bike and skate rental. At McKinley Marina, and at McKinley Beach, adjacent to the marina, are boat rentals. **Lake Park** has a lawn bowling area and lots of room to play in the lovely wooded area on top of the bluffs. Scenic Lincoln Memorial Drive runs along the lakeshore through the parks. For information about the parks, contact the Milwaukee County Parks Department, 414-257-6100.

Several boat tour companies offer the chance to see Milwaukee's harbor and lakefront from the water. Kids especially like going under the low bridges and seeing the huge freighters in the harbor as the tour boat travels along the river, into the harbor and out into Lake Michigan. **Celebration of Milwaukee** offers both meal and sightseeing tours on a passenger yacht (more formal than the other tour lines); **Edelweiss** offers meal cruises on two boats modeled after European river yachts; and **Iroquois Boat Line** provides 45-minute sightseeing cruises on a 150-passenger ship.

Celebration of Milwaukee, 502 N. Harbor Dr.; phone 414-278-1113. Cruises daily April through early October. $.

Edelweiss, 1110 Old World Third St.; phone 414-272-3625. Lunch, brunch, and dinner cruises daily April through October. $.

Iroquois Harbor Cruises, on Milwaukee River downtown at the Clybourn Street bridge; phone 414-332-4194. Tours twice daily late June through August. $.

Another way to view the skyline from the lake is to chase those lunker trout and salmon on a **Lake Michigan charter fishing** expedition. The lake in the Milwaukee area offers excellent fishing. Your friendly charter captain will provide all the equipment and expertise needed, and he'll even clean your catch. Trips from three hours to a full day are available.

Contact A A-hoy Lucky Boy Charters, 5600 W. Burnham St., Milwaukee; phone 414-543-9003 or 414-645-2379. Or try Jack's Charter Service, 2545 S. Delaware Ave., Milwaukee; phone 414-482-2336 or 800-858-5225 (outside Milwaukee). Or Wishin "N" Fishin, 1244 S. 34th St., Milwaukee; phone 414-835-6570.

Nature-loving kids and parents need not leave Milwaukee to find interesting nature walks, nature programs and wildlife. **Wehr Nature Center** has 200 acres of restored prairie, woodlands, wetlands, and a small lake, all linked by nature trails. There's a nature center with exhibits, and scheduled hikes, lectures, and other events throughout

the year. Wehr is in Whitnall Park, the largest of Milwaukee County's parks. Whitnall also contains Boerner Botanical Gardens, a golf course, playgrounds, picnic areas, and trails. **Schlitz Audubon Center** is on the shore of Lake Michigan, and features trails that wind along the beach, through wooded ravines, onto the bluffs, and through open fields. The nature center houses exhibits and has scheduled hikes, lectures, and other programs throughout the year.

Wehr Nature Center, 9701 W. College Ave. (take I-94 south from downtown to College Ave., then west); phone 414-425-8550. Open 8-4:30 daily. Call for schedule of special events. Free, $ for some events.

Schiltz Audubon Center, 1111 E. Brown Deer Rd. (take I-43 north from downtown to Brown Deer Rd., then east); phone 414-352-2880. Open 9-5 Tuesday-Sunday. Closed Thanksgiving weekend, Christmas Day and New Year's Day. Call for schedule of special events. $.

Milwaukee has a thriving music, dance, and theater community, and those involved in the performing arts always include offerings of interest to children. The **Milwaukee Symphony** presents a variety of programs geared to children and families, including Family Concerts, Summer Nights (outdoors in the park), Pops Concerts, and Classical Conversation Concerts. The **Milwaukee Youth Symphony** is composed of musicians ages 8 to 19 who give concerts geared to kids. The **Milwaukee Ballet** performs a wonderful *Nutcracker* each Christmas, but also gives other performances that older children will enjoy. **First Stage Milwaukee** mounts a number of plays for children each season.

The Symphony, Ballet, and First Stage all appear at the Performing Arts Center, 929 Water St., downtown. In addition, the PAC hosts many local and out-of-town performers and troupes. Contact the box office, 414-273-7206 or 800-472-4458 (WI only) for information about upcoming performances. $.

Older children will enjoy many of the plays performed by the **Milwaukee Repertory Theater**, one of the top regional theater companies in the U.S. The company presents both modern plays and the classics on their main stage and experimental theaters. The Rep presents an outstanding production of *A Christmas Carol* each December.

Theater and box office 108 E. Wells St., downtown; phone 414-224-9490. Season runs mid-September through late April. Evening and matinee performances Tuesday-Sunday. $.

The **Riverside Theater** and the **Pabst Theater** both have continuing series of performances by touring singers, musicians, comedians, dancers, theater companies, and other entertainers.

Riverside, 116 W. Wisconsin Ave., downtown; box office phone 414-224-3000. $.

Pabst, 144 E. Wells St., downtown; box office phone 414-286-3663. $.

Milwaukee has more **professional sports** teams than most cities of its size. The **Milwaukee Brewers** play American League baseball from mid-April through late September at County Stadium, off I-94 just west of downtown; phone 414-933-9000.

The **Milwaukee Bucks** pro basketball team hits the boards at the Bradley Center, as do the amateur but top-notch college players of the **Marquette University Golden Eagles**. The professional hockey players of the **Milwaukee Admirals** freeze the court before they play on it. The **Milwaukee Wave**, a professional soccer team, also plays at the Bradley Center. At 1001 N. 4th St., just north of downtown.

For ticket information:
Bucks 414-227-0500
Golden Eagles 414-288-7127
Admirals 414-227-0550
Wave 414-962-WAVE
Bradley Center ticket information 414-227-0400

Auto racing fans turn out in force at the **Milwaukee Mile** race track for top competition in Indy-car, stock car, motorcycle, and other fast and noisy racing events. Big time racing. In State Fair Park at I-94 and 84th Street west of downtown; phone 414-453-8277. Racing throughout the summer.

THINGS TO DO IN THE SUBURBS

Eagle

Take I-94 west from Milwaukee to Oconomowoc, then Hwy 67 south to this village in southwest Waukesha County.

Kettle Moraine State Forest Southern Unit covers nearly 20,000 acres of lakes, wooded hills, and undulating fields. The forest provides hiking, horseback riding, bicycling, cross-country skiing, snowmobiling, scenic auto tours, swimming, picnicking, camping, and other outdoor activities. The visitor center has a slide presentation about the forest and the glaciers that shaped the land, plus naturalist programs and hikes from April through October.

Visitor center on Hwy 59 three miles east of Eagle; mailing address S91 W39091, Hwy 59, Eagle, WI 53119; phone 414-594-6200. Handicap-accessible hiking, picnic, and camping facilities. Open daily. $ for some developed use areas.

Old World Wisconsin is one of the best outdoor historical museums in the U.S. More than 50 structures originally built by immigrants to the state have been moved here. Farm houses, barns, churches, blacksmith shops, an inn, schools, even a Finnish sauna, have been restored to their original look and have been grouped into homesteads and villages. Costumed guides work the homesteads and operate the village businesses, growing crops, raising livestock, spinning and weaving, cooking and sewing just as Wisconsin's early immigrants did. Kids can talk to the "farmers" and "innkeepers" who operate the homesteads and businesses. Visitors can walk the 576-acre grounds or take one of the trams that make regular stops throughout the park. Special events are held throughout the season—a Civil War encampment, a children's day, a theresheree, and others. In addition to the Danish, Finnish, German, Polish, and other homesteads and the Yankee village, the park has a restaurant, gift shop, and exhibit area. Bring a picnic or buy your lunch, but plan to spend several hours. Even if you take the tram around the grounds, there's a lot of walking on unpaved paths. This is not the place for strollers.

Just south of Eagle on Hwy 67; mailing address S103 W37890 Hwy 67, Eagle, WI 53119; phone 414-594-6300. Partially wheelchair accessible. Open 10-4 Monday-Friday and 10-5 Saturday-Sunday May 1 through October, except in July and August, when it's open 10-5 daily. $.

Kettle Moraine Ranch offers pony and horseback rides, including rides through parts of the Kettle Moraine State Forest, plus covered wagon rides, and a petting zoo with more than 60 farm animals to pet and feed. There's also a western town with general store, saloon, snack bar, and other traditional wild west emporiums. The ranch has special seasonal events such as an October pumpkin hunt.

W379 S9446 Hwy S, Eagle; phone 414-594-2122. Open Saturday and Sunday in April and May, daily Memorial Day weekend through November. $.

Waukesha

Take I-94 west from Milwaukee to this fast-growing suburban city of 60,000.

Waukesha is the eastern terminus of the **Glacial Drumlin State Trail**, a 51-mile trail on the bed of a former railroad right-of-way. The trail passes through a number of small towns between Waukesha and its western end in Cottage Grove, a Madison suburb. The trail is open to bicyclists, hikers, cross-country skiers, and snowmobilers.

Trailhead on McArthur Rd., off St. Paul Ave. (County Hwy X); mailing address N846 W329 County Hwy C, Delafield, WI 53018; phone 414-646-3025. Open daily. $ for bicycling.

Oconomowoc-Hartland

These small lake communities are the center of a beautiful area of lakes, summer homes, golf courses, parks, and scenic drives. Take I-94 west and exit at either Hwy 83 (Hartland) or Hwy 67 (Oconomowoc).

The **Oconomowoc City Beach Park** offers a lovely sand beach with lifeguard, picnic area, playground, boat rentals, boat launch, and snacks. There are even Wednesday evening band concerts. A perfect place to spend a warm summer afternoon with the kids.

On Lac La Belle, in the 300 block of West Wisconsin Avenue, in downtown Oconomowoc. Open daily. For information, contact the Oconomowoc Recreation Department, 414-569-2199. $ for swimming.

Honey Acres has as its star attraction a hive of bees. Actually, lots of hives, because Honey Acres produces more than two million pounds of honey annually. The museum operated by Honey Acres shows bees at work in hives (safely behind glass), and explains bee society, honey-making, and the history of beekeeping. You can sample different kinds of honey. A unique experience for kids.

On Hwy 67 twelve miles north of Oconomowoc; phone 414-474-4411. Wheelchair accessible. Open 8:30-3 daily. Free.

Kettle Moraine Railway provides 50-minute rides on a restored steam train. The area is very scenic.

On Hwy 83 five miles north of Hartland; mailing address Box 247 North Lake, WI 53064; phone 414-782-8074. Train leaves the North Lake depot Sundays at 12:30, 2, and 3 from the first Sunday in June through the third Sunday in October. Trips also run on Labor Day and on the first two Saturdays in October. $.

Hartford

Take I-94 west to Hwy 83, then north 20 miles to this picturesque community.

Hartford Heritage Auto Museum showcases the Kissel, a luxury car built in Hartford from 1906 to 1931. Also on display are more than 75 other rare, mint-condition antique cars as well as exhibits of automobile artifacts such as engines and license plates. There's also a display of vintage motorcycles and another featuring antique outboard motors. This is a look-don't-touch musuem, but for kids who like cars, it's a must-see.

147 N. Rural St., Hartford, WI 53027; phone 414-673-7999. Wheelchair accessible. Open 10-5 Monday-Saturday and noon-5 Sunday May 1 through September, closed Monday, Tuesday and holidays the rest of the year. $, kids under 8 free.

Pike Lake State Park is popular for swimming, hiking, and cross-country skiing. The scenic park also has picnic areas, a campground, and summer weekend naturalist programs and hikes.

3544 Kettle Moraine Rd., off Hwy 60 east of Hartford; phone 414-670-3400. Open daily. $.

Winter Fun

Milwaukee, of course, goes full tilt through the winter, with cultural events and most attractions open and operating. This section covers fun that's unique to winter. Downhill skiing in the Milwaukee area is offered at three nearby areas—Alpine Valley in East Troy (see Southeast

Gateway, p. 54), at Crystal Ridge in Franklin in southern Milwaukee County, and at Little Switzerland northwest of Milwaukee near Hartford.

Crystal Ridge is a small family-oriented ski area with eight runs on a 200-foot hill. The hill offers rentals and lessons and has a chalet with a cafeteria. Off 76th St. (County Hwy U); mailing address 7900 W. Crystal Ridge, Franklin, WI 53132; phone 414-529-7676.

Little Switzerland is also a family-oriented ski area with 16 runs on a 200-foot hill. The hill offers rentals and lessons and has a chalet with snack bar. Twenty miles northwest of Milwaukee on County Hwy AA off Hwy 41; mailing address 105 Hwy AA, Slinger, WI 53086; phone 414-644-5020.

Cross-country skiers should head directly to the **Milwaukee County Zoo**, which has three miles of groomed beginner and intermediate trails, rental equipment, warming shelter, and lots of animals.

There's also excellent cross-country skiing at **Old World Wisconsin** (Friday, Saturday, and Sunday only) and in Kettle Moraine State Forest Southern Unit, with 4.8 miles of groomed trails. Pike Lake State Park has more than eight miles of groomed trails. (See Things to Do above for address and phone for each.)

A number of Milwaukee County Parks have groomed cross-country ski trails. **Whitnall Park** has more than two miles of easy trails, plus rentals, lessons, and a warming house. There's also an outdoor ice skating rink and a toboggan slide (with toboggan rentals). 5879 S. 92nd St., Milwaukee; phone 414-425-7303. **Brown Deer Park** has more than four miles of groomed trails as well as a sledding hill and an outdoor ice skating rink. The park has ski rentals and a warming shelter with a snack bar. 7835 N. Green Bay Ave. (Hwy 57), Brown Deer (northwest of downtown); phone 414-352-8080 or 414-352-7502. For information about skiing and other winter activities in Milwaukee County parks, call the parks department at 414-257-6100.

The **Pettit National Ice Center** is the Olympic training facility for speed skaters. There's also public skating. In Wisconsin State Fair Park, off I-94 west of downtown (exit at 84th Street). Phone 414-266-0100.

Eble Ice Arena offers public indoor ice skating year-round, including skate rentals. It's at 19486 Bluemound Road, in Brookfield, about five miles west of the Milwaukee County Zoo (and near a Kopps Frozen Custard shop for after-skating treats). Phone 414-784-5155.

Wilson Recreation Center has indoor ice skating year-round. It's at 4001 S. 20th St. (take I-94 south from downtown to W. Howard, then west); phone 414-281-4610. The Milwaukee County Parks Department has a number of outdoor ice skating rinks each winter. Location varies depending on budgets and ongoing work at the parks. Contact the Department at 414-257-6100 for the location of outdoor rinks.

Milwaukee is alleged to have more bowling alleys per capita than any other city of its size. That may or may not be true, but bowling is a favorite Milwaukee winter pastime. The six **Red Carpet Bowling Centers** have open bowling throughout the week. Call them at 414-358-3530 for the location nearest you.

Events

DECEMBER-JANUARY. **Winterfest** goes on practically all winter, with special activities including world championship snow sculpting, theater festivals, fun runs and other athletic events, and musical entertainment. Each weekend highlights different activities. From mid-December through January, downtown Milwaukee. Call 414-273-FEST or 800-837-FEST for information.

JULY. The world-famous **Great Circus Parade** is a must for families. This re-creation of a 19th-century circus parade features beautiful antique circus wagons from Circus World museum pulled by matched teams of horses. There are bands, clowns, animals, jugglers, and much fun. In the few days before the parade the public can visit the lakefront grounds where the parade is being organized to see the wagons and animals, clown shows, exhibits, and even some circus performances. Parade held in downtown Milwaukee in mid-July. Phone 414-273-7877. Tickets needed in advance for the best parade route seating.

JUNE-SEPTEMBER. Milwaukee **lakefront festivals**. All summer, it's one terrific festival after another. All are held at the Henry Maier Festival Park or on the adjoining Summerfest Grounds on Harbor Drive at the end of Wisconsin Avenue. For information and specific dates contact the Greater Milwaukee Convention & Visitors Bureau (see Tourist Information below) or call the number listed with each festival. Beginning in late June and continuing through early September, the major lakefront festivals, in order:

Summerfest—big name musical stars, rides, food, continuous entertainment on 10 stages throughout the grounds. Late June-early July. Phone 800-837-FEST.

Festa Italiana—Italian food, entertainment, bocce tournament, flag throwing, art exhibits, and spectacular fireworks. Mid-July. Phone 414-223-2180.

German Fest—dancing, entertainment, German food. Late July. Phone 414-464-9444 or 800-355-9067.

African World Festival—dancing, music, food. Early August. Phone 414-372-4567.

Irish Fest—top Irish musicians and dancers, games, food, children's area. Mid-August. Phone 414-476-3378.

Mexican Fiesta—great food, fast dancing, colorful costumes. Late August. Phone 414-383-7066.

Indian Summer—celebrating Native American heritage with a pow-wow, cultural exhibits, entertainment, food. Early September. Phone 414-774-7119 or 414-383-7425.

Other big festivals and events held elsewhere in Milwaukee include:

JUNE. **RiverSplash!** celebrates the slowly revitalizing Milwaukee River with gondola and water taxi rides, lots of music and other entertainment on outdoor stages, canoe races, fireworks, and clowns and other entertainers for kids. Held the first weekend in June along the Milwaukee River in downtown Milwaukee from Michigan Street north. Phone 414-332-9401.

JULY. **Greek Festival** celebrates the heritage of Milwaukee's Greek community with a major dancing, entertainment, and food extravaganza. Held in early July at the Frank Lloyd Wright-designed Annunciation Greek Orthodox Church, 9400 W. Congress St., Wauwatosa; phone 414-461-9400.

AUGUST. The **Wisconsin State Fair** has something for everyone—big name entertainers, stock car races, a huge midway, plenty of food, ongoing entertainment, and, of course, thousands of animals. Kids (and parents) can find something they like here, from a chance to talk to Smokey the Bear at the Department of Natural Resources building, to watching huge draft horses parade, to riding a thrilling carnival ride. Held for ten days in early August at State Fair Park, I-94 and 84th St.; phone 414-266-7000 or 800-844-FAIR.

AUGUST. **Maritime Days** lets you tour ships and Coast Guard boats and sample food from more than 35 local restaurants while you enjoy five stages of entertainment. There are lots of activities for kids including face painting, jugglers and mimes, and arts and crafts activities. Held for five days starting the last Monday in August at Veterans Park at the downtown Milwaukee lakefront. Phone 414-223-7500.

NOVEMBER. **Holiday Folk Fair** celebrates Milwaukee's diverse ethnic heritage with a giant festival to kick off the end of the year holidays. There are folk dancers from around the world, musicians and singers, cultural exhibits, an international marketplace where you can get started on your Christmas shopping, and, of course, more ethnic goodies than you can possibly eat. But give it a try. Held in mid-November at the Milwaukee Center,

500 W. Kilbourn Ave., downtown Milwaukee. Phone 414-225-6225.

Shopping

There are a number of regional malls in the Milwaukee area. The two best are Grand Avenue and Mayfair. There are also many specialty shops and unique shopping areas.

Grand Avenue has been a catalyst in the revival of downtown Milwaukee. This classy enclosed mall has more than 150 stores and restaurants ranging from large department stores to merchants selling handmade crafts from carts. Much of the mall consists of renovated older buildings, making for a more interesting and creative look than the average mall. Stores of special interest to kids are Puzzlebox, with wonderful toys, Celebrate Wisconsin, with unique Wisconsin souvenirs, GapKids casual clothing, and other stores with selections for both children and adults. The mall has a number of restaurants and the unique Speisegarten food court with more than a dozen eating establishments. Worth browsing. Along the 100, 200, and 300 blocks of West Wisconsin Ave. Phone 414-224-0655. Open 10-7 Monday-Friday, 10-6 Saturday, 11-5 Sunday (some store hours may vary).

Mayfair is the area's largest mall, with more than 160 department stores, boutiques, shops, and restaurants. If you can't find it at Grand Avenue, try Mayfair. 2500 N. Mayfair Rd. (at North Ave. and Hwy 45), Wauwatosa; phone 414-771-1300. Open 10-9 Monday-Friday, 10-6 Saturday, 11-6 Sunday.

Cedarburg, north of Milwaukee, has a wonderful shopping district along Washington Avenue in the historic downtown. Along a six-block stretch you'll find antique, craft, gift, toy, and clothing stores, most of them in historic buildings. Many stores are aimed at adults, but there are a number that kids will find particularly enticing. At the **Ornamental Iron Shop**, located in Cedar Creek Settlement, a group of shops that occupy an 1864 woolen mill, you can watch a blacksmith create wrought iron items. The **Cedar Creek Winery**, also in the Settlement shops, gives tours and samples (kids get soda). The

Settlement shops are at the corner of Washington Avenue and Bridge Road at the north end of town. South of the Settlement shops along Washington Avenue you'll find **T. Bear, Friends and Toys** (phone 414-376-0815), with a wide selection of stuffed animals plus games, Brio toys, books for kids, and much more. Across the street **Cedarburg Books** sells books for kids and adults (phone 414-377-4140). A little farther south you'll find **B.J. Becks's**, a major toy store. In between kids' stores, browse in the galleries, antique shops, and craft stores that cater to the older set. To get to Cedarburg take I-43 north from Milwaukee, exit at Hwy 57, then head west. Follow the signs to the historic downtown. Cedarburg stores are open daily. Hours change depending on the season.

Treats

Milwaukee is famous for frozen custard. Even if you've tried this super-rich ice cream elsewhere, you'll find the Milwaukee variety is richer, creamier, and just better than anywhere else. It's a continuing debate in Milwaukee as to whether Kopp's, Gille's, or Leon's makes the best frozen custard in town. Try all three just to be sure you don't miss anything. All three make it fresh daily, and they have a changing flavor of the day.

Kopp's Frozen Custard has three locations. They serve a full menu of burgers, fries, shakes, and other fast food specials as well as the custard. Everything's good. Bluemound Rd. and Brookfield Rd. (six miles west of the zoo), phone 414-789-1393; 7631 W. Layton Ave., phone 414-282-4080; and 5373 N. Port Washington Rd., phone 414-961-2006.

Gille's Drive-In also serves good burgers, hot dogs, fries, and other fast food specials along with really great frozen custard. Take-outs only. 7515 W. Bluemound Rd.; phone 414-453-4875. About one mile east of the Milwaukee County Zoo. Closed in winter.

Leon's Frozen Custard is worth a visit after dark. It's one of the last of the neon encrusted drive-ins. You'll see it from blocks away. They also serve hot dogs but their real focus is the custard. Take-out only. Great sundaes.

3131 S. 27th St. (Hwy 41); phone 414-383-1784. Leon's is about two and a half miles directly south of the Mitchell Park Conservatory (the Domes).

Chocoholics head directly to **Ambrosia Chocolate**, Milwaukee's local chocolate factory, where you can choose from the state's largest selection of chocolates and candy. Made fresh daily. 1048 Old World Third St. downtown; phone 414-271-5774. Open 9-5 Monday-Saturday.

While you're strolling along Washington Avenue in Cedarburg, you'll probably notice **Beerntsen's Candy Shop** in the Stagecoach Inn (phone 414-377-9512). Go in and get some of the best homemade chocolate in Wisconsin. If you're in the mood for ice cream, just stoll up the street to **The Chocolate Factory Ice Cream Parlor** (414-377-8877). Famous for their hot fudge sundaes. A little farther up the street is **Mary Jane's Confectionery** (phone 414-375-8665), one of the largest candy stores in the area, offering chocolates, hard candies, and their signature hand-dipped strawberries and raspberries. All these shops are open daily, so you never have to go without sugar.

Where to Stay

There are many fine hotels and motels throughout the Milwaukee area. With the exception of motels near the airport, this listing is limited to lodgings near the attractions, events, and shopping areas mentioned in this chapter.

AIRPORT AND SOUTH

Holiday Inn-South/Airport, 6331 S. 13th St. (south of downtown on I-94, exit on College Ave., then east), Milwaukee 53221; phone 414-764-1500 or 800-HOLIDAY. Holidome with indoor pool, wading pool, sauna, playground, games area, exercise room, cable TV with free movies, restaurant, coin laundry. Kids under 18 free with parents. Five minutes to the airport.

The Grand Milwaukee Hotel, 4747 S. Howell Ave. (Hwy 38), Milwaukee 53207; phone 414-481-8000 or

800-558-3862. Large hotel with plenty of entertainment—movie theaters, bowling alley, indoor tennis courts, health club, indoor and outdoor pools, sauna, whirlpool, playground, game room, cable TV with free movies, restaurant. Suites available. Kids free with parents. Five minutes to the airport.

DOWNTOWN AND LAKEFRONT

Holiday Inn City Centre, 611 W. Wisconsin Ave., Milwaukee 53203; phone 414-273-2950 or 800-HOLIDAY. Moderate priced motel within easy walk of museums, Grand Avenue Mall, restaurants, Bradley Center, theaters, Milwaukee River. Amenities include outdoor pool, cable TV with free movies, restaurant. Kids free with parents.

Ramada Inn-Downtown, 633 W. Michigan St., Milwaukee 53203; phone 414-272-8410 or 800-228-2828. Moderate priced motel within easy walk of museums, Grand Avenue Mall, restaurants, Bradley Center, Milwaukee River, theaters. Outdoor pool, cable TV with free movies, restaurant. Kids free with parents.

Hilton Hotel, 509 W. Wisconsin Ave., Milwaukee 53203; phone 414-271-7250 or 800-445-8667. Elegant 1920s-era hotel with completely modernized and very comfortable rooms plus lots of amenities including indoor pool, exercise room, cable TV with free movies, restaurant, shops. Easy walk to Grand Avenue mall, museums, theater, Bradley Center, Milwaukee River, restaurants. Kids free with parents.

Hyatt Regency Milwaukee, 333 W. Kilbourn Ave., Milwaukee 53203; phone 414-276-1234 or 800-233-1234. A modern luxury hotel with excellent rooms, cable TV with free movies, health club (adults only), large central atrium with several restaurants plus another one on top of the hotel that revolves. Enclosed walkway to Grand Avenue mall. Easy walk to Bradley Center, museums, theater, Milwaukee River. Kids free with parents.

The Pfister Hotel, 424 E. Wisconsin Ave., Milwaukee 53202; phone 414-273-8222 or 800-558-8222. An elegant older luxury hotel with both renovated and new wings.

Indoor pool, health club, cable TV with free movies, shops, restaurants. Easy walk to lakefront, Milwaukee River, theaters, Grand Avenue Mall. Short cab ride or longer walk to museums.

Park East Hotel, 916 E. State St., Milwaukee 53202; phone 414-276-8800 or 800-328-7275. A moderate priced hotel with cable TV and VCRs, exercise room, good restaurant. One block from lakefront parks. Short cab ride or a long walk to Bradley Center, Grand Avenue Mall, museums, Milwaukee River, theaters. Hotel has a free shuttle to many events.

WEST AND SUBURBS

Best Western Midway Motor Lodge-Hwy 100, 251 N. Mayfair Rd., Wauwatosa, 53226; phone 414-774-3600 or 800-528-1234. Moderate priced motel with indoor pool, whirlpool, sauna, games area, cable TV with free movies, restaurant. Kids free with parents. Convenient to the zoo, Mayfair mall, State Fair Park, County Stadium.

Ramada Inn-West, 201 N. Mayfair Rd. (Hwy 100), Milwaukee 53226; phone 414-771-4400 or 800-531-3965. Moderate priced motel offering indoor pool, sauna, whirlpool, playground, games area, exercise room, cable TV with free movies, restaurant. Near zoo, Mayfair mall, State Fair Park, County Stadium.

Milwaukee Marriott Brookfield, 375 S. Moorland Rd., Brookfield 53005 (exit I-94 at Moorland Road); phone 414-786-1100 or 800-228-9290. Luxury motel offering indoor pool, exercise room, cable TV, restaurant. Adjacent to large shopping center, five minutes to the zoo, State Fair Park, ten minutes to County Stadium and downtown.

Holiday Inn Sun Spree Resort, 1350 Royale Mile Rd. (exit I-94 at Hwy 67), Oconomowoc 53066; phone 414-567-0311 or 800-558-9573. A large luxury resort with lodging choices from single rooms to three-bedroom villas. Facilities include indoor and outdoor pools plus a swimming beach on nearby Silver Lake, playground, indoor and outdoor tennis courts, cross-country and downhill skiing, ice skating, exercise room, spa, golf, movie theaters, rental bicycles, shops, restaurants. Kids stay free with parents. Short drive to Old World Wisconsin, Kettle Moraine State Forest, Honey Acres, Kettle Moraine Steam Train. Twenty minute drive to Milwaukee County Zoo, State Fair Park, County Stadium.

Best Western Harborside Motor Inn, 135 E. Grand Ave., Port Washington 53-74; phone 414-284-9461 or 800-528-1234. Comfortable moderate priced motel downtown in this small city on the shore of Lake Michigan. The motel is on the harbor with great lake views. Amenities include indoor pool, whirlpool, sauna, game room, several restaurants within a few blocks. Twenty-minute drive to Milwaukee, near Cedarburg.

Where to Eat

MILWAUKEE

Gille's, **Kopp's** and **Leon's** should be on your list for burgers, hot dogs, and frozen custard (see Treats above for addresses). And don't forget lunch and dinner cruises (see Things to Do above).

The **Grand Avenue Mall's Speisgarten** has more than a dozen food vendors ranging from burgers and pizza to Greek specials. A good place to go when everyone in the family wants something different. On the third floor of the Grand Avenue Mall, 300 block of W. Wisconsin Ave., downtown. Open mall hours (see Shopping above).

Historic **Turner Restaurant** serves good basic food—burgers, chicken, beef, soups—in beautifully restored Turner Hall. Their Friday night fish fry is a Milwaukee tradition and their German specialties are excellent. 1034 N. 4th St., downtown; phone 414-273-4844. Open Tuesday-Sunday for lunch and dinner.

Buca is a fun Italian restaurant that serves almost everything on its large menu family-style. The portions are huge. The restaurant is often noisy and busy, especially on weekends. It's quite popular with families. The food is good, the decor '50s (red vinyl, velvet drapery, jugs of wine as decoration). The menu includes pizza, pasta, chicken, and veal plus salads and great desserts. Any restaurant that has a shrine to Frank Sinatra has to be good. They don't take reservations, but call ahead and they'll put your name on the waiting list so by the time you get there your table will almost be ready. 1233 N. Van Buren, just north of downtown; phone 414-224-8672. Open daily for dinner.

John Ernst Cafe, Milwaukee's oldest restaurant, serves authentic German dishes in a wonderfully decorated dining room. Children's menu. 600 E. Ogden Ave., just north of downtown; phone 414-273-1878. Open Tuesday-Sunday for lunch and dinner.

Jack Pandl's Whitefish Bay Inn is a Milwaukee tradition. Serving great burgers, fish, steaks, ribs, and German specialties. Leave room for the homemade desserts. Children's menu. 1319 E. Henry Clay St. (take Lake Drive north to 5200 block, it's on the corner); phone 414-964-3800. Open daily for lunch and dinner.

Atotonilco is named for the hometown of its Mexican owners. The large menu in this informal neighborhood restaurant includes dinners with such specialties as pollo con mole as well as standards like tacos and burritos. There's no children's menu, but many items such as tacos can be ordered a la carte. Good Mexican food, moderately priced. 1100 S. 11th St., corner of 11th and W. Washington St., just south of downtown. Phone 414-384-2678. Open daily for lunch and dinner.

South of downtown is where the good Mexican restaurants are located, and **La Fuente** is one of the best. Large menu. Real Mexican food prepared by real Mexicans. 625 S. 5th St.; phone 414-271-8595. Open daily for lunch and dinner.

Three Brothers serves excellent Serbian food, which is sort of a mix of Italian, Greek, and Turkish. It's a neighborhood, family-run restaurant that is locally known for its great food. Specialties include roast lamb, veal dishes, roast goose, chicken, and burek. They also make outstanding desserts. Food ranges from spicy to mild, and rice is a staple. 2414 S. St. Clair St. (south of downtown on

I-794 over the harbor bridge); phone 414-481-7530. Open for Tuesday-Sunday for dinner. No credit cards.

SUBURBS
The **Settlers Inn** in Cedarburg serves up a variety of sandwiches, burgers, homemade soups, salads, and deli specialties, plus a Friday night fish fry. Outstanding desserts. Children's menu. Open daily for lunch and dinner. W63 N657 Washington Ave., Cedarburg; phone 414-377-4466.

Its an easy drive up the Lake Michigan shore to **Smith Brothers Fish Shanty** and its famous fresh seafood. Great Lakes and other fresh water fish is the specialty, but the menu also includes ocean fish, shrimp, shellfish, and whatever is in season. Save room for dessert. Children's menu. The interesting nautical decor in this lakeside restaurant will keep the kids entertained while the chef works his magic. This restaurant is a 10-minute drive from Cedarburg. On Hwy 33 at the waterfront in Port Washington; phone 414-284-5592. Open daily for lunch and dinner.

The **Kettle Moraine Inn** is a good place to rest up after a hike in the forest. The atmospheric inn serves great burgers and fries, sandwiches, soup and chili, and for dinner offers homemade pizza, chicken, fish, seafood, spaghetti, and steaks. There's a pool table, pinball, and darts to keep the kids occupied. At the intersection of Hwys 67 and 59 in downtown Eagle; phone 414-594-2121. Open daily for lunch and dinner. Full dinner menu Friday and Saturday only.

Extended Hours Grocery Store

Farwell Foods
1940 N. Farwell Ave.
Milwaukee
414-273-1273
Just north of downtown

Emergency

For fire, police, or ambulance, dial 911.

Tourist Information

Greater Milwaukee Convention & Visitors Bureau
510 W. Kilbourn Ave.
Milwaukee, WI 53203
414-273-3950, 414-273-7222, or 800-231-0903
Taped events message 414-799-1177

5

Sheboygan, Manitowoc, and Two Rivers

Including Elkhart Lake and Kettle Moraine State Forest Northern Unit

Stroll and swim along miles of sparkling Lake Michigan beaches. Tour a World War II submarine. Thrill to world-class auto racing. Hike the wooded trails of the Kettle Moraine State Forest. This area of port cities, farming communities, and forests offers a variety of family activities with a focus on outdoor fun.

Sheboygan, Manitowoc, Two Rivers, and the area to the west were settled by sturdy Dutch, German, and Scandinavian people who established dairy farms, a commercial fishing industry, shipyards, and factories. Today the area still depends on farming and on manufacturing companies such as Kohler (plumbing fixtures) and Mirro (aluminum cookware). While commercial fishing is today limited, Lake Michigan charter fishing for salmon and trout caters to visitors from throughout the world.

PLEASE NOTE: The area code for ALL phone numbers in this chapter, except the one noted in the text, changes from 414 to 920 in October 1997.

Sheboygan and Vicinity

Including Elkhart Lake and Kettle Moraine State Forest Northern Unit

Most visitors to this manufacturing center and lake port city of 48,000 arrive via I-43, which runs north-south, or on Hwy 23, which runs east-west.

Things to Do

Kohler-Andrae State Parks. These two adjoining parks provide a beautiful beach, hiking, off-road biking, skiing, and horseback riding trails, picnic area, nature trails, and a nature center with interpretive programs, and some spectacular scenery from the dunes. There's also a campground with both tent and trailer sites.

1520 Old Park Rd., Sheboygan, off County Hwy KK, four miles south of Sheboygan; phone 414-451-4080. Wheelchair-accessible camping and picnic facilities. Open year-round. $.

Jaycee Quarry Park has a swimming area with bathhouse, paddleboat rentals, playground, frisbee golf, picnic areas, hiking and cross-country ski trails, and the dreaded 208-foot-long Aqua Avalanche waterslide. The best city park for kids.

On Business Hwy 42 northeast of downtown. For information, call the Sheboygan Parks Department, 414-459-3440. Open year-round. $ for boat rental, waterslide.

The **Boardwalk** along the Sheboygan River is the best place to view commercial and pleasure boats and to see the weathered shanties built by commercial fishermen during the heyday of Great Lakes fishing. New and restored buildings along the Boardwalk house restaurants, retail stores, and shops catering to boaters. Kids enjoy the watching boats and feeding the ducks and seagulls.

On Riverfront Dr. Open daily year-round. Free.

Sheboygan is a center for **Lake Michigan charter fishing**. More than a dozen charter captains offer half or full-day trips to fish for lake trout and salmon. Pulling in a fighting two-foot-long salmon is a real thrill. And your charter captain will clean and freeze your catch.

Contact the Sheboygan County Convention & Visitors Bureau, phone 414-457-9495 or 800-457-9497, for a list of charter captains.

Road America is one of the premier auto racing tracks in the U.S. Kids love the noise, the speed, and the specialty cars and motorcycles that race on the four-mile course that winds through scenic Kettle Moraine country. Top drivers compete in a number of events each season, including a vintage car race, Grand Prix auto races, Indy-car races, and high-powered motorcycle races.

N7390 Hwy 67, Elkhart Lake, 20 miles northeast of Sheboygan, take Hwy 23 to Hwy 67; phone 414-876-3366 or 800-365-RACE. Racing early June through August. $, children 12 and under admitted free with adult.

The **Kettle Moraine State Forest Northern Unit** stretches for more than 25 miles through the hilly glacial topography west of Sheboygan. The glaciers that created this dramatic landscape left behind steep hills, forested valleys, and sparkling lakes. The 28,000-acre forest is part of the Ice Age National Scientific Reserve, and the Henry Reuss Ice Age Visitor Center is located one-half mile south of Dundee on Hwy 57 (phone 414-533-8322). The Center features exhibits and films depicting the effect glaciers had on the land. A naturalist at the center leads hikes and gives lectures and programs during the summer. The forest also has many miles of hiking, off-road biking, and cross-country ski trails, horseback riding trails, and snowmobile trails, plus beaches, picnic areas, and campgrounds. Mauthe Lake and Long Lake are the two major developed recreational areas in the forest, with beaches, picnic areas, camping, and nearby trails.

For information, contact Forest Superintendent, N1765 Hwy G, Campbellsport, WI 53010; phone 414-626-2116. Wheelchair accessible camping and picnic facilities available. Open year-round. $ for camping and for some developed areas. [The area code for this phone number does NOT change in October 1997.]

Old Wade House and **Jung Carriage Museum**. The Wade House was a stagecoach inn built in 1851 to serve traffic on the heavily traveled plank road between Sheboygan and Fond du Lac. Wade House, a blacksmith shop, and an adjoining home have been restored, complete with costumed guides who explain life in the mid-19th century. Visitors are encouraged to join in activities such as cooking or doing chores. Special events such as dances are held throughout the season, and visitors are also encouraged to take part in these. A short ride by horse-drawn carriage brings visitors to the Jung Carriage Museum, a collection of nearly 100 restored carriages and wagons. Kids particularly enjoy the fire-fighting equipment, omnibuses, and fancy passenger carriages.

On Hwy 23, twenty miles west of Sheboygan in Greenbush; mailing address Old Wade House, Box 34, Greenbush, WI 53026; phone

414-526-3271. Open 9-5 daily May through October. Last tour begins one hour before closing.

Winter Fun

Jaycee Quarry Park has nearly 10 miles of groomed cross-country ski trails designed for novice and intermediate skiers, including a lighted loop for night skiing. For trail information, contact the Sheboygan Parks Department (see Things to Do above).

Kettle Moraine State Forest Northern Unit offers some of the finest cross-country skiing in Wisconsin, with 33 miles of groomed trails for skiers of all skill levels. The Greenbush trails are especially popular. The forest also has 58 miles of snowmobile trails. For information and trail maps, contact the Forest Superintendent (see Things to Do above).

Where to Stay

Harbor Inn, 905 S. 8th St., Sheboygan; phone 414-452-2424. A small motel on the riverfront. Cable TV, VCR and video rental, free continental breakfast, harbor overlook. Short walk to restaurants.

Pinehurst Inn, 600 Hwy 32 North, Sheboygan Falls; phone 414-467-4314. A small motel five miles west of downtown Sheboygan. Indoor pool, whirlpool, cable TV, free continental breakfast, restaurant, handicap-accessible rooms available.

The American Club, Highland Dr., Kohler; phone 800-344-2838. Take Hwy 23 west to County Hwy Y, south to Highland Dr. One of Wisconsin's premier resorts, and priced to match, The American Club has just about everything any kid or parent could want—indoor pool, health club, lake with swimming beach, rental boats, ice skating, cross-country ski trails, a wildlife preserve with nature programs, a golf course, eight restaurants, shops, and the best bathrooms in the state in the form of top-of-the-line Kohler products. Rooms also have cable TV and free movies, and many have refrigerators. There are also a number of family events each year, including Independence Day and Christmas celebrations. The resort, the core of which is the refurbished living quarters of turn-of-the-century Kohler Company workers, is on the National Register of Historic Places.

Where to Eat

Citystreets serves traditional American fare—beef, seafood, chicken—as well as lighter dishes. On the historic riverfront. 712 Riverfront Dr.; phone 414-457-9050. Open for lunch Monday-Friday; open for dinner Monday-Saturday.

Randall's Frozen Custard serves homemade custard on homemade cones, plus steak sandwiches and Sheboygan brats on hard rolls. Sounds like a well-balanced meal. 3827 Superior Ave., Sheboygan; phone 414-458-9699. Open daily for lunch and dinner.

Emergency

For fire, police or ambulance, dial 911.

Tourist Information

Sheboygan County Convention & Visitors Bureau
712 Riverfront Dr., Suite 101
Sheboygan, WI 53081
414-457-9495
800-457-9497

Elkhart Lake Chamber of Commerce
104 S. East St.
Elkhart Lake, WI 53020
414-876-2922

Manitowoc and Two Rivers

Stroll a powdery beach, tour a submarine, munch a scrumptious chocolate pig, dine with a neon penguin. These adjoining lakeside cities are a real find for family vacations.

Manitowoc and Two Rivers, with a combined population of 47,000, have a rough-and-tumble history as commercial fishing and shipbuilding centers. Exit I-43 onto either Hwy 151 or Hwy 42 for a relaxing visit to these charming and historic cities.

Things to Do

The **Wisconsin Maritime Museum** has excellent displays depicting more than a century of Lake Michigan maritime history. The full-size section of a clipper ship under construction shows how wooden sailing vessels were built. The museum has a large collection of model ships, and craftsmen are often at work on new models. Other exhibits show the history of the outboard motor, of military ships and yachts built in Manitowoc shipyards, and best of all, there's a tour of the World War II submarine *USS Cobia*, an example of the type of subs built in Manitowoc during the war. The museum also sponsors special events throughout the year. This museum is a must-see. The exhibits are interesting, clearly explained, and carefully laid out.

75 Maritime Dr., Manitowoc; phone 414-684-0218. Wheelchair accessible except for submarine. Open 9-8 daily Memorial Day through Labor Day, 9-5 daily Labor Day through Thursday before Memorial Day. Cobia tours early April through October only. $.

The carferry **Badger** travels between Manitowoc and Luddington, Michigan. You can take the four-hour one-way ride, and spend time in Michigan, or the family can take a round-trip overnight cruise (without your car). The 410-foot Badger carrys 620 passengers and 175 autos. It offers staterooms for overnights, a restaurant, a small maritime museum, game and video arcade, movies and activities for kids, gift shop, and bingo. A must for any kid interested in boats.

Sails from the harbor in Manitowoc; office at 900 S. Lakeview Dr., Manitowoc; phone 800-841-4243. Daily sailings from Manitowoc and Luddington mid-May through mid-October. $.

Lincoln Park, Manitowoc's largest city park, encompasses wooded terrain on a bluff overlooking the lake. The park has picnic areas, tennis courts, playgrounds, and wooded walking trails. It also includes the **Lincoln Park Zoo**, whose residents include bear, buffalo, deer, bald eagles, and other animals native to the area as well as animals from the Arctic, Africa, and Europe. This small but attractive zoo gives them room to roam in natural surroundings.

1200 block of North 8th St., Manitowoc; phone 414-683-4537. Open year-round. Free.

Zunker's Antique Car Museum has more than 40 beautifully restored antique autos as well as antique bicycles and motorcycles, a large license plate collection, and a doll collection. The museum is a family operation in tight quarters, so things aren't organized very well. Plus, there are big "Do Not Touch" signs all over the place. But for kids (and parents) who like vintage cars, this collection is worth a visit.

3722 MacArthur Dr. (south of Hwy 42 on County Hwy R to Broadway, east to MacArthur), Manitowoc; phone 414-684-4005. Open 10-5 daily early May through September. $.

Watch the bread rise and learn about commercial baking with a tour of **Natural Ovens of Manitowoc**, producer of whole grain breads, muffins, cookies, rolls, and energy drink mix. Adjoining the Ovens is the **Natural Ovens Farm & Food Museum**, with a petting area where kids can pet sheep, rabbits, and chickens, and watch the Belgian horses. The museum also has exhibits of antique farm implements and equipment, old farm buildings, a blacksmith shop, and a trail to a pond.

Ovens at 4300 County Hwy CR, Manitowoc; phone 414-758-2500. Tours at 9, 10, and 11 on Monday, Wednesday, Thursday, and Friday. Free.

Museum at 4024 Hwy CR; phone 800-558-3535. Open 9-3 Monday-Saturday, animals fed at 10:30a.m. Free.

The **Capitol Civic Center** is a 1200-seat refurbished 1920s movie palace that is now the performing arts center of Manitowoc. The Civic Center hosts a variety of traveling productions, including musicians, dance, comedy, and drama, throughout the year. A family theater series offers theatrical performances specifically for young people.

917 S. 8th St., Manitowoc; phone 414-683-2184. Performances throughout the year. $.

Manitowoc and Two Rivers are the center of a large **Lake Michigan charter fishing** industry. More than 30 charter boat operators will be happy to take you and your family on a half or full-day Lake Michigan fishing expedition in search of trout and salmon. They'll also clean and freeze anything you catch.

For a list of charter boats or other information about charter fishing, contact Two Rivers Charter Fishing Hotline, 2010 Rogers St, Two Rivers; phone 800-533-3382.

Neshotah Park Beach is a beautiful white sand beach on Lake Michigan with lifeguards, bath house, and concession stand. The remainder of the park has picnic areas, playgrounds, and tennis courts.

On Zlatnik Dr., Two Rivers; phone 414-793-5592. Park open year-round, lifeguard daily early June through Labor Day. Free.

The **Rogers Street Fishing Village Museum** and the adjoining **Great Lakes Coast Guard Museum** are on the site of one of the earliest commercial fishing villages on Lake Michigan. Exhibits trace the history of commercial fishing from open boats to large trawlers. Tour historic buildings, board fishing vessels, climb the (rather short) 1886 Two Rivers harbor lighthouse. At the Coast Guard Museum the Shipwreck & Rescue exhibit honors the heroic crews that saved (or tried to save) boats in peril on the Great Lakes.

2102-2022 Rogers St., Two Rivers; phone 414-793-5905. Open daily 10-4 late May through October, noon-4 Tuesday-Saturday November through late May. Free, donation requested.

Just north of Two Rivers, **Point Beach State Forest** stretches for five miles along the Lake Michigan shore. The beach is one of the finest on Lake Michigan, and not to be missed for swimming, wading, and building sand castles. Also in the forest are picnic areas, hiking, off-road biking, and cross-country ski trails, snack bar, and campground. During the summer, a naturalist conducts hikes and gives lectures about the lake and the shoreline flora and fauna.

9400 County Hwy O, Two Rivers; phone 414-794-7480. Handicap-accessible picnic and camping facilities. Open year-round. $.

Point Beach Energy Center has an excellent series of hands-on exhibits about electricity. Kids can take a computer energy quiz, operate a solar-powered model train, and grab a globe of static electricity. There's also a picnic area and nature trail. Next door to the Point Beach Nuclear Power Plant.

6600 Nuclear Rd., Two Rivers (eight miles north on Hwy 42); phone 414-755-6400 (if outside Two Rivers, call collect). Open 9-4:30 daily April through October, 10-4:30 Monday-Friday and noon-4:40 Saturday and Sunday November through March. Closed major holidays. Free.

The Manitowoc-Two Rivers area has some wonderful opportunities for **bicycling**. The City of Manitowoc has both paved bike paths and marked bike routes along quiet streets. South of Manitowoc, Hwy LS provides a more hilly lakeshore ride. Sandy Bay Road from Two Rivers to Point Beach State Forest is scenic and uncrowded, as is the road in the state forest. Continue north on Sandy Bay Road to Lake Shore Road for a longer ride along the lake.

Winter Fun

Point Beach State Forest has 11 miles of groomed cross-country ski trails for novice and intermediate skiers. It's great fun to ski along the top of the dunes and look down on Lake Michigan crashing against the beach. (See Things to Do above). $.

Woodland Dunes Nature Center has eight miles of groomed trails on flat to gently rolling terrain. The center offers ski rentals and a warming house and snack bar.

On Hwy 310 just west of Two Rivers; phone 414-793-4007. Open daily 10-4 during ski season. $.

Hidden Valley is a small downhill ski and snowboarding area that offers ski rentals and lessons as well as a snack bar and warming chalet. The longest of the seven runs is 2,600 feet with a vertical drop of 200 feet. The area caters to families. Special Saturday morning kids lessons.

Take Hwy 310 west to Hwy R, north to Hidden Valley Rd,; phone 414-863-2713 or 414-682-5475. $.

Events

JUNE The **Experimental Aircraft Association's local Fly-In and Air Show** is the largest free air show in the Midwest, featuring military, civilian, and vintage aircraft. Get close to really interesting planes, then watch them do their stuff in the air. Held in early June at the Manitowoc

airport. Phone 414-682-9227 or the Visitor & Convention
Bureau at 800-627-4896 for date and details.

Treats

If you don't do anything else in Manitowoc, go to
Beerntsen's. This master confectioner makes the best
chocolates in the area, maybe the best in Wisconsin. And
their hard candies and ice cream aren't bad, either. The
store still has the old-fashioned soda fountain and black
walnut candy cases it's always had. And it still has the
wood booths and beveled glass mirrors in the dining
area. The hardest part is choosing which delectable
morsel to buy. So why not buy an assortment and try
them all? Beerntsen's is famous for its solid milk chocolate pigs, bowling balls, tennis rackets, and other fanciful
shapes. 108 North 8th St., Manitowoc; phone 414-684-
9616. Open 10-10 daily.

Cedar Crest Ice Cream has been churning out the
creamy stuff since 1965. You'll see why they're doing a
booming business when you stop into their ice cream parlor (which is right next to the factory, so you know it's
fresh). The parlor has over two dozen flavors to tempt
you, not to mention old-fashioned thick shakes and malts,
plus delicious sundaes. At 2000 S. 10th St., Manitowoc,
phone 414-682-5577. Open daily. Look for the giant fiberglass Guernsey out front.

Rentals

Ecology Sports rents bicycles and canoes in summer
and cross-country skis in the winter. 712 Chicago St.,
Manitowoc; phone 414-684-4061.

Where to Stay

Inn on Maritime Bay, 101 Maritime Dr., Manitowoc;
phone 414-682-7000 or 800-654-5353. A wonderful motel
on the harbor next to the marina and a block from the
Maritime Museum. Indoor pool, whirlpool, sauna, cable
TV, refrigerators available, handicap accessible rooms
available, good restaurant, easy walk to downtown and to
lakefront park. Boat rental adjacent. Neighboring YMCA

has indoor tennis, health club, and pool, with special day pass rates for motel guests.

Holiday Inn, 4601 Calumet Ave., Manitowoc, at intersection of I-43 and Hwy 151; phone 414-682-6000 or 800-HOLIDAY. A top-notch motel with excellent rooms, indoor pool, whirlpool, sauna, exercise room, game room, cable TV, playground, suites available, handicap-accessible rooms available, restaurant. The motel is three miles from the Manitowoc lakeshore.

Lighthouse Inn, 1515 Memorial Dr., Two Rivers; phone 414-793-4524 or 800-228-6416. This modern lakeside motel has an indoor pool, whirlpool, sauna, cable TV with free movies, very good restaurant. Great lake views. Kids under 18 stay free with parents.

Campers will find the wooded campsites at **Point Beach State Forest** to be convenient and well-maintained. Of the 127 campsites, 66 have electrical hookups. Winter camping is also available. Contact the Superintendent, Point Beach State Forest, 9400 County Hwy O, Two Rivers; phone 414-794-7480.

Urban campers flock to the **Seagull Marina & Campground** in Two Rivers near the commercial fishing docks. The campground has 55 tent and RV sites with electric hookups, showers, game room, a fishing pier, boat launch ramp and boat dock, and a beach on Lake Michigan. Two blocks to downtown Two Rivers. 1400 Lake St., Two Rivers; phone 414-794-7533.

Where to Eat

The Penguin is one of the last of the true diners—covered with neon outside, and inside a menu based on good, inexpensive, basic food. Stay in the car and a car hop will take your order, or go inside for a booth or counter seat. Big breakfasts, good burgers, lots of sandwiches, plate lunches, and dinners, all topped off by homemade frozen custard. 3900 Calumet Ave. (Hwy 151), Manitowoc; phone 414-684-6403. Open daily for breakfast, lunch, and dinner.

Lighthouse Inn on the Lake specializes in traditional American food—soups, sandwiches, beef, chicken, and seafood—that's tasty and well-prepared. Children's menu. 1515 Memorial Dr., Two Rivers; phone 414-793-4524. Open daily for breakfast, lunch, and dinner.

Extended Hours Grocery Store

Copps 24 Hour Food Center
3415 Custer St.
Manitowoc
414-682-6827

Emergency

For fire, police, or ambulance, dial 911.

Tourist Information

Chamber of Commerce
1515 Memorial Dr. (Hwy 42)
Manitowoc, WI 54221
414-684-3537
800-262-7892

or stop at the Visitor Information Center
I-43 at Hwy 151 (exit 149)
414-683-4388
800-627-4896

REMEMBER: The area code for ALL phone numbers in Sheboygan, Manitowoc, Two Rivers, and Elkhart Lake, and some of the phone numbers for the Kettle Moraine State Forest Northern Unit (noted in the text), changes from 414 to 920 in October 1997.

6

Lake Winnebago and the Fox Cities

Including Appleton, Neenah, Menasha, Kaukauna, Oshkosh, Green Lake, Fond du Lac, Chilton, and Horicon

Nature calls brilliantly from the Fox River Valley, from the broad waters of Lake Winnebago, the state's largest inland lake, to the expansive Horicon Marsh, one of our most instructive and entertaining wildlife laboratories. Here is a chance for you and your children to watch a muskrat busy about its haystack marsh house, thrill to the coming of tens of thousands of honking wild geese, or see a blue heron stalk its breakfast among the cattails. The area also has man-made attractions where kids can feed a zebra, see the world's smallest airplane, or learn about Harry Houdini. And you'll surely find some real bargains at the outlet mall.

Lake Winnebago and Horicon Marsh are the natural features that dominate this region. Lake Winnebago is ten miles wide and 30 miles long, with a surface area of 137,708 acres. Horicon Marsh, 32,000 acres of marshland sometimes called "The Everglades of the North," is best known for the annual fall goose migration. Rivers—the Rock flowing through Horicon Marsh, and the Fox and Wolf flowing into, and in the case of the Fox, also out of Lake Winnebago—also influenced settlement and the development of industry in the area.

The eastern shore of Lake Winnebago from Menasha south to Fond du Lac is lined with homes and farms. Small towns with names like Pipe and Jericho dot the countryside. The area is primarily rural, with farming the economic mainstay. With the exception of High Cliff State Park, visitor facilities are minimal, consisting of boat launching areas and local parks.

On the lake's more developed west shore are the cities, parks, and attractions of most interest to visitors. Hwy 41, which skirts the western shore, is the route by which most visitors arrive in the region. Hwy 151 touches the south end of the lake at Fond du Lac then turns north along the lake's east shore.

> PLEASE NOTE: All the phone numbers in this chapter change from area code 414 to area code 920 in October 1997

The Fox Cities— Appleton, Neenah, Menasha, and Kaukauna

The communities bordering the Fox River as it flows from Lake Winnebago north to Green Bay began as trading outposts in the 17th century. Logging, sawmills, and farming dominated the economy through the early 20th century. As the logging boom subsided, the area switched to papermaking, and today the world's highest concentration of paper mills lines the Fox River between Neenah and Green Bay. The Fox Cities, with a population of nearly 175,000, are also regional centers of finance, insurance, and education.

Things to Do

Fox Cities Children's Museum offers 27,000 square feet of hands-on exhibits, workshops, and live entertainment for kids from toddler to teen. Kids can "drive" a fire engine, operate a construction crane, try on 19th century clothes, walk through a giant model of a human heart, see live performances by jugglers, mimes, storytellers, musicians, magicians, and lots more. They'll be happily (and educationally) occupied for hours. A top-notch children's attraction.

10 College Ave., in the second level of the Avenue Mall, downtown Appleton; phone 414-734-3226. Wheelchair accessible. Children under 17 not admitted without an adult. Open 10-5 Monday-Thursday, 10-8 Friday, 10-5 Saturday, noon-5 Sunday. $.

Outagamie Museum-Houdini Historical Center
exhibits demonstrate the role of changing technologies in
Appleton area history. Exhibits include a 1940 physician's
office, an 1890 bathroom and a 1930s burglar-proof bank
as well as displays of equipment used in agriculture, in
the home, and in manufacturing. The Houdini Historical
Center, on the second floor, has an extensive collection of
items used by the famous magician and Appleton native
Harry Houdini, including many of his handcuffs, leg
irons, and picklocks. The Houdini collection also includes
posters, photos, and Houdini memorabilia. The museum
has regulalry scheduled demonstrations and hands-on
exhibits for kids. The Houdini Historical Center offers a
series of magic shows plus interactive magic exhibits.

330 E. College Ave., Appleton; phone 414-735-8445. Wheelchair
accessible. Open 10-5 Tuesday Saturday, noon-5 Sunday. Also open 10-
5 Monday in June, July, and August. $.

Funset Boulevard, a Hollywood-theme indoor family
entertainment center, features over 100 games and attractions, including a carousel, kiddie rides, playground with
a huge soft play area, virtual reality center, arcade,
bumper cars, miniature golf, laser tag, and eight movie
theaters. There's also a restaurant. Everything you need to
keep the kids occupied on a cold or rainy day.

3916 W. College Ave., just off Hwy 41, Appleton; phone 414-993-
0909. Open 11-11 Friday and Saturday, 11-10 Sunday-Thursday. $.

At **Simon's Specialty Cheese**, you can not only take
home some of Wisconsin's finest, you can watch cheese
being made through the big viewing window. There's
also a video explaining the process.

Hwy 41 and County Hwy N, Appleton; phone 414-788-6311.
Wheelchair accessible. Open 8-6 Monday-Friday, 8-5 Saturday. Free.

The **Wisconsin Timber Rattlers** professional class A
baseball team (a farm team for the Seattle Mariners) enter-
tains fans throughout the season at the Fox Cities Stadium, 2400 N. Casaloma Dr., just outside Appleton in the
town of Grand Chute. Phone 414-733-4152. Games early
April through August, call for schedule. $.

The **Gordon Bubolz Nature Preserve** has an earth-
sheltered nature center with exhibits and nature programs about the preserve's white cedar forest and its

animal inhabitants. The 762-acre preserve has eight miles of scenic hiking-ski trails plus a trout pond.

4815 N. Llynndale Dr., Appleton; phone 414-731-6041. Open 8-4:30 Tuesday-Saturday, 12:30-4:30 Sunday. Free.

Activities at **Plamann County Park** will keep your children happily occupied for hours. They can visit the Children's Farm to see and learn about (but not feed) farm animals such as pigs, lambs and miniature horses. They can take a turn through the 18-hole frisbee golf course (so can you), or they can enjoy the swimming beach, playground, hiking trails, and tennis courts. Take a picnic and spend the day.

1300 block of Broadway Dr., Appleton; phone 414-832-4790 Wheelchair accessible. Open daily year-round, but swimming beach and children's farm open summer only. (Children's Farm open daily 9-4:30 May through September). $ for swimming.

High Cliff State Park, an 1,100-acre state park on the northeastern shore of Lake Winnebago, sits atop the 200-foot-high cliffs of the Niagara Escarpment, an ancient limestone ridge. The park has hiking, ski, off-road bike, and horseback riding trails, plus picnic areas, an observation tower with a wonderful view of the lake and surrounding countryside, a swimming beach, marina, boat launching, and camping. In summer, a naturalist offers guided hikes. A small museum explains the history of the area and the limestone quarry that used to occupy part of what is now the park.

N7475 High Cliff Rd., seven miles west of Menasha on Hwy 55/114. Phone 414-989-1106. Wheelchair accessible camping and picnic facilities. Open daily. $.

The **University of Wisconsin-Fox Valley Center Planetarium** offers a half-dozen different shows throughout the school year. Join your kids on a journey to Mars, learn about the Star of Bethlehem, find out what's happening in the night sky, even learn what the Hubble Space Telescope's seeing out there.

1478 Midway Rd., Menasha (from Hwy 41, exit at Hwy 441, go east to Midway Rd.) Phone 414-832-2848 or 414-832-2600. Shows scheduled weekly (usually Sunday evening) throughout the school year. Call for schedule. $.

Speed and noise combine at the **Wisconsin International Raceway**, where stock car and drag races run

April through October at the raceway at Hwy 55 & Hwy KK, Kaukauna. Phone 414-766-5577. $.

Winter Fun

For cross-country skiing, **High Cliff State Park** has four-plus miles of groomed trails. Great views. The **Gordon Bubolz Nature Preserve** has eight miles of groomed trails plus a warming shelter and ski rentals. $.

The **Tri-County Ice Arena** has public skating October through March. Just west of Hwy 41 at 700 West Shady Lane, Neenah. Phone 414-731-9731.

Shopping

You can find anything you need at the massive **Fox River Mall**, the region's largest. With 140 stores, plus restaurants, you need never come out. There's a Disney Store, a Gap Kids, lots of other clothing, toy, game and book stores, an arcade, a movie theater, restaurants, and a food court. It's at 4301 W. Wisconsin Ave., Appleton, at the intersection with Hwy 41; phone 414-739-4100. Open 10-9 Monday-Friday, 10-8 Saturday, and 11-6 Sunday.

Barnes and Noble Books, 4625 Michaels Dr., behind the Fox River Mall, phone 414-830-6960, has a large selection of books for all ages. It has an especially nice children's section with storytelling and other events scheduled frequently. Open daily.

The **Avenue Mall** in downtown Appleton is anchored by the local Herberger's Department Store and also houses the Fox Cities Children's Museum. There are also clothing stores, book and gift shops, candy and gourmet food stores, specialty shops, and a food court. It's at 10 College Avenue in downtown Appleton; phone 414-738-4325. Open daily.

Conkey's Books, 226 College Ave., Appleton, phone 414-735-6223, has a large selection of books, games, and gifts. Outstanding children's section. It also has a coffee house. Open daily.

Treats

Vande Walle's Candies has been tickling the Fox Cities' sweet tooth since 1975. Their rich, creamy caramels are a favorite, as are the caramel pecan patties, English toffee, fudge, nut clusters and—you get the picture. They also make bakery products and ice cream, so your entire family can go on a total sugar jag. Try chocolate cake with chocolate ice cream and chocolate fudge on the side. There's also a self-guided tour of the operation on weekdays. 400 Mall Dr., Appleton, right behind the Fox River Mall; phone 414-738-7799. Open 7 a.m.-9 p.m. Monday-Friday, 7a.m.–6p.m. Saturday, 10-6 Sunday.

Where to Stay

Paper Valley Hotel and Conference Center, 333 W. College Ave., downtown Appleton; phone 414-733-8000. Excellent facility with 294 rooms and suites. Amenities include cable TV, indoor pool, whirlpool, miniature golf, a large indoor game and recreation area, exercise room, coffee shop and full service restaurants, and shops. Handicap accessible rooms available. Children under 18 stay free with parents.

Woodfield Suites, 3730 W. College Ave., Appleton, at intersection with Hwy 41. Phone 414-734-7777. All suites come with microwave, refrigerator, cable TV. Some full kitchens. Indoor pool, whirlpool, sauna, steam room, exercise room, game room, play area, restaurant.

Holiday Inn of Appleton, 150 Nicolet Rd., Appleton, west off Hwy 41 on College Ave. to Nicolet. Phone 414-735-9955 or 800-HOLIDAY. Typical Holiday Inn, with indoor pool, whirlpool, sauna, exercise room, game room, restaurant. Handicap accessible and non-smoking rooms available. Children stay free with parents.

Where to Eat

Dos Bandidos Mexican Restaurant (which also serves pizza) is housed in the historic Between the Locks building, which also is home to a microbrewery that produces a dozen varieties of Adler Brau. Parents can quaff a great glass of beer while the kids partake of pizza or a whole host of Mexican specialties. Adler Brau also produces a terrific root beer. 1004 S. Olde Oneida Street, Appleton (take Appleton Street south from downtown, cross the bridge, take the first left). Open Monday through Saturday for lunch and dinner, Sunday for dinner; phone 414-731-3322.

Frank's Pizza Place is where the local college students buy their homemade pizza. Frank's also has an extensive Italian menu including lasagna, spaghetti, and sandwiches. They deliver anything on the menu. 815 W. College Ave., Appleton; phone 414-734-9131. Open daily for dinner.

Emergency

For fire, police, or ambulance, dial 911.

Tourist Information

Fox Cities Convention & Visitors Bureau
3433 W. College Ave.
Appleton, WI 54914
414-734-3358.

Oshkosh

This community of 55,000 was settled in the 1830s at the spot where the Fox River flows into Lake Winnebago, and was named Oshkosh after the chief of the local Menominee tribe. Oshkosh grew into a bustling sawmill and lumber shipping center during the logging era of the late 1890s. Today, the city has a diverse economic base, led by Oshkosh B'Gosh clothing company, the city's most famous business. Oshkosh is also home to the Miles Kimball direct mail company, Oshkosh Truck, a 10,000-student campus of the University of Wisconsin, and is the county seat of Winnebago County.

Except during August, when thousands of aircraft land at Wittman Field for the Experimental Aircraft Association's annual fly-in, virtually all visitors arrive by car on U.S. Hwy 41.

Things to Do

The **Experimental Aircraft Association Museum** is one of the outstanding family attractions in Wisconsin. It is worth a special trip. The museum displays experimental aircraft ranging from some of the earliest craft to a replica of the Voyager, the first plane to fly non-stop around the world without refueling. On display are the world's smallest airplane, racing planes, aerobatic planes, and antique and classic planes. There's a World War II hanger with a B-17 bomber and fighter planes. The enthralling film *On the Wing* is shown throughout the day, and a number of videos tell the story of individual planes. Visitors can take a video trip through the Amazon basin in a 1930s experimental plane. In summer the Pioneer Airport is open, with vintage planes and a hanger. Weather permitting, visitors can fly in a restored 1929 Ford Tri-Motor airliner or an open-cockpit bi-plane. There's also a Cessna Restoration Center where EAA craftsmen build and restore small planes—and you can watch and ask questions. Gift shops and vending machines.

3000 Poberezny Dr. (Hwy 44 exit off Hwy 41); phone 414-426-4818. Wheelchair accessible. Open 8:30-5 Monday-Saturday, 11-5 Sunday. Closed major holidays. $.

Menominee Park, on the shore of Lake Winnebago, is one of the loveliest city parks in Wisconsin. Bring a picnic and spend an afternoon here. Kids (and parents) can ride the miniature train or the carousel, rent paddleboats and canoes on the lagoon, or try the bumper boats. In addition to picnic areas with restrooms, there are several playgrounds, a swimming beach with lifeguards and a bath house, tennis courts, snack bars, boat launch ramps, and paved bike paths. In addition, the park has a wonderful small zoo, where children can feed the goats, ducks, and even the zebra.

Entrance at corner of Hazel and Merritt streets. Phone 414-236-5082 or 414-236-5080. Open daily. Zoo open late May through mid-September. Admission free; boat rental $.

The **Grand Opera House**, a restored theater, is the venue for a performing arts series and other live entertainment throughout the year. Many of the events are kid-oriented. 100 High Ave.; box office phone 414-424-2350. Performances year-round.

The **Pioneer Princess**, a 63-foot luxury passenger yacht, accommodates 49 passengers on cruises on Lake Winnebago and the Fox River. Tours last 90 minutes to two hours. Many include a full meal or special treat such as an ice cream social.

Docked at the Pioneer Marina, 1000 Pioneer Dr.; phone 414-233-1980 or 800-683-1980. Cruises daily Memorial Day through Labor Day, less often in April, May, September, and October. $.

Exhibits at the **Oshkosh Public Museum** focus on local history, including the fur trade, Indian tribes and the logging era, as well as the natural history of the area. Exhibits of clothing from the turn of the century, jewelry, china and glassware and decorative arts, painting and sculpture round out the collection. The Apostles Clock, a massive 1895 handcrafted timepiece, "performs" every hour on the hour. The museum is housed in a 1907 lumber baron's mansion on a large lot, and families are welcome to picnic on the grounds.

1331 Algoma Blvd.; phone 414-424-4730. Wheelchair accessible. Open 9-5 Tuesday-Saturday, 1-5 Sunday. Closed holidays. Free, donation requested.

Settlers Mill Adventure Golf has 18 holes of challenging miniature golf, complete with lots of water hazards and tricky shots. There's also a game room with video games, foosball, and pinball. At 3025 S. Washburn St., adjoining the Horizon Outlet Mall; phone 414-426-4221. Open daily May through October.

Events

JULY. **Sawdust Days** honors Oshkosh's history as a sawmill town. Menominee Park fills up with a carnival, arts and crafts displays, entertainment stages, food vendors, folks in period costume, and a midway. Held in early July. Phone 414-235-5584 for information.

AUGUST. The **Experimental Aircraft Association Convention and Aviation Exhibition** (known locally as the EAA Fly-in) runs for a week in early August. The 12,000 or so aircraft, ranging from tiny home-built planes to Stealth bombers, make Wittman Field the busiest airport in the world for the duration of the fly-in. Visitors can wander among the planes parked in the grass around the airport. There are also daily air shows, exhibits, seminars, and workshops. Phone 414-426-4800 for information.

Shopping

Horizon Outlet Center is an all-outlet mall with more than 60 stores. Buy books, clothing, glassware, shoes, luggage, and just about anything else you can think of. Oshkosh B'Gosh has an outlet here. There's even a toy discount store. 3001 S. Washburn St., at the intersection of Hwys 41 and 44. Phone 414-231-8911 or 800-866-5900. Open 10-9 Monday-Friday, 10-8 Saturday, 11-6 Sunday.

Treats

Hugh's Homaid Chocolate is a family enterprise that produces amazingly wonderful hand-dipped candies, and they still work out of the family's basement. 1823 Doty St., phone 414-231-7232. Irregular hours. Call before you go. It's worth the effort.

Where to Stay

Pioneer Inn, 1000 Pioneer Dr.; phone 414-233-1980 or 800-683-1980. This large resort complex on Lake Winnebago features indoor and outdoor pools, a wading pool, miniature golf, game room, cable TV, rental boats and bikes, tennis courts and a playground. There are also daily activities for families and for kids by themselves. Lovely grounds. Two restaurants.

Oshkosh Hilton, 1 N. Main St.; phone 414-231-5000 or 800-445-8667. Downtown on the river. Indoor pool, whirlpool, game room, exercise room, restaurant. Kids stay free with parents.

The **Circle R. Campground**, 1185 Old Knapp Rd.; phone 414-235-8909, is just two miles south of Wittman Field. This full service campground has all hookups, a store, recreation room, playground, showers, laundry and dump station. Open May through October.

Where to Eat

Wisconsin Farms Restaurant specializes in organically-fed beef, but also has a large menu that includes vegetarian fare. Their homemade soups and cheesecakes are especially good. Close to Horizon Outlet Center and EAA Museum. 2450 S. Washburn St. (Hwy 44 exit off Hwy 41); phone 414-233-7555. Wheelchair accessible. Open daily for breakfast, lunch, and dinner.

Lara's Tortilla Flats serves authentic Mexican food, everything from tacos to combo plates. It's all good. Children's menu. 715 N. Main St.; phone 414-233-4440. Open Monday through Saturday for lunch and dinner, Sunday for dinner.

Ardy & Ed's Drive-In is one of the very last of its kind— a drive-in with roller skating car-hops. The typical drive-in menu includes burger baskets, sandwiches, root beer floats and ice cream treats. Continuous '50s music. It's an experience. Dine in your car or at an outdoor picnic table. 2413 S. Main St.; phone 414-231-5455. Open daily for lunch and dinner March through September.

Extended Hours Grocery Store

Copps 24 Hour Food Center
1200 Koeller Rd.
414-233-0740

Emergency

For fire, police, or ambulance, dial 911.

Tourist Information

Oshkosh Convention & Tourism Bureau
2 North Main St.
Oshkosh, WI 54901
414-236-5250
800-876-5250

Green Lake

Beautiful Green Lake, the deepest in Wisconsin, was well known to 19th-century travelers, and it is still the focus of the thriving vacation community of Green Lake. This peaceful rural area offers tranquil, low-key family vacations.

Things to Do

The **Green Lake Conference Center**, owned by the American Baptist Assembly, occupies 1,100 beautifully tended acres on the shore of Green Lake. The church offers the property for conferences and retreats, but it is also open to the public for hiking, boating, bicycling, golf, and cross-country skiing. There's an indoor swimming pool, canoe, paddleboat, sailboat, kayak, and powerboat rentals, bike rentals, tennis, and beautiful wooded hiking trails. Restaurant and picnic areas. You can stay overnight, or pay a day use fee to use the facilities. A gem.

On Hwy 23 just west of village of Green Lake; phone 414-294-3323 or 800-558-8898. Open daily. Call for information about activities.$.

The **Escapade** is a 60-foot catamaran-style yacht that offers one-hour cruises on Green Lake, which is seven miles long and two miles wide. The cruises include commentary by the captain about the history of the lake, which has the oldest resort community west of Niagara Falls, and interesting sites along the shore.

Cruises leave from the Heidel House, 643 Illinois Avenue just east of the village of Green Lake; phone 414-294-3344 or 800-444-2812 for information and reservations. Cruises weekends in May, September, and October; daily Memorial Day-Labor Day. $.

Any kid who's ever looked longingly at a horse will love a trip to **Larson's Clydesdales**. Owner Judy Larson, who raises and shows national champions, gives a charming, folksy tour of the farm, explaining how the gentle giants are prepared for a show, including grooming, harnessing, and everything else you ever wanted to know about the behind-the-scenes work of a horse show. The hour-plus tour ends with a Clydesdale strutting his stuff in the show ring. Kids can pet the horses, and there are also plenty of friendly cats and dogs on this working farm.

Ten miles southeast of Green Lake; take Hwy 23 east to Ripon, then Hwy 49 south to Reeds Corner Rd., turn east (right) to the Clydesdale sign. Phone 414-748-5466. Judy offers tours and a Clydesdale show Monday through Saturday afternoons May through October. Reservations required. $.

Winter Fun

The **Green Lake Conference Center** (See Things to Do above) offers 16 miles of groomed cross-country ski trails for beginning through advanced skiers. There's a warming house, snack bar, and ski rentals, as well as an indoor heated pool and changing area.

Treats

Bayview Landing Ice Cream Parlor is the place to cool off after a tough day on the lake. Cones, sundaes, shakes, and malts, plus candy and gourmet coffees. At 496 Bayview Court, adjoining Lakeside City Park in downtown Green Lake on the water. Phone 414-294-3066. Open daily April through October.

Where to Stay

Green Lake Conference Center, Hwy 23, Green Lake, 54941; phone 414-294-3323 or 800-558-8898. This beautiful facility is owned by the American Baptist Assembly, but is open to the public. Visitors are offered the entire range of lodging and camping. The Roger Williams Inn and two other lodges provide lakeshore hotel accommodations (and dining on the American Plan). In addition, there are housekeeping cabins (seasonal), camping for trailers and tents, and even large houses for rent. Houses, cabins, and camping areas are either in the woods or along the lake shore. Lodging and camping are spread throughout the spacious grounds, so there's no feeling of being crowded. Guests are given the run of the place (see Things to Do above). Kids and young adults under 21 stay free with parents in the lodges.

Heidel House Resort, Illinois Avenue, Green Lake, 54941; phone 414-294-3344 or 800-444-2812. A full-service resort on the shore of Green Lake, the Heidel House offers beautifully appointed rooms and suites in several buildings. Amenities include indoor and outdoor pools, swimming beach, playground, tennis courts, exercise room, game room, boat rentals, and a dining room. Camp Heidel, a summer activities program for kids, provides plenty for fun for the kids while you're having your own good time. There's also a golf course across the road.

Oakwood Lodge, 365 Lake St., Green Lake, 54941; phone 414-294-6580 or 800-498-8087. A historic bed and breakfast on the water in a home that was built in the 1860s as a vacation lodge. Eleven guest rooms, nine with private baths; several two-room suites that are perfect for families. Private pier and swimming area. Wonderful breakfast in the dining room at your convenience. Great screened porch. Large yard for the kids to play.

Tourist Information

Green Lake Area Chamber of Commerce
Box 386
Green Lake, WI 54941
414-294-3231
800-253-7354

Fond du Lac

French fur traders referred to this area as the "fond" or farther end of Lake Winnebago. The community grew in the late 1800s as a lumbering and milling town. Today this city of 38,000 is a thriving manufacturing center and is also the home of Marian College, a two-year University of Wisconsin center, and the Moraine Park Technical Institute.

Things to Do

Lakeside Park on Lake Winnebago is a beautifully landscaped 400-acre municipal park with a variety of recreational facilities including the lighthouse that is the city's symbol. Kids can climb the lighthouse for a view of the lake. The park also contains playgrounds, a petting zoo, mini-train, carousel and other rides, and aqua bike, paddleboat, and canoe rentals as well as picnic areas. A lovely way to spend a summer afternoon. In December the park is aglow with thousands of Christmas lights and decorations.

At the north end of Main St.; phone 414-929-2950. Lighthouse open daily mid-April through mid-October, zoo, rides and rentals open daily Memorial Day weekend through Labor Day. Park grounds open daily year-round. Park grounds free, rides and rentals·$.

The **Wild Goose State Trail** runs 34 miles along the west side of Horicon Marsh on an abandoned railroad right-of-way from Fond du Lac to Clyman Junction southwest of Horicon. Lovely scenery, and lots of wildlife during spring and fall.

Begins south of Fond du Lac off Rolling Meadows Drive just south of the Hwy 41-151 intersection. For information, call the Fond du Lac County Planning and Parks Department, phone 414-929-3135, or the Dodge County Planning Department, phone 414-386-3705. Open daily for biking, hiking, and winter snowmobiling. $.

The **Little Farmer** has a little of everything—playground, petting zoo, pick-you-own strawberries and apples, fresh bakery, lots of farm animals, hayrides, and live concerts throughout the season. They've even got several miles of nature trails. All on a working farm.

Eight miles north of Fond du Lac on Hwy 151; phone 414-921-4784. Open June-July for strawberries, August-December for apples, concerts, crafts, hayrides, other activities. $.

Events

JUNE. **Walleye Weekend** celebrates Fond du Lac's favorite Lake Winnebago game fish. While the centerpiece of the festival is a walleye fishing tournament, there's plenty to occupy landlubbers. The world's largest fish fry happens on Friday night, along with live musical accompaniment. On Saturday and Sunday there's the milk carton boat regatta, stage shows, lumberjack shows, strolling entertainers, and food. Held at Lakeside Park the second weekend in June. Free admission. Call 800-937-9123 for information.

Where to Stay

Ramada Hotel, One Main St.; phone 414-923-3000 or 800-2-RAMADA. Beautiful downtown hotel renovated and restored to its original 1920s style. Amenities include indoor pool, whirlpool, cable TV with free movies, exercise room, restaurants.

Holiday Inn, 625 Rolling Meadows Dr., at intersection of Hwys 151 and 41; phone 414-923-1440 or 800-HOLIDAY. A large Holidome with indoor pool, whirlpool, sauna, game room, miniature golf, exercise room, cable TV and free movies, restaurant.

Where to Eat

For 50 years, **Schreiner's** has been a Fond du Lac institution. And no wonder. The family-owned restaurant serves excellent, moderately priced meals, and makes its own bread, pastries, soups, and desserts. Everyone in the family will find something to their liking on the large traditional menu that focuses on sandwiches, beef, chicken, and seafood dishes. Children's menu. 168 N. Pioneer Rd., at the intersection of Hwys 41 and 23; phone 414-922-0590. Open daily for breakfast, lunch, and dinner.

Extended Hours Grocery Store

Copps 24 Hour Food Center
330 N. Peters Ave.
414-922-7320

Emergency

For fire, police, or ambulance, dial 911

Tourist Information

Fond du Lac Convention & Visitors Bureau
19 W. Scott St.
Fond du Lac, WI 54935
414-923-3010
800-937-9123

Chilton

This small community east of Lake Winnebago in Calumet County is a farming community whose largest business is Kaytee, one of the nation's largest bird seed companies.

Things to Do

The **Kaytee Avian Education Center** is an outgrowth of the company's research on bird feed and nutrition. They keep birds around anyway, so why not show them off? The result is a first-rate avian showcase. The center has birds from all over the world—parrots, macaws, finches—dozens of species. The tropical bird room, where warm-weather birds fly freely, observed by visitors on a "rainforest walkway," lets visitors get quite close to exotic birds. Kids will love the nursery, where baby birds are hand-fed and cared for. Kids can also hold and pet some of the birds, and there's a wonderful show with trained birds going through their paces. There are lots of hands-on exhibits for younger kids as well as exhibits about bird classification and bird habitats for older children. Outdoors, there's a large prairie area where Kaytee products attract native birds for visitors to watch. A great place to spend an afternoon.

585 Clay St., Chilton (look for the big Kaytee silos); phone 414-849-2321 or 800-669-9580. Open 9-5 Thursday, Friday, Saturday. $ (kids under 5 free).

Horicon

This community of 3,800, twenty-five miles south of Fond du Lac, is best known as the gateway to the 32,000-acre Horicon Marsh, which stretches north of the city for 15 miles. Visitors arrive in the city of Horicon on Hwy 33. Hwy 26 runs along the western side of Horicon Marsh, Hwy 49 runs through the north end of the marsh, and County Hwys Z and Y and Hwy 28 run along the marsh's eastern edge.

Things to Do

Horicon Marsh is best known for fall goose viewing. Every October, more than 200,000 geese pass through the marsh on their way south. Wild Goose Parkway, a signed 50-mile loop around the marsh, has several good goose-viewing areas on the route. Along the east edge of the marsh, the Department of Natural Resources office at the end of Palmatory Drive (turn north off Hwy 33 in Horicon) has a viewing area and a hiking trail through a section of the marsh. There's also a good view from the Horicon Marsh International Education Center at N7725 Hwy 28, just northeast of the village of Horicon. The center offers naturalist programs on spring and fall weekends and information about the marsh is available on weekdays (phone 414-387-7860). Further north, the Federal Fish and Wildlife Service (phone 414-387-2658) has six miles of nature trails going into the marsh as well as a viewing platform over the marsh. The trails are located off Hwy 49 on the east side of the marsh. Perhaps the best known viewing area is along Hwy 49. The privately-run **Marsh Haven Nature Center**, on Hwy 49 at the north end of the marsh (phone 414-324-5818), has nature trails, an observation deck, and nature programs. A visit to the marsh is also worthwhile in spring and summer. The spring migration, when thousands of geese and ducks visit the marsh on their way north, occurs in April. Rental canoes and boat tours can get you into the heart of the marsh to see geese, ducks, herons, and egrets as well as muskrats, turtles, and other residents. Tours of the marsh leave from the **Blue Heron Landing**, at the bridge on Hwy 33 in downtown Horicon.

One-hour tours operate daily (except late July) May through October. Two-hour tours of a large heron and egret rookery operate weekends in May, June, and July. Phone 414-485-4663 for schedules. $.

At the Blue Heron landing you can also rent canoes with shuttle service (and guide, if requested) for exploring the marsh canoe trails. Phone 414-485-4663. Rental operates daily (except late July) April through September. $.

Join the **Wild Goose Trail** off Hwy 33 just west of the village of Horicon for a ride along the west edge of Horicon Marsh (see Things To Do—Fond du Lac, above).

Emergency

For fire, police, or ambulance, dial 911.

Tourist Information

Horicon Chamber of Commerce
Box 23
Horicon, WI 53032
414-485-3200

REMEMBER: The area code for ALL the phone numbers in Appleton, Neenah, Menasha, Kaukauna, Oshkosh, Green Lake, Fond du Lac, Chilton, and Horicon changes from 414 to 920 in October 1997.

Wild Goose Facts

- The geese you see at Horicon marsh are migrating from their summer home near Hudson Bay to their winter quarters in Tennessee, Missouri, and southern Illinois. The geese will return to Hudson Bay in April to mate, lay eggs, and raise their goslings. They begin the flight south when the weather turns cold and the Hudson Bay food supply begins to decline.
- Geese stop at Horicon for a week or two to rest and feed before continuing their flight south.
- Geese mate for life.
- There are several subspecies of Canada goose, which look similar but come in different sizes, ranging from three to eighteen pounds. The geese that migrate through Horicon Marsh weigh an average of seven to ten pounds at maturity and have a wing span up to five feet.
- Geese prefer a diet of leaves, buds, grasses, roots, and seeds from both aquatic and terrestrial plants. The geese at Horicon marsh fly out early each morning to feed, often on corn left after the harvest in farm fields. They return each evening to the safety of the marsh.
- During migration, geese average 40 mph in flight, though they can fly as fast as 70 mph with a tailwind. They fly at altitudes up to 9,000 feet.
- Scientists believe geese fly in a "V" formation while migrating because flying behind and to one side of the goose in front reduces air resistance and makes for easier flying. The lead goose will drop back periodically, to be replaced by one from back in the "V," one that presumably is more rested due to the benefits of flying behind another goose.

7

Green Bay

Have your picture taken in a Packer uniform, then kick a winning field goal. Celebrate a Victorian Christmas. Watch a pow-wow. Feed a deer.

Family fun in Green Bay means history, amusement parks, outdoor activities, and, of course, the Green Bay Packers.

Green Bay is one of the oldest communities in Wisconsin. Because of its strategic importance on the Great Lakes-Mississippi River trade route, in the mid-1600s the French built a fort and trading settlement to guard the area. In 1761, the British, victorious in the French and Indian War, claimed the site. Americans took possession of the area after the War of 1812, and in 1816 built Fort Howard to stake a permanent claim.

With the opening of the Wisconsin Territory, settlers from Germany, Norway, Belgium, Denmark, Poland, and other northern European countries began to arrive. In the late 19th and early 20th century, Green Bay was the logging, commercial fishing and transportation center of northeast Wisconsin.

Today, this city of 100,000 is a center of papermaking, food processing, meat packing, transportation, higher education, and, of course, professional football.

In the 1970s and '80s, Green Bay's downtown was redeveloped into City Centre, a convention, shopping and entertainment district, with parks, riverwalks, museums, hotels, restaurants and a major shopping mall.

Most visitors arrive by car, on either I-43 or Hwy 41. Scheduled air service is provided at the modern Austin Straubel Airport.

PLEASE NOTE: The area code for ALL the phone numbers in Green Bay and the surrounding area changes from 414 to 920 in October 1997.

Things to Do

Bay Beach Amusement Park has a number of rides including a ferris wheel, bumper cars, a miniature train, and a tilt-a-whirl. The park also has a giant slide, a toddlers' wading pool, pony rides, playgrounds, an arcade, picnic areas, and a snack bar. There are also go-kart tracks, bumper boats, and miniature golf across the street from the amusement park. Children of all ages will find something to enjoy here.

1313 Bay Beach Rd.; phone 414-448-3365. Partially wheelchair accessible. Open 10-6 daily early May until Memorial Day weekend, 10-9 daily Memorial Day weekend through last weekend in August, 10-6 weekends in September. Park admission is free; many rides cost 10 cents, most cost only 20 or 30 cents.

Down the street (an easy walk) from Bay Beach Amusement Park, the **Bay Beach Wildlife Sanctuary** is a nature center with exhibits, gift shop, picnic area and snack bar. Over six miles of hiking trails crisscross the sanctuary's 700 acres of woodland, wetlands, and meadows. A small zoo features native Wisconsin animals such as bobcats, bald eagles, and deer. There's also an Observation Building which houses an animal rehabilitation unit and the Birds of Prey exhibit. A highlight of any child's trip to the sanctuary is a chance to feed the resident ducks and geese, who appear to survive entirely on handouts from visitors. Corn for bird feeding can be purchased at the Observation Building.

1660 E. Shore Dr.; phone 414-391-3671. Zoo and nature center wheelchair accessible. Open daily 8-8 mid-April to mid-September, 8-5 daily remainder of the year. Free.

Green Bay is Titletown, and many visitors plan their entire visit around the Green Bay Packers. Start with the **Green Bay Packer Hall of Fame**, a must-see for any kid (or parent) who even vaguely enjoys football. Exhibits highlight Packer history, outstanding players and coaches, and the history of professional football. Kids will enjoy the videos of great moments in Packer history, the film of football bloopers, and the computer football trivia quizzes. There's also a kicking and passing area where kids can try their skill with the pigskin. And, of course, there are those Super Bowl trophies. There's a large gift shop for those who need a Packer jacket, T-shirt, pennant, or other souvenir. From mid-July through late August, the **Packers practice** on their indoor and outdoor practice fields on Packer Drive across Oneida Street from Lambeau Field and behind the Packer Hall of Fame. There's generally a heavy morning workout and a more casual afternoon practice. Many practices are open to the public. Ninety-minute **Lambeau Field tours** are offered daily in June, July, and August (with occasional breaks for pre-season games and other events). Tours include the press box, the field, the sky boxes, and a video about day-to-day operations of the Packers. Tours begin from the Hall of Fame. For information about tours and training camp, call the Hall of Fame.

Hall of Fame, 855 Lombardi Ave.; phone 414-499-4281. Wheelchair accessible. Open 10-5 daily September through May, 9-6 daily in June, July, August. $. Stadium tours $. Training camp free. Check out the Hall of Fame website at http://www.packer.com/hall_of_fame.html.

In the late 1970s, more than 25 historic Green Bay area buildings area were moved to or reconstructed on the 48-acre site of **Heritage Hill State Park**. The park is divided into four areas with buildings from 1672, 1836, 1871, and 1905 that range from a replica of a Jesuit missionary's bark chapel to a 1905 Belgian settler's farmhouse. Costumed guides help you and your kids get the feel of life in fur trading posts, in frontier forts, in small towns, and on the farm. There's a picnic area, snack bar, and a tram to provide transportation around the park. Many special events are held in the park throughout the year and are great times for a family visit. There's a Civil War reenactment in June, a Childhood Past weekend in July, and a French and Indian War encampment and an ethnic festival in September. The annual Spirit of Christmas Past features sleigh rides, musical performances, and, of course, plenty of decorated Christmas trees.

2640 S. Webster Ave.; phone 414-448-5150 or 800-721-5150. Partially wheelchair accessible. Open weekends 10-4:30 May and September, open 10-4:30 Tuesday-Saturday, Sunday noon-4:30 Memorial Day through Labor Day, open the last Friday-Sunday in November and the first two weekends in December. $ (kids under 5 free).

At the **Neville Public Museum**, an excellent series of exhibits show the history of the Green Bay area, including the main exhibit "On the Edge of the Inland Sea," which chronicles the 12,000-year history of the Green Bay area since the glaciers receded. Science and art exhibits as well

as traveling exhibitions are also housed in the museum.
Because the museum has few hands-on exhibits and only
a few videos, younger children may not be amused.

210 Museum Place; phone 414-448-4460. Wheelchair accessible.
Open noon-4 Sunday, 9-4 Tuesday, Thursday, Friday, Saturday,
9-9 Wednesday. Closed Monday and major holidays. Free, donation suggested.

Great Explorations Children's Museum has plenty of
hands-on activities, including a gas station with a gas
pump, an exposed car engine and a gear display, a police
station where kids can hunt for clues to solve a "crime,"
an Operation Station where kids can "operate" on a torso
and check their vital signs, and a Green Bay Packer
"locker room" with a football toss area and a Packer
trivia test. There's also an indoor playground with
tubes and slides, an exhibit that shows how TV signals
get to your TV at home, and many more fun things
for kids. The museum also hosts a series of changing
exhibits. This museum is only two blocks away from the
Neville Museum.

Second level of Port Plaza Mall, downtown Green Bay; phone 414-
432-GEXP. Wheelchair accessible. Open Monday, Wednesday, Thursday 10-5, Tuesday and Friday 10-8, Saturday 10-6, Sunday noon-5.
Closed major holidays. Children under 17 not admitted without an
adult. $ (free for kids under 2).

The romance of railroading comes alive at the **National
Railroad Museum**. The museum's entrance hall houses
exhibits of railroad history as well as a large layout of
model trains, a slide show on the history of rail passenger
service, and a gift shop. Exhibited on the museum
grounds are 80 restored locomotives and rail cars, including Dwight Eisenhower's World War II staff car and the
world's largest steam locomotive. In summer, visitors can
take a 20-minute train ride in a restored 1910 passenger
car. Many of the cars and locomotives on display are
housed indoors, so a trip to this museum is a possible
rainy day activity.

2285 S. Broadway; phone 414-435-7245 or 414-437-7623. Exhibit hall
wheelchair accessible. Open 9-5 daily (closed Thanksgiving, Christmas,
New Year's Day). $ (train ride offered summer only).

The **Oneida Nation Museum** tells the story of the
"People of the Standing Stone," one of the six nations of
the Iroquois confederacy, who migrated to Wisconsin

from upstate New York in the 1820s. Exhibits focus on tribal arts and crafts, spiritual beliefs, and daily life of the Oneida, as well as the history of the tribe. A hands-on area allows children to examine war clubs, beadwork, baskets, a ceremonial drum, and many other objects. A replica longhouse and stockade village give visitors the feel of 19th century Oneida life. The museum also has a picnic area, nature trail, and gift shop.

On the Oneida Reservation, seven miles west of Green Bay, at W892 Hwy EE. Phone 414-869-2768. Wheelchair accessible. Open 9-5 Tuesday-Friday, 10-2 Saturday-Sunday. $.

Waterboard Warriors Waterski Show provides jumping and other daredevil thrills at 7 p.m. every Tuesday and Thursday in June and July, and at 6:30 on Tuesday and Thursday in August. At the north corner of the Brown County Fairgrounds, on the Fox River just off Broadway in the city of DePere. Phone 414-494-8185. Free.

The **NEW Zoo**, located in the 1,600-acre Brown County Reforestation Camp, is one of the most modern in the Midwest. It is divided into four sections that include animals such as lynx, otter, wolves, and fox from Wisconsin, prairie-dwelling animals such as sandhill cranes and prairie dogs, and many animals from throughout the world, including lions, wallabies, llamas, and baboons. There's also a Children's Zoo with deer, goats, sheep, Galapagos tortoise and other domestic and wild animals for kids to view and pet. The visitor center has a gift shop and concession area. On the grounds of the Reforestation Camp are trout ponds, picnic and playground areas, an observation tower, and hiking and cross-country ski trails.

North Eastern Wisconsin (NEW) Zoo, 4378 Reforestation Rd. (8 miles NW of Green Bay, take U.S. Hwy 41 to Hwy B, west to Hwy IR, north on Hwy IR to the Zoo and Camp); phone 414-434-6814. Partially wheelchair accessible. Zoo open daily: 9-6 April through October, 9-4 November through March. Free.

Winter Fun

For cross-country skiing, try the **Brown County Reforestation Camp**, with more than sixteen miles of groomed trails and a warming house. Trail fee charged. For information, contact Brown County Parks at 414-448-4466. The **Bay Beach Wildlife Sanctuary** also has

six miles of groomed cross-country ski trails, with a warming house and snack bar. Both areas have beginner and intermediate trails and the Reforestation Camp has advanced trails.

For indoor fun, the **De Pere Ice Recreation Center**, 1450 Fort Howard Ave., phone 414-339-4097, in neighboring De Pere, has public ice skating on weekends. Or try roller skating at **Rola-Rena Roller Skating**, 731 Morris Ave., phone 414-494-6152. Open daily year-round. Younger kids will enjoy some time at the local **Discovery Zone**, 2763 S. Oneida St., phone 414-496-3401.

Events

JULY. The **Oneida Pow-wow and Festival of Performing Arts** features Native American foods, crafts, dancing, and athletic events. Held in early July on the Oneida Reservation adjoining the city of Green Bay. Call 414-869-2214 for information. $.

AUGUST. **Artstreet** features over 150 artists' displays, live performance stages with free continuous entertainment, a children's area, and food vendors in Green Bay's annual salute to the arts. Held the last weekend in August in the City Centre area. Phone 414-435-2787 for information. Free.

Shopping

The **Port Plaza Mall** in downtown Green Bay has 120 stores, everything from major department stores to tiny specialty shops. Toy stores, candy shops, book stores, clothing stores, drug stores, and restaurants are all found within the covered confines of this mall, which is within easy walking distance of the major downtown hotels and directly across the river from the Neville Public Museum. This mall is also the home of Great Expectations Children's Museum (see Things to Do, above). Phone 414-432-0641. Open 10-9 Monday-Friday, 10-6 Saturday, 11-5 Sunday.

Treats

Beerntsen's sells the best fresh homemade chocolates, plus other kinds of candy, peanuts and popcorn. It's at

200 Broadway, just a block from the Neville Public Museum. Phone 414-437-4400.

Storheim's Frozen Custard is the place to go for outstanding freshly made frozen custard. They also serve burgers and other sandwiches, if you want a complete meal. Their three locations mean you're never far from creamy dairy products. At 2276 E. Mason St., phone 414-465-1415; 108 N. Oakland Ave. (corner W. Walnut and N. Oakland), phone 414-432-4284; and 1860 W. Mason St., phone 414-498-2070.

Where to stay

Regency Suites, 333 Main St.; phone 414-432-4555 or 800-236-3330. This all-suites hotel offers an indoor pool, whirlpool and sauna, game room, exercise room, cable TV, and free breakfast in the courtyard restaurant. Every suite has two rooms, a refrigerator, wet bar and microwave. The hotel is connected by skywalk to the Port Plaza Mall, and is close to many attractions. Children stay free with parents. Handicap accessible rooms available.

Holiday Inn City Centre, 200 Main St.; phone 414-437-5900 or 800-HOLIDAY. Located on the Fox River and convenient to downtown attractions. Amenities include indoor pool, whirlpool and sauna, cable TV, and restaurant. Handicap accessible rooms available. Children under 18 stay free with parents.

Best Western Downtowner, 321 S. Washington St.; phone 414-437-8771 or 800-252-2952. Amenities include cable TV, indoor pool, kiddie pool, whirlpool and sauna, game room, billiard and ping-pong tables, putting green, and a restaurant. Free continental breakfast Monday-Friday. Free cribs. Children under 16 stay free with parents. Handicap accessible rooms available.

Midway Motor Lodge, 780 Packer Dr.; phone 414-499-3161 or 800-528-1234. Convenient to the Packer Hall of Fame, Lambeau Field, and the Packer practice fields as well as Heritage Hill and the National Railroad Museum, this motel offers cable TV, an indoor pool, game room, ping-pong and billiards as well as a restaurant. Children under 12 stay free with parents.

Holiday Inn Airport, 2580 S. Ashland; phone 414-499-5121 or 800-HOLIDAY. This 147-room Holidome offers plenty for children—indoor pool, whirlpool, game area and billiards, cable TV, and a restaurant. Children stay free with parents. Handicap accessible rooms available.

Camping is available at the **Brown County Fairgrounds** (on the Fox River off Broadway in De Pere) from May through mid-October. Showers, dump station, picnic area, boat launch. Tent and trailer sites. Phone 414-448-4466.

The nearest full-service campground is **Happy Hollow Campground**, 10 miles south of Green Bay on Hwy 41. Facilities include showers, swimming pool, playground, ice cream parlor, recreation hall, laundry and store. There's also a nature trail, and free kids crafts activities and movies for kids. Phone 414-532-4386. Open year-round. Good Sam discounts apply.

Where to eat

Green Bay residents swear by **Chili John's**, which has been famous for its many varieties of chili for 75 years. The tables are formica, the decor minimal, but the chili, burgers, hot dogs, and Mexican dishes keep the customers coming. At 519 S. Military, phone 414-494-4624. Open daily for lunch and dinner.

The **Bay Family Restaurant** also offers good, hearty homemade soups and desserts, a full menu of sandwiches and dinners and a children's menu. The Bay Family Restaurant has two locations. The original is in the Bay Motel, 1301 S. Military Ave., phone 414-494-3441. The other is at 1245 E. Mason St., phone 414-437-9020. Both are open daily for breakfast, lunch, and dinner.

Kroll's is another Green Bay tradition that features plenty of high-cholesterol food in an informal atmosphere. In this case, Kroll's is famous for their hamburgers, which include a pat of butter on top of the patty (dieters can ask for margarine). The burgers, sandwiches, plate lunches (and even salads) are hearty and good. Two locations: 1658 Main St., phone 414-468-4422; and Kroll's West at 1990 South Ridge Rd. (across from Lambeau Field), phone 414-497-1111. Both are open daily for lunch and dinner.

Extended Hours Grocery Store

Lindy's Markets
2080 University Ave.; 414-432-5233
2020 S. Webster St.; 414-437-2101

Emergency

For fire, police, or ambulance, dial 911.

Tourist Information

Green Bay Area Visitor & Convention Bureau
Box 10596
Green Bay, WI 54307-0596
414-494-9507

REMEMBER: The area code for all phone numbers in Green Bay and surrounding areas changes from 414 to 920 in October 1997.

8

Door County

Door County, the "thumb" of Wisconsin that extends into Lake Michigan to form Green Bay, is the perfect place for family vacations. The beautiful landscape and the lovely communities that dot these shores provide a scenic backdrop for family activities ranging from amusement parks to bird watching. In Door County you can balance your vacation time between rambunctious entertainment and quiet "quality time" to relax and enjoy your children.

Door County's picturesque villages and towns began as fur trading, commercial fishing, logging, farming, and shipping centers, founded by immigrants from Germany, Poland, Scandinavia, Belgium, and Iceland.

Sturgeon Bay, at a point on the peninsula where traders and explorers portaged about a mile between Lake Michigan and Green Bay, was founded in 1850 on the site of French trading posts. In 1882, the Sturgeon Bay Ship Canal opened, allowing ship traffic bound to and from the city of Green Bay to avoid the difficult voyage around the entire Door Peninsula. Since then, Sturgeon Bay has been the economic and political center of Door County.

By the turn of the century, tourism had become an important industry, as visitors from Chicago, Milwaukee, and other large cities arrived by passenger ship and railroad to enjoy the cool summer breezes, the clear air, and the 250 miles of Door Peninsula shoreline, with its lovely beaches and dramatic limestone cliffs. Today, tourism, farming, and shipbuilding in the Sturgeon Bay shipyards are the county's economic base.

Virtually all visitors to Door County arrive by car, on either Hwy 57 from the city of Green Bay, or on Hwy 42 from the south. The two highways merge a few miles south of Sturgeon Bay, cross the ship canal bridge, then split. Hwy 42 follows the Green Bay (western) side of the peninsula, while Hwy 57 meanders along the Lake Michigan (eastern) side. The highways meet again in Sister Bay.

Hwy 57 ends there, while Hwy 42 continues north to Gills Rock and Northport at the tip of the peninsula, and the ferry to Washington Island. From Sturgeon Bay to Gills Rock is only about 45 miles.

> PLEASE NOTE: The area code for ALL phone numbers in Door County changes from 414 to 920 in October 1997.

Things to Do

Door County is best known for adult diversions such as visiting art galleries, antiquing and shopping, and fine dining. The kids, though, need never be bored. Not with five state parks, ferries and other boat rides, amusement parks, ice cream parlors and just hanging out on the beach to keep them occupied.

The Farm is chock full of baby farm animals that can be held and fed, plus there are plenty of farm activities such as milking demonstrations. There's also a pioneer homestead, vegetable and herb gardens, nature trails and a picnic area. The Farm's log buildings are filled with pioneer farm implements and home furnishings. The Farm does a good job of entertaining your kids while educating them about farming and farm animals.

Four miles north of Sturgeon Bay on Hwy 57; phone 414-743-6666. Wheelchair accessible. Open 9-5 daily Memorial Day weekend through Labor Day. $.

The **Door County Maritime Museum** explains the history of shipbuilding and commercial fishing in Door County. Exhibits include antique engines, a restored pilothouse, antique boats, lots of model boats, and artifacts from sunken ships. There's a 1907 pilot house where kids can "get behind the wheel" of a Great Lakes boat. One room is devoted to the history and operation of lighthouses. There's also a workshop where visitors can watch craftsmen making small boats using old-fashioned techniques.

At 120 N. Madison St. in Sturgeon Bay. Phone 414-743-5958. Open 10-6 daily May through October, 10-5 daily November through April. $.

Sunset Park is one of the Sturgeon Bay's largest city parks, and one of the best for family outings. There's a swimming beach, playground, tennis and basketball courts, and picnic areas. There's also a herd of resident seagulls and ducks just waiting for a handout. Be sure to bring bread or other duck treats. On the west edge of town on N. Third Ave. Open daily. Free.

Potawatomi State Park is often overlooked by Door County visitors because it is off the beaten path. Big mistake. The park offers hiking, ski, and off-road biking trails, summer naturalist programs, picnic areas, boat launching, downhill skiing, snowmobiling, and wonderful views of Green Bay and Sturgeon Bay from the park's magnificent bluffs and observation tower.

Four miles SW of Sturgeon Bay off Hwy 42/57 at 3740 Park Rd.; phone 414-746-2890. Handicap-accessible camping and picnic facilities. Open daily. $.

Kurtz Corral offers horseback rides and hayrides, three miles east of Carlsville on County Hwy I (phone 414-743-6742). **Herb's Horses**, two miles south of Egg Harbor on Division Rd. (phone 414-868-3304), has trail rides and a pony ring for smaller children.

Frank Murphy County Park is a real gem. This 14-acre park on the shore of Green Bay between Sturgeon Bay and Egg Harbor is beautiful and relatively uncrowded. You'll find a 1,600-foot beach, playground, boat launch ramp, volleyball court, fishing pier, and a picnic area with water and toilets. Everything you need for a lazy afternoon by the water. On Hwy B four miles south of Egg Harbor. Open daily. Free.

Whitefish Dunes State Park and adjoining **Cave Point County Park** provide some of the most varied and spectacular scenery on the Door Peninsula. Whitefish Dunes protects the largest sand dunes in Wisconsin, including one that rises nearly 100 feet above the beach. Many visitors swim or just relax on the flawless beach (no lifeguards), while others hike (or ski) the 11 miles of trails. Naturalists offer guided nature hikes and educational programs throughout the summer. Just up the shore the beach gives way to rocky limestone outcrops of which

Cave Point is the most spectacular. Visit on a day when
the wind is out of the east and watch the waves crash
against the rocks. Reach Cave Point by a short trail from
the Whitefish Dunes parking lot, or drive in during the
summer. Both parks have picnic areas.

Both parks can be reached via Cave Point Dr., off Hwy 57 at south
edge of Jacksonport, or via Clark Lake Rd. off Hwy 57 if approaching
from Sturgeon Bay. Whitefish Dunes mailing address 3701 Clark Lake
Rd., Sturgeon Bay; phone 414-823-2400. Open daily year-round. Cave
Point free. Whitefish Dunes $.

Thumb Fun Park and Waterworks offers a smorgasbord of more than 25 rides and attractions, including go-
karts, miniature golf, bumper boats, train rides, five
heated water slides, an antique carousel and kiddie rides,
plus a haunted house. Thumb Fun has a restaurant and
snack bars, picnic area, showers and changing rooms
and locker rental.

One mile north of Fish Creek on Hwy 42; phone 414-868-3418. Partially wheelchair accessible. Open daily Memorial Day weekend
through Labor Day. $.

Peninsula State Park is one of the most popular in
Wisconsin, and no wonder. Just about any outdoor activity available in Door County is found within Peninsula's
3,763 acres—bike paths, hiking, ski and off-road bike
trails, beaches, boat landings, fishing pier, nature center
and naturalist-led hikes, picnic areas, camping, an observation tower, a historic lighthouse, and even a golf
course. Plus, the scenery is magnificent, from the rocky
shore to the marvelous beach to the dramatic bluffs.
A must-see. If nothing else, just drive through.

On Hwy 42 between Fish Creek and Ephraim; mailing address Box
218, Fish Creek; phone 414-868-3258. Limited handicap accessible facilities, check at visitor center. Open daily. $.

If the kids are up for a little nightlife, the Fish Creek area
offers a couple of great options. If you're in the mood for
the movies, head for the **Skyway Drive-In**, where you
can sit in the car, eat popcorn and hotdogs, watch a first
run movie, and tell your kids about the good old days
before VCRs. On Hwy 42 just north of Fish Creek; phone
414-854-9938. Double feature weekends in May, nightly
movies June through Labor Day. If live entertainment is
to your taste, take the family to a performance of the
American Folklore Theater. This professional musical

troupe performs comedy, storytelling, and folk music in original shows that weave together history and culture. Sounds like it could be educational, but don't let that scare you—it's great fun. Who wouldn't want to see a musical review called *Lumberjacks in Love*? The group performs nightly except Sunday mid-June through August in the Peninsula State Park amphitheater, then weekends through mid-October in the Fish Creek Town Hall and the Ephraim Village Hall. Phone 414-869-2329.

Those with serious miniature golf aspirations will want to stop at **Pirate's Cove Adventure Golf** for a workout on the water hazards, rocks, and other obstacles. Eighteen holes of challenging fun.

On Hwy 42 just south of Sister Bay; phone 414-854-4929. Open daily May through October. $.

If one miniature golf course doesn't satisfy your golf lust, try **Johnson's Park**, right next door to Pirate's Cove. Johnson's has a challenging miniature golf course plus a go-kart track, a kiddy track for the smallfry, batting cages, and an arcade.

On Hwy 42 just south of Sister Bay; phone 414-854-4715. Open daily May through October. $.

Carole's Corral and Vacationland Farm has a great petting zoo where kids can pet goats, lambs, deer, and other cute animals, and feed ducks and baby farm animals. They can also work off some excess energy on the playground, or ride a pony. The farm also has trail rides and Wednesday evening cookout and hayride (July and August only, reserve in advance). There's a restaurant adjacent, or bring your lunch and enjoy the farm's picnic area.

On Hwy 57 one-half mile south of Sister Bay; phone 414-854-2525. Open daily May through October. Open by reservation for winter sleigh rides. $.

Newport State Park is managed as a wild area, with limited development along its 11 miles of Lake Michigan shoreline. A beautiful beach and 23 miles of hiking trails through the woods mean you and you kids can get away from the crowds. There are 16 walk-in primitive campsites, as well as ski trails and easy off-road bike trails.

Take Hwy 42 east from Ellison Bay to Newport Lane.; phone 414-854-2500. Handicap-accessible picnic facilities. Open daily. $.

Three boat lines provide service to Washington Island. Kids love the half-hour trip. The **Washington Island Ferry** takes cars, buses, RVs, bicycles, and other vehicles as well as people. **C.G. Richter Passenger Cruises** and the **Island Clipper** carry passengers and bikes. If you're on the island without transportation, you can rent bikes (see Rentals below) or take one of the narrated tours.

The Ferry leaves from the dock at Northport, at the end of Hwy 42. Phone 414-847-2546 or 414-854-4146. It operates daily year-round, with over 20 trips a day in the summer, fewer in winter. $.

Richter Cruises and Island Clipper leave from Gills Rock. Richter phone 414-847-2546; Clipper phone 414-854-2972. Both operate daily late May through mid-October. $.

The **Washington Island Cherry Train** and the **Viking Tour Train** schedule departures from the island ferry dock to coincide with boat arrivals. The narrated 90-minute tram tours stop at several local points of interest, including galleries, the shore and harbors, and museums. The driver narrates and explains the history of Washington Island. Very scenic.

At the Washington Island dock. Cherry Train phone 414-847-2039. Viking Train phone 414-854-2972. Both trains have several tours daily Memorial Day weekend through mid-October. $.

Rock Island State Park was once the estate of millionaire inventor Chester Thordarson. Today the 905-acre island is entirely owned by the state, which maintains the park for hiking, swimming, and primitive camping. The park is absolutely lovely, with its sweeping beaches, dramatic bluffs and deep woods. It is accessible only by boat. The passenger ferry *Karfi* takes visitors on the 20-minute trip to Rock Island from Jackson Harbor on Washington Island. No bikes or motor vehicles are allowed on the island. If you visit, bring enough food. The park has no store. You can easily take the boat to Rock Island, spend a few hours, and return before dark.

Karfi berthed in Jackson Harbor, at the northeast corner of Washington Island. Phone 414-847-2252. Many round trips to Rock Island daily, mid-May through mid-October. $.

Rock Island State Park phone 414-847-2235. The park is open all year, but there's a ranger there May through October only, and you'll have to make your own way there by boat or across the ice when the *Karfi* isn't running. Camping fee.

Everyone ought to try **charter fishing** at least once. It's quite a thrill to pull in a two-foot-long trout or salmon. Charters operate on both Lake Michigan and Green Bay. The bay has calmer waters. All charters are similar in that all equipment and bait is provided and you can stay out for three to eight hours. If you should catch anything, the charter captain will clean and freeze your fish for you.

Some of the most popular charter operators are Snug Harbor Marina in Sturgeon Bay (414-743-2337), Lynn's Charter Fishing in Baileys Harbor (414-854-5109), Hub's Charter and Cruises in Sister Bay (414-854-2113), and Capt. Paul's Charter Fishing in Gills Rock (414-854-4614). Or check with the Door County Chamber of Commerce (see Tourist Information below) for an operater located near where you're staying.

For kids who like being on the water, but don't want to spend their time staring at a fishing line, Door County is the home of the state's largest concentration of excursion boats. The **Boat House** in Fish Creek (phone 414-868-3745) offers several one-hour sailboat cruises and a 90-minute sunset sailboat cruise daily in summer, weather permitting, on a 27-foot catamaran. **Bella Sailing Cruises** offers two-hour sailing trips out of Ephraim (phone 414-854-2628), and the **Ephraim Sailing Center** has catamaran cruises and sailing lessons at the South Shore Pier in Ephraim (phone 414-854-7245). If you want to captain your own boat, see Rentals below.

Because Door County has many miles of paved, lightly traveled local roads, **bicycling** has become a very popular visitor activity. Some of the best biking roads are Cave Point Drive south of Jacksonport, Glidden Drive south of Whitefish Dunes park, County Hwys B & G from Sturgeon Bay to Egg Harbor, the bike path at Peninsula State Park, Beach Road north of Sister Bay, and Garrett Bay Road and Cottage Road from Ellison Bay to Gills Rock. The Chamber of Commerce has a map of bike routes available at many sport shops or from the Chamber (see Tourist Information below). Bike rentals are plentiful (see Rentals below).

Winter Fun

Families are increasingly discovering the delights of a Door County winter vacation. The area boasts some of Wisconsin's best and most scenic cross-country ski trails, snowmobile trails, sleigh rides and, yes, shopping and

other indoor sports. The ferry to Washington Island runs all winter, if a view of the ice-covered shore is on your list of must-sees.

For cross-country skiing, take your family to **Peninsula State Park**, with 19 miles of groomed and tracked trails; **Potawatomi State Park**, with 17 miles of trails (this park is especially popular with skilled skiers due to the hilly terrain); **Whitefish Dunes State Park**, with 11 miles of trails, including an easy trail to Cave Point, which wears a spectacular ice coating in winter; or **Newport State Park**, with 23 miles of ungroomed but easy trails. The **Wagon Trail Resort**, south of Ellison Bay on County Hwy Z (phone 414-854-2385), maintains three miles of beautiful groomed trails.

For thrill-seekers, part of the **Peninsula State Park** golf course becomes a sledding hill when the snow flies.

In winter, the Door County stables turn to sleigh rides. **Carole's Corral**, just south of Sister Bay on Hwy 57 (phone 414-854-2525), has trail rides and sleigh rides, both by appointment. Also providing both trail rides and sleigh rides by appointment is **Kurtz Corral**, three miles east of Carlsville on County Hwy I (phone 414-743-6742).

For indoor activities, try knocking down pins at the **Sister Bay Bowl**. On Hwy 42 in Sister Bay; phone 414-854-2841 for open bowling hours.

Shopping

Door County shopping leans heavily to arts and crafts, antiques, boutiques and gift shops—nothing for a kid to get too excited about. With a little looking, though, your kids can learn to love shopping.

Dancing Bear, 15 N. Third Ave. in downtown Sturgeon Bay (phone 414-746-5233) sells Brio and other great toys, books for kids, stuffed animals, and rustic home furnishings and accessories for the parents. Open year-round.

Book World, also on N. Third Ave. in Sturgeon Bay, sells books and games for kids plus books and magazines for the adults in your party. Open year-round.

One of the best T-shirt and souvenir shops is **Door County Gifts**, which offers caps, shirts, shorts, and other items that are a cut above the standard Door County souvenir wear. Children's sizes from 6 months to 14. In Sturgeon Bay at 160 N. Third Ave., phone 414-743-7459.

Lili Peuchen, at the **Main Street Shops** in Egg Harbor (phone 414-868-2252), is the peninsula's premier children's clothing store. The place to go for upscale clothes. The Main Street Shops also has T-shirt and sportswear shops, Grandma's Attic doll store, a gourmet food and cookware shop, and a variety of gift and craft shops. Open year-round.

Spielman's Kid Works, in the Top of the Hill Shops just north of Fish Creek off Hwy 42 (phone 414-868-2469) sells wooden toys, kid-size furniture, rockers and riding toys, plus books, puppets, puzzles and games. Open May through December.

The **Fish Creek Kite Company** (phone 414-868-3769) just north of Fish Creek on Hwy 42, next to Thumb Fun Park, is worth a visit just for the colors and shapes on display in the form of the hand-made kites, wind socks, and banners. Open daily in warm weather.

Passtimes Books has an excellent selection of children's books as well as Door County books, magazines, literary classics, and the latest bestsellers. The store is on Hwy 42 in downtown Sister Bay, phone 414-854-2127. Open daily.

Treats

Vacations are for indulgence.

The Sister Bay branch of the **Door County Library** allows visitors to borrow books, for free. It's right downtown on the shore next to the village park. The Ephraim branch of the library, on Hwy 42 in the old village hall, also trusts visitors and will let you check out books.

Food for the soul is fine, but what about the body? The **Door County Confectionery** has branches at 140 N.

Third Ave. in Sturgeon Bay, in the Main Street Shops in Egg Harbor, Founders Square in Fish Creek, and on Hwy 42 at the south end of Ephraim. Terrific chocolates and fudge. They're especially proud of their Bear Paws, and you will be too after you've tried them.

Chocoholics who visit Door County head immediately for the **Chocolate Chicken**, in Harbor Square on Hwy G in Egg Harbor. Choose from a variety of hand dipped milk- and bitter-sweet chocolates, fudge, cookies, or cake. There's gourmet coffee and espresso for the adults.

The **Fudge House** in Founders Square, Fish Creek, claims to have sold more than 500,000 pounds of its various flavors. And they're only open from May through October. They must be doing something right.

Not Licked Yet Frozen Custard, on Hwy 42 at the north end of Fish Creek, has terrific home-made frozen custard. Plus you can get a complete drive-in menu of hot dogs, burgers, fries, malts, the entire experience. Plus picnic tables and resident ducks. Open daily May through October.

Ephraim's local ordinances prohibit alcohol and dancing. Perhaps that's why the town is a hotbed of another sinful indulgence—ice cream. Either **Anne's Ice Cream Cabin** or **Wilson's Restaurant and Ice Cream Parlor** will send you and the kids into a blissful sugar high—and it's all legal. Both are on Hwy 42 in town. Anne's is open mid-May through mid-October. Wilson's is open mid-April through mid-October.

If you're in the Sister Bay area, be sure to stop at the **Door County Ice Cream Factory & Sandwich Shoppe**, at Hwy 42N and Beach Rd. Watch them make your ice cream, then choose from 30 flavors, or try a sundae, malt or one of their specialty desserts. By the way, they also serve good sandwichs and soup. Open Memorial Day weekend through mid-October.

Everyone who's been there raves about **Grandma's Country Bakery** and all the great pecan rolls, pies, bread, and other indulgences that come from the kitchen.

It's at the Wagon Trail Resort, on County Hwy Z south of Ellison Bay. Definitely worth the trip.

Rentals

Door County is designed for visitors. You need nothing except the clothes on your back and a credit card. Anything else is for rent.

BICYCLES

Island Clipper Bike Rental, at the dock, Washington Island; phone 414-854-2972. **Nor Door Sport & Cyclery**, on Hwy 42 in Fish Creek; phone 414-868-2275. **Edge of Park**, on Hwy 42 in Fish Creek; phone 414-868-3344. **Nicolet Beach Rentals**, at the Nicolet Campground in Peninsula State Park; phone 414-854-9220. **Bay Bikes & Boards**, 20 N. Third Ave., Sturgeon Bay; phone 414-743-4434.

BOATS, MOTORS, SAILBOARDS, SAILBOATS

The Boat House, in Fish Creek (phone 414-868-3745), rents motor boats, canoes, kayaks, and paddleboats. **Nicolet Beach Rentals**, at the Nicolet Campground in Peninsula State Park (phone 414-854-9220) rents sailboats, canoes, kayaks, paddleboats, hydro bikes, and windsurfers. **South Shore Boat Rentals** in Ephraim (phone 414-854-4324), rents paddleboats, pontoon boats, and motorboats. The **Ephraim Sailing Center** (phone 414-854-4336) rents sailboats and windsurfers and also offers sailing lessons. The **Wagon Trail Resort**, south of Ellison Bay on County Hwy Z (phone 414-854-2385) rents canoes and sea kayaks, motorboats, pontoon boats, paddleboats, and rowboats. They also offer sea kayak lessons and excursions (phone 414-854-9616).

WINTER EQUIPMENT

Door County Sales in Sturgeon Bay (phone 414-743-7297) rents snowmobiles, as does **Harbor Marine & Motor Sports** in Baileys Harbor (phone 414-839-2930). **Mac's Sport Shop** in Sturgeon Bay (phone 414-743-3350) rents cross-country skis. Mac's branch in Sister Bay (phone 414-854-5625) rents snowshoes, ice skates, and snow tubes. **Nor Dor Sport & Cyclery** of Fish Creek (phone 414-868-2275) rents cross-country skis, snowshoes, ice skates, and tubes for snow tubing.

Where to Stay

Door County has thousands of rooms available for visitors. On any given summer or fall weekend, they're almost all booked, so reserve well ahead for weekends. In winter, many lodging facilities close, but there's still a good choice of full service resorts, motels, and inns.

Bay Shore Inn, 4205 Bay Shore Dr., Sturgeon Bay; phone 414-743-4551. A modern condominium resort with indoor and outdoor pools as well as a beach, playground, game room, tennis court, bicycles, sailboats and paddleboats. The resort offers one- and two-bedroom suites with kitchens. Kids six and under stay free. Located just north of Sturgeon Bay on County Hwy B, on Green Bay. Open year-round.

For good basic lodging without a lot of frills, try renting a cabin. **Birmingham Cottages**, 4709 N. Bay Shore Dr. (Hwy B), Sturgeon Bay (phone 414-743-5215), are simply furnished but comfortable two-bedroom cottages on the shore of Green Bay. Beach, picnic area, boats, playground, wooded grounds. Open mid-April through October.

Glidden Lodge, 4670 Glidden Dr., Sturgeon Bay; phone 414-746-3900 On Lake Michigan seven miles north of Sturgeon Bay on Hwy 57, then east on Hwy T. A modern condo resort on wooded grounds in a quiet setting. Close to Whitefish Dunes State Park. Beach, indoor pool, tennis courts, game room. Open year-round.

The Bare's 5918 Hwy 57, Jacksonport; phone 414-823-2525. A B&B that caters to families. Four guest rooms, each with private bath, in a modern home. Large wooded grounds with walking trails. Full breakfast served. Open year-round.

Baileys Harbor Yacht Club, 8115 Ridges Rd., Baileys Harbor; phone 414-839-2336 or 800-927-2492. The original yacht club burned ten years ago, and the new condominium complex that rose from the ashes is one of Door County's best new resorts. With Toft's Point nature preserve on one side and the harbor on the other, this resort offers plenty of peace and quiet with all the amenities.

There are more than 50 luxury condo units in three lodges, plus fully furnished housekeeping cabins or rustic cottages with no cooking facilities. In addition to hiking and cross-county ski trails at the doorstep, guests have at their disposal tennis courts, indoor and outdoor pools, a beach, marina, and bike, canoe and kayak rental.

Alpine Resort, Hwy G, Egg Harbor; phone 414-868-3000. On the shore of Green Bay, with golf course, outdoor pool, beach, rowboats, tennis courts, bicycles. Children's activities in summer. Babysitting available. Choose either a motel room or cottage. Restaurant at the lodge. Open late May through late October. Mailing address: Box 200, Egg Harbor 54209.

Mariner Motel & Cottages, 7505 Mariner Rd., Egg Harbor; phone 414-868-3131. Four miles south of Egg Harbor on Hwy G. Small resort on well-landscaped grounds on the shore of Green Bay. Choose motel rooms or cottages. Private shoreline (rocky) and pier, outdoor pool, free canoes and bikes for guests, TV. Quiet and secluded. Open early May through October.

The Shallows, 7353 Horseshoe Bay Rd., Egg Harbor; phone 414-868-3458 or 800-257-1560. Four miles south of Egg Harbor on Hwy G. Lovely, quiet and secluded small resort on the shore of Green Bay. Choose motel room, suites, townhouse or cottage. Private shoreline (rocky), outdoor pool, tennis court, bicycles, boats. Babysitting available. Open May through early October.

Fish Creek Motel and Cottages, on Spruce Street in Fish Creek (phone 414-868-3448), offers modern motel rooms in two buildings, as well as three fully-furnished housekeeping cottages—a studio and two two-bedroom units with screened porches on spacious grounds. And it's all within a block or two of all the Fish Creek shopping, restaurants, waterfront, and entertainment. Open mid-April through October. Mailing address: Box 125, Fish Creek 54212.

Peninsula Motel, 4020 Hwy 42, Fish Creek; phone 414-868-3281. A 17-unit motel at the entrance to Peninsula State Park. Basic lodging at a reasonable price. The clean, modern motel has limited amenities, but you can ski, hike, bike, or snowmobile right from the door. Ski and bike rentals adjacent. Open year-round.

Homestead Suites, Hyw 42, Fish Creek; phone 414-868-3748 or 800-686-6621. Modern lodging at the entrance to Peninsula State Park. Choose basic accommodation in a motel room or rent a suite with microwave, coffeemaker, and refrigerator. Indoor pool, whirlpool, and sauna for guests. Mailing address: Box 730, Fish Creek 54212. Open year-round.

Twin Oaks Country Lodge, W3397 Hwy 42, Fish Creek; phone 414-854-2633. Between Fish Creek and Ephraim, on a side entrance to Peninsula State Park. Basic 12-unit motel with outdoor pool, game room, cable TV, free bikes. Not fancy, but clean and moderately priced. Open May through October.

Evergreen Beach Motel, 9944 Hwy 42, Ephraim; phone 414-8542831. This 42-room motel provides clean, modern accommodations. The motel has a private beach and dock (the waters of Green Bay are across the road from the motel) as well as an outdoor heated pool. Each of the 42 rooms has a balcony overlooking the harbor. Open May through October.

Eagle Harbor Inn and Cottages, 9914 Hwy 42, Ephraim; phone 414-854-2121. The antique-filled Inn is an adults-only B&B, but the six one- and two-bedroom cottages on the grounds welcome families. All cottages are fully furnished and have double whirlpools, fireplaces, kitchens, and private decks. The inn and cottages are across the road from the water. There's a commons building with a pool, fitness room, and sauna, plus an outdoor play area and picnic area on the grounds. Open year-round.

Little Sister Resort, 360 Little Sister Rd., Sister Bay; phone 414-854-4013. One-half mile off Hwy 42 south of Sister Bay. Thirteen one-to-three-bedroom cottages and six chalets are scattered throughout 20 wooded acres on the Green Bay shore. Beach, boats, bikes, tennis court, playground, and an indoor whirlpool. Modified

American Plan available mid-June through late August. Lodging only May through mid-June and September and October.

Helm's 4 Seasons Resort, 414 Mill Rd., Sister Bay; phone 414-854-2356. Modern resort complex located on the water in the heart of Sister Bay. Choose from motel rooms or housekeeping apartments. Amenities include cable TV, coin laundry, video games, indoor pool. Adjacent to city park with beach, playground. Easy walk to public tennis courts, shops, restaurants. Open year-round.

One of the best family resorts in Door County is the **Wagon Trail Resort**, 1041 County Hwy ZZ, Ellison Bay; phone 414-854-2385 or 800-99-WAGON. Choose from a room in the main lodge or a fully furnished vacation home or cottage on the 200-acre wooded grounds. Indoor pool, game room, TV, playground, tennis court, cross-country ski trails and ski rentals, rental bicycles, motorboats, canoes, boat ramp. Excellent family restaurant. Near Newport State Park. Open year-round.

A number of fine campgrounds operate in Door County. Two state parks, **Rock Island and Newport**, offer rustic camping only. **Peninsula State Park** and **Potawatomi State Park** provide full service campgrounds with showers and electrical hookups. Newport, Peninsula and Potawatomi offer winter camping, if you and your kids are especially rugged.

Quietwoods North Camping Resort, 3668 Grondin Rd., Sturgeon Bay; phone 414-743-7115, or 800-9-TO-CAMP. Two miles southwest of Sturgeon Bay adjacent to Potawatomi State Park. A large campground with 250 sites. Full hookups, dump station, flush toilets, showers, plus a camp store, laundry, and LP sales. Amenities include a playground, two outdoor heated pools and a wading pool, game room, miniature golf, and planned family activities. Rental trailers are available.

Camp-tel Family Campground, 8164 Hwy 42, Egg Harbor; phone 414-868-3278. Limited to families. The campground has wooded sites, a store, laundromat, showers, dump station, propane for sale. Amenities include an outdoor pool, TV room, game room, and playground. Open mid-May through mid-October.

Spike Horn Campground, 8705 Cana Island Road, Baileys Harbor; phone 414-839-2430. Offers 49 beautiful wooded and shoreline sites along the scenic shore of Lake Michigan. Showers, electrical hookups. Amenities include a beautiful beach, boats, hiking trails. Lovely spot for a quiet camping vacation.

Wagon Trail Campground, 1190 County Hwy ZZ, Ellison Bay; phone 414-854-4818. Operated by the same people who run the Wagon Trail Resort. An outstanding campground with 130 sites, near Lake Michigan. Separate RV and tent areas, full hookups, dump station, store, laundry, flush toilets, showers. Amenities include a game room, hiking trails, playground, recreation field, boat rentals, and beach. They also rent trailers and camping cabins. Open year-round.

For families that want more privacy and peace and quiet, or more space, than they can find in a resort or campground, renting a cabin or house for a week or two is the easy, and often more inexpensive, way to vacation. **Door County Vacation Rental Company**, 4133 Main St., Fish Creek, phone 800-826-7772, can help you find just the place. They are agents for rental cabins and cottages scattered throughout Door County.

Where to Eat

There are few places in Door County where children are unwelcome or would feel out of place. This listing focuses on eating establishments with good food, moderate prices, and an informal atmosphere.

The **Pudgy Seagull** entices families with moderate prices for their excellent homemade soups, chicken dishes, spaghetti, sandwiches, hearty breakfasts, and homemade desserts. 113 N. Third Ave., downtown Sturgeon Bay; phone 414-743-5000. Open daily for breakfast, lunch, and dinner.

The **Village Cafe** is one of those places you'll want to return to regularly, as, of course, local residents do.

Wonderful breakfasts, great soups, outstanding burgers, and homemade desserts and pastries. Fish boils weekends during the summer. At 7918 Hwy 42 at north edge of Egg Harbor; phone 414-868-3342. Open daily for breakfast and lunch May through October; also open weekend evenings late June through early October for fish boils.

For those on the other side of the peninsula, the **Sandpiper** in Baileys Harbor is the place for good family dining. The restaurant specializes in homemade whitefish chowder, soups and desserts, burgers and sandwiches, and does some great things with baked chicken. Fish boils throughout the week mid-May through October. On Hwy 57 at the north end of Baileys Harbor; phone 414-839-2528. Open daily April through October for breakfast, lunch, and dinner.

Perhaps the most famous restaurant in Door County is the **White Gull Inn**. And with good reason—the restaurant serves wonderful food. It is often crowded, so bring something to occupy the kids while you wait. You can make a reservation for dinner. Excellent breakfasts with homemade muffins, pastries, pancakes and French toast, great sandwiches, and amazing dinners. Children's menu. Fish boils offered regularly all year. 4225 Main St., Fish Creek; phone 414-868-3517. Open daily for breakfast, lunch, and dinner.

The **Second Story at Ephraim Shores** is a dependable family restaurant with hearty breakfasts, homemade soups, sandwiches and burgers, salads, and dinners featuring fish and seafood, pork, and beef dishes. It really is on the second story and it has a great view of the harbor. Open daily for breakfast, lunch, and dinner May through October.

Al Johnson's Swedish Restaurant is another well-known Door County eating establishment. It's the restaurant with goats on the roof! From the excellent Scandinavian fruit soup to the baked chicken specials, there's something for everyone in the family. Virtually everything is homemade. Al's is often crowded, especially on weekends, and they don't take reservations, but the wait is worth it. At 702-712 Hwy 42 in Sister

Bay; phone 414-854-2626. Open daily for breakfast, lunch, and dinner.

The **Sister Bay Cafe** serves up delicious Norwegian-style meals in a cozy cafe at the water's edge in downtown Sister Bay. Homemade waffles, potato pancakes, burgers, sandwiches, cold plates and salads, Norwegian farmers stew, seafood, steaks, Norwegian meatballs like mom used to make, and Scandinavian specials. It's all good. 611 Hwy 42; phone 414-854-2429. Open daily for breakfast, lunch, and dinner April through October, weekends in November and December.

The **Sister Bay Bowl** provides bowling and dining, in any order. The restaurant serves good, basic food in an unpretentious atmosphere—sandwiches as well as fish, chicken, and steaks. Children's menu. Hwy 42 at south edge of Sister Bay; phone 414-854-2841. Dinner served nightly mid-April through January 1, weekends in January, February, and March. Lunch served daily mid-June through mid-October.

The **Wagon Trail Restaurant** starts with Grandma's Bakery for bread, pies, pastries, and everything kids and parents love (including world-class pecan sticky buns), then builds with a salad bar, hearty sandwiches, homemade soups, and dinner menus featuring beef, chicken, pork, ribs, and steaks. Yum. Fish boils year-round. Swedish breakfast buffet. No reservations. At the Wagon Trail Resort, 1041 Hwy ZZ, Ellison Bay; phone 414-854-2385. Open daily for breakfast, lunch, and dinner.

The **Viking Restaurant** is famous for its nightly fish boils during the summer. The rest of the menu is just as good—buttermilk pancakes, chili, whitefish chowder, chicken, steaks, pork, and good sandwiches. This is the restaurant that popularized the Door County fish boil. They've been boiling them since the early 1960s. Children's menu. On Hwy 42 in Ellison Bay; phone 414-854-2998. Open daily for breakfast, lunch, and dinner. Fish boils nightly May through October.

While waiting for a boat to Washington Island, try the **Shoreline Restaurant** at the dock in Gills Rock. Watch the boats and the birds while you eat. The food is good and inexpensive. Try the excellent whitefish dishes, or stick with steaks, homemade soup, or a good burger or sandwich. And the breakfasts will stick to your ribs too. On Hwy 42 in Gills Rock; phone 414-854-2950. Open daily May through October for breakfast, lunch, and dinner.

On Washington Island, the place to eat is **Findlay's Holiday Inn** (no relation to the national chain). The wonderful Norwegian-style dining room serves hearty Scandinavian breakfasts, great lunches and terrific dinners. Homemade soup, bread, and desserts. Friday night fish fry, Saturday specials. At Detroit Harbor near the ferry dock; phone 414-847-2526. Open daily for breakfast, lunch, and dinner.

Extended Hours Grocery Stores

Econo Foods
1250 N. 14th Ave.
Sturgeon Bay
414-743-8896

Pick n' Save
1847 Egg Harbor Rd.
Sturgeon Bay
414-743-8830

Emergency

For fire, police or ambulance, dial 911.

Tourist Information

Door County Chamber of Commerce
Box 406
Sturgeon Bay, WI 54235
414-743-4456
Web site http://doorcounty.org

REMEMBER: The area code for ALL phone numbers in Door County changes from 414 to 920 in October 1997.

9

Central Wisconsin

Including Wausau, Marshfield, Wisconsin Rapids, Stevens Point, and Waupaca

Watch hawks soaring below you. Learn how birds' feathers work. See how paper is made. Talk to lumberjacks. Canoe a quiet stream. All these family activities, and more, await you in Central Wisconsin.

Though most of Central Wisconsin is flat—part of the Central Sands agricultural area—the hills around Wausau include Rib Mountain, the third highest point in the state. The Wisconsin River and the Waupaca chain of 22 lakes provide plenty of fishing, swimming, canoeing, and other water sport opportunities.

Central Wisconsin communities originally developed as trading, logging, and farming centers. Today they are known for papermaking, manufacturing, farming and food processing, and as centers of medicine and higher education.

Wausau

This city of 35,000 began as a logging center during the great boom of the late 19th century. Today, it is a year-round recreation center and is also a commercial hub for a large area of central Wisconsin. Visitors may arrive in Wausau via scheduled airline at the Central Wisconsin Airport just south in Mosinee. Most, however, arrive by car on I-39 (Hwy 51), which runs north-south, or on Hwy 29, which runs east-west.

Things to Do

The **Leigh Yawkey Woodson Art Museum** permanent collection is devoted largely to nature and representations of plants, animals, and natural scenes. Birds are a special focus of the collection. Many of the exhibits include beautiful and delicate porcelain and glass, enough to keep any parent on edge during a visit. However, the museum offers a number of special exhibitions and children's programs that aim to bring both birds and the museum's collection to life for the younger set. The museum also has a wonderful outdoor sculpture garden with both fanciful and realistic sculptures. The garden is worth a visit on its own.

700 N. Twelfth Street; phone 715-845-7010. Open 9-4 Tuesday-Friday, noon-5 Saturday-Sunday. Closed holidays. Free.

The **Grand Theater** is a beautifully restored 1920s opera house that is now used for local and traveling theater companies, musicians, dance and other entertainment. Many of the events are family oriented.

415 Fourth St.; phone 715-842-0988. Performances year-round. $.

Rib Mountain State Park has one of the most spectacular settings in Wisconsin—on top of a huge quartzite rock that rises 650 feet above the surrounding countryside. Your kids will love climbing the observation tower, where they can look down on hawks riding the air currents below, hiking the scenic trails and watching for squirrels, deer and other animals, and picnicking at one of the shaded areas on top of the mountain. The park also has a campground (no electricity), and there's a major downhill ski area as well, but no cross-country ski trails, although some park trails are designed for snoeshoeing in the winter. This is one of the most scenic of Wisconsin's state parks.

5301 Rib Mountain Dr.; phone 715-842-2522 or 715-359-4522 (off season). Open daily mid-April through mid-October, ski hill open daily early December through mid-March. $.

The **Mountain-Bay State Trail** runs for 83 miles between Wausau and Green Bay on an abandoned railroad bed that has been surfaced with crushed limestone. The Wausau-Marathon County portion of the trail goes past farms and through forests. A good choice for family cycling because it's off the highway and it's flat.

Trailhead behind the Weston Municipal Center, 5500 Schofield Ave., Schoefield (south suburb of Wausau). For information, contact the Marathon County Park Dept., 715-847-5235. $ for riders over 16.

Dells of the Eau Claire County Park is one of the most beautiful spots in Wisconsin. The wooded 190-acre park surrounds the rocky gorge carved out over the eons by the Eau Claire River. Visitors can swim at the beach and picnic area upstream from the dells themselves, or picnic and hike next to the roaring waters. There's also a playground and a campground.

Take Hwy Z 15 miles east from Wausau, then follow the signs on Hwy Y. For information, contact the Marathon County Parks Dept.; phone 715-847-5235. Park open daily. Free. Camping May through October. $.

Winter Fun

Rib Mountain has the highest vertical drop, 624 feet, of any Wisconsin downhill ski area. One of the state's best downhill facilities, the area has 13 runs for skiers of all skill levels, plus a large chalet, ski lessons, rentals, and a snack bar. There are ski lessons for kids, and kids ski free on weekdays when accompanied by an adult.

On County Hwy NN just west of I-39; mailing address Box 1349, Wausau 54402; phone 715-845-2846. Open daily early December through mid-March, snow conditions permitting.

Slyvan Hill/American Legion County Park offers three miles of beginner-intermediate groomed cross-country ski trails plus a small downhill ski area with runs up to 1,800 feet served by four rope tows. Downhill lessons for kids Saturdays in January. A good choice for beginning skiers. Chalet and warming house available. Cross-country skiing free, fee for downhill skiers. There's also a sledding hill near the cross-country ski trails. On Horseshoe Spring Rd., on the northeast side of Wausau. Contact the Marathon County Parks Dept., phone 715-847-5235, for information and hours.

The **Marathon Park Indoor Rink** offers ice skating from late October to mid-February. Skate rental and lessons are available. Skating hours vary, phone 715-847-5367 for information. Park is at intersection of Hwy 52 and 17th St.

Open bowling is offered by **Mountain Lanes**, 1401 Elm, just off 17th Ave. (phone 715-845-4331) and by **Day's Bowl-A-Dome**, 1715 Stewart Ave. (phone 715-848-2292).

Shopping

Downtown Wausau has a very attractive mall with large department stores as well as small specialty shops, bookstores, gift shops, and restaurants. It's easy to enjoy a couple of hours of browsing and snacking.

On the outskirts of town, at the intersection of I-39 (Hwy 51) and Business Hwy 51, is the **Cedar Creek Factory Stores** complex, with more than 30 factory outlet stores, a **Discovery Zone** (phone 715-355-8205), a six-screen movie theater (phone 715-355-1080), and several restaurants. If you can't find it here, you don't need it. Open daily. For mall information, phone 715-355-0011.

Events

FEBRUARY. The **Badger State Winter Games** bring amateur athletes from across the state to compete in cross-country skiing, ski jumping, snowshoeing, curling, speed skating, and other winter sports. The Games are geared to athletes of all ages and abilities. Why not join in with your family? Held annually in early February. For information, contact Badger State Games, Box 1377, Madison, WI 53701; phone 608-251-3333. Entry fee.

JUNE. The **Great Wisconsin River Logjam** celebrates the Wausau area's history as a logging and trading town. The focus of the festival is on lumberjack contests such as log rolling and canoe jousting, and on costumed lumberjacks and fur traders in an authentic encampment. There's also a Civil War encampment, plus plenty of children's games and activities, world class white-water kayak races, and an air show. A big event with lots of family activities, plenty of food and fun. Held in late June. Contact Wausau Area Convention and Visitors Council (see Tourist Information below) for details. $ for some events.

AUGUST. The **Wisconsin Valley Fair** is one of the three largest regional fairs in the state. This big event has everything—rides, a midway, entertainment ranging from singers to stock car races, and, of course, plenty of farm animals and animal judging. Held in early August at Marathon Park (on Stewart Ave. just east of I-39 exit).

Contact Wausau Area Convention and Visitors Council (see Tourist Information below) for information. $.

Where to Stay

Wausau Inn & Conference Center, 2001 N. Mountain Rd. (intersection of I-39 and County Hwy NN); phone 715-842-0711 or 800-928-7281. Indoor pool, whirlpool, game room, cable TV, cribs available, good restaurant, handicap accessible rooms. Near Rib Mountain ski area. Kids under 18 stay free with parents.

Ramada Inn, 201 N. 17th Ave. (exit I-39 to Hwy 52, east to 17th St.); phone 715-845-4341 or 800-754-9728. Indoor and outdoor pools, whirlpool, game room, cable TV, cribs available, handicap accessible rooms, restaurant. Kids stay free with parents.

Campers can head to either **Rib Mountain State Park** (30 sites with no electricity but great scenery) or to the **Dells of the Eau Claire County Park**. The Dells park has 25 wooded sites, 16 with electricity, for tents and RVs. No showers. For Rib Mountain, contact the park (See Things to Do above). For the Dells of the Eau Claire, contact the Marathon County Parks Dept., 500 Forest St., Wausau; phone 715-847-5235. Both parks open for camping May through October.

Where to Eat

Michael's serves good food with a menu focus on fresh seafood, veal, and steaks, all moderately priced. Children's menu. 2901 Rib Mountain Dr. (east off I-39 on County Hwy N); phone 715-842-9856. Open Monday-Saturday for dinner.

2510 Restaurant is a family-style restaurant with a large menu that's sure to have something for everyone in the family. Featured items include steaks, prime rib, barbeque ribs, seafood, chicken, Mexican and Italian entrees, and sandwiches. There's also a bakery on the premises that makes fresh homemade desserts and breakfast items. Children's menu. 2510 W. Stewart Ave.; phone 715-845-2510. Open daily for lunch and dinner. The adjoining bakery and deli is open daily for breakfast.

Extended Hours Grocery Store

County Market
220 South 18th Ave.
715-845-8846

Emergency

For fire, police, or ambulance dial 911

Tourist Information

Wausau Area Convention and Visitors Council
300 Third St.
Wausau, WI 54403
715-845-6231
800-236-9728

Marshfield

This city of 20,000 is best known as the home of the excellent medical center, the Marshfield Clinic. Major thoroughfares are Hwy 10, which runs east-west through the city, and Hwy 13, which runs north-south.

Things to Do

Wildwood Park & Zoo houses a well-maintained small zoo whose residents include buffalo, elk, and deer roaming in large enclosures, as well as grizzly bears, monkeys, mountain lion, timber wolf, wild sheep, and a variety of other animals. The adjoining park has playgrounds, picnic areas, tennis courts, swimming pool, and a small lake where kids can feed the ducks, geese, and swans. Green and shaded, a very pleasant park to spend an afternoon.

On Roddis Ave., just off Hwy 13 at south end of town; phone 715-384-4642. Wheelchair accessible. Park open 8:30 a.m.-10:30 p.m. daily. Zoo open 8-7:30 daily early May through mid-October, open 8-2:45 daily mid-October through April. Pool open daily early June through August. Park and zoo free, pool $ for age 3 and up.

Wisconsin Rapids

Papermaking is synonymous with this city of 19,000 on the banks of the Wisconsin River. Visitors come via Hwy 13, which runs north-south through the city, or on Hwy 54, which runs east-west.

Things to Do

The city maintains a number of parks and pathways along the river, some of which have playgrounds and picnic areas. A stroll or bike ride along the river through downtown and the stately neighborhoods will take you through some of the most scenic areas of the city.

A tour of **Consolidated Paper's No. 16 Paper Machine Complex** will amaze you and the kids, as you watch giant rolls of paper spin off the papermaking machines. Educational and fun. Kids must be accompanied by an adult.

Entrance at 4th and Fremont Sts. at midpoint of complex, parking across the street; phone 715-422-3789. Tours year-round at 10 Wednesday, Thursday, and Saturday; tour time two hours. Free.

Sandhill Wildlife Area is managed as a public demonstration area. A 14-mile unpaved road called the "Trumpeter Trail" winds through the area. Points of interest are described in a free nature guide. Three observation towers accessible from the trail give visitors an opportunity to see the resident buffalo herd, a large marsh with geese, sandhill cranes, and other wild residents, and, finally, a panoramic view of the countryside from a tower atop a 200-foot quartzite bluff. Hiking trails are also marked throughout the area. In winter, 17 miles of ungroomed cross-country ski trails are open for public use.

Off Hwy 54 seventeen miles west of Wisconsin Rapids; mailing address Sandhill Wildlife Area, Box 156, Babcock, WI 54413; phone 715-884-2437. Trumpeter Trail open from late April through early November. Free.

Winter Fun

Public ice skating rinks are located at **Mead Athletic Field**, 17th Ave. and Chase St.; **Ward Johnson Park**, 3100 North Ave.; **Witter Field**, 8th Street North and

Franklin St.; and **Robinson Park** off Hwy 54. For information, contact the Wisconsin Rapids Recreation Department, 715-421-8240.

Treats

Herscleb's Dairybest churns out homemade ice cream using Grandpa Herscleb's 1939 recipe. High-butterfat heaven. They also serve food, but save most of your calories for dessert. Corner of 16th St. and Hwy 54; phone 715-423-1760. Open daily.

Where to Stay

Mead Inn, 451 E. Grand Ave. (Business Hwy 13); phone 715-423-1500. An excellent downtown motel with an indoor pool, game room, cable TV, exercise room, handicap-accessible rooms, and two restaurants.

Extended Hours Grocery Store

Copps 24 Hour Food Center
900 E. Riverview Expressway
715-423-1620

Emergency

For fire, police, or ambulance, dial 911

Tourist Information

Wisconsin Rapids Area Chamber of Commerce
1120 Lincoln St.
Wisconsin Rapids, WI 54494
715-423-1830

Stevens Point

This former Wisconsin River trading post is today best known as the home of Sentry Insurance and of the University of Wisconsin-Stevens Point. The city is at the center of the Central Sands agricultural area which is known for the production and processing of potatoes and other vegetables.

Visitors to this city of 43,000 usually arrive on I-39 (Hwy 51) which runs north-south, on Hwy 10, which runs east-west, or via scheduled airline to the Central Wisconsin Airport a few miles north in Mosinee.

Things to Do

Rainbow Falls Family Park has miniature golf, three go-kart tracks, bumper boats, water slides, wave pool, a kiddy wading pool and playground, and more. Also be sure to visit the adjoining outlet mall where there's an indoor **Rainbow Kids** play area with video games, ball pits, mazes, and lots of other stuff for kids to climb on and in, slide down, crawl through, and bounce on.

At intersection of I-39 and County Hwy B just south of Stevens Point; Rainbow Falls phone 715-345-1950; Rainbow Kids phone 715-345-7845. Rainbow Falls open daily 10-dark mid-May through early September; open 11-6 weekends in early May and September. Rainbow Kids open daily. $.

The **Schmeekle Reserve**, a UW-Stevens Point research and teaching area just north of the campus, is open to the public for activities including hiking, bicycling, and canoeing (short portage to the lake required). A boardwalk takes visitors through a large marsh. The Visitor Center has natural history exhibits and a naturalist to answer questions.

Visitor Center at the reserve entrance on North Point Dr.; phone 715-346-4992. Reserve open daily year-round. Visitor Center open 9-5 Monday-Friday and noon-5 Saturday and Sunday May through October; open 8-4 Monday-Friday and noon-4 Saturday and Sunday November through April. Free.

Pfiffner Pioneer Park provides a bike trail, boat launch ramp and dock, picnic area and playground on Crosby Avenue at the Wisconsin River just north of downtown. Bukolt Park, just up the shore from Pfiffner Park at Bukolt Avenue and the river, has picnic areas, playground and a beach for river swimming. Bukolt Park, Schmeekle Reserve and Pfiffner Pioneer Park are part of the unique 24-mile **Green Circle**, a trail linking scenic and natural areas in and around Stevens Point. The Circle offers bicycling, hiking, bird watching, and other outdoor activities along its route. Contact the Stevens Point Parks and Recreation Department (715-346-1531) for a Green Circle map and other information.

Winter Fun

Ice skaters flock to the indoor skating rink at **Goerke Park**, at Main St. and Michigan Ave. For open skating hours, call 715-346-1576.

Treats

Sweet Treats is the place for ice cream, chocolate, jelly beans, hard candies, and lots of other normally forbidden (or at least rationed) goodies. Here's the place to indulge. 919 Main St., phone 715-341-4990. Open daily.

Shopping

Gepetto's Workshop is a wonderful toy store featuring high quality dolls, stuffed animals, toy soldiers, games, books, puzzles, and much more. 1121 Main St.; phone 715-341-8640. Open 10-5 Monday-Saturday, open Friday evening until 8.

Play 'N Learn has the largest selection of teaching materials and educational toys in the area. 1008 Main St.; phone 715-344-4882. Open 10-8 Monday-Friday, 9-4 Saturday, and noon-4 Sunday.

The **CenterPoint Mall** downtown shopping district has more than 30 stores offering a wide selection of clothing, books, toys, and other items. The mall is on Hwy 10 in downtown Stevens Point; phone 715-344-1599. Open 10-9 Monday-Friday, 9:30-5 Saturday, 11-5 Sunday.

Where to Stay

Best Western Royale Inn, 5110 Main St. (Hwy 10); phone 715-341-5110 or 800-528-1234. Indoor pool, whirlpool and sauna, game room, cable TV, handicap accessible rooms, and a 24-hour restaurant that serves good food.

Holiday Inn, 1501 North Point Dr. (off Business Hwy 51 North); phone 715-341-1340 or 800-922-7880. A Holidome with indoor pool, whirlpool and sauna, kids playpark, game room, cable TV, video machine rental, exercise room, restaurant, lounge with live entertainment.

Lake DuBay Shores Campground is a large, forested campground with full hookups, showers, recreation hall, playground and children's activities, nature trail, store, and a beach and boat dock on Lake DuBay, which is an impoundment of the Wisconsin River. The only drawback to this popular campground is that the campsites are a bit small and close together. Not a problem if you don't mind being close to your neighbor. 1713 DuBay Dr., Mosinee, WI 54455 (on Hwy 34 two miles west of I-39); phone 715-457-2484. Open all year.

Where to Eat

The **Hot Fish Shop**, a Stevens Point tradition, serves excellent fresh seafood, soups, salads, and desserts. The extensive menu also includes sandwiches, and beef, chicken, and veal dishes. 1140 Clark St.; phone 715-344-4252. Open daily for lunch and dinner.

Emergency

For fire, police or ambulance, dial 911.

Tourist Information

Stevens Point Convention & Visitors Bureau
23 Park Ridge Dr.
Stevens Point, WI 54481
715-344-2556
800-236-INFO
24-hour activities and events information 715-341-6566

Waupaca

This resort area developed around a chain of 22 lakes and the beautiful Crystal River. The area is most easily reached on Hwy 10, which runs east-west, and on Hwy 22, which runs north-south.

Things to Do

The **Chief Waupaca**, a 60-foot sternwheeler, and the 54-foot motor yacht *Lady of the Lakes* provide one and one-half hour narrated tours on the Waupaca chain of lakes. Meals are available on some of the cruises. Both vessels dock at Clearwater Harbor.

On County Hwy QQ, off Hwy 22 south of Waupaca; phone 715-258-2866. Cruises daily Memorial Day weekend through Labor Day. $.

A visit to the Chain O' Lakes wouldn't be complete without a trip through several of them on the famous Crystal River. **Ding's Dock** has been providing rental canoes, along with shuttle service and changing rooms, for decades. The Crystal is easily canoed, although there are a few fast spots (but no real rapids). And it's shallow. If you tip over you can just stand up. Ding's offers a three-hour scenic trip on the river and two lakes. Not recommended for kids under 6.

N2498 Columbia Lake Dr. (Hwy Q), off Hwy 22 south of Waupaca; phone 715-258-2612 or 800-236-7577. Open daily May through September.

Waterslide & Go-karts water park has everything needed to keep the kids happy—two water slides, go-karts, mini go-karts, playground, an arcade, and snack bar and picnic areas where you can relax while the kids play.

At intersection of Hwys 10 & 22 & K; phone 715-258-8122 or 800-944-2908. Open 10-8 daily Memorial Day weekend through Labor Day. $.

Tom Thumb Mini Golf is the area's first miniature golf course, with 18 holes, many featuring devious mechanical hazards designed to ruin that hole-in-one. Not as large and technologically sophisticated as the mega-mini-golf courses that are around now, (reminiscent of the '50s, according to their promotional brochure) but adequate to keep you and the kids entertained for an hour or so. Shady location on the lake.

On Whispering Pines Rd. (Hwy 22 south of Waupaca to Rural Rd., west to Whispering Pines Rd.); phone 715-258-8737. Open 10-10 Monday-Saturday, 11-10 Sunday, Memorial Day weekend through Labor Day. $.

Hartman Creek State Park contains four of the Waupaca chain's 22 lakes. The park offers swimming, boating (no motors allowed), 14 miles of hiking trails, a playground, picnic areas, and a campground. In summer, a naturalist leads hikes and gives lectures about the park's flora, fauna, and Indian archeological sites.

The park is popular for cross-country skiing and snow-mobiling in winter.

N2480 Hartman Creek Rd.(south of Waupaca on Hwy 22, west on Rural Rd.); phone 715-258-2372. Handicap accessible camping and picnic facilities. Open daily year-round. $.

South Park, a beautiful Waupaca city park, encompasses 15 shaded acres on Mirror Lake and Shadow Lake. Facilities include a swimming beach with bath house, playground, picnic areas, boat launch, fishing pier, and lots of room to run around. A perfect place to while away a summer afternoon. At the end of S. Main St. Open daily.

Winter Fun

South Park has an outdoor ice skating rink and a sledding hill. Or try cross-country skiing at **Hartman Creek State Park**.

Treats

Katie McCann's Coffee House has excellent gourmet coffees and teas, plus ice cream, pastries, and great desserts. On Hwy QQ in downtown King (south of Waupaca off Hwy 22), phone 715-258-4995.

Rentals

Chain O'Lakes Marine rents canoes, motorboats, pontoon boats, pedal boats, sailboats, and waverunners. On County Hwy QQ at Clear Water Harbor; phone 715-258-8840.

Ding's Dock rents canoes, motorboats, and pontoon boats. On County Hwy Q; phone 715-258-2612.

Becker Marine rents canoes, pedal boats, rowboats, motorboats, and pontoon boats. On Hwy Q (off Hwy QQ); phone 715-258-9015.

Where to Eat

Clear Water Harbor, the starting point for the boat tours of the chain of lakes, has a waterside dining room that serves great burgers and sandwiches plus soups, salads, and homemade desserts. There's also a Friday fish fry.

Eat outdoors on the deck and watch the boats on Taylor Lake. Mom and Dad can get a beer or cocktail from the bar, too. Open daily May through September for lunch and dinner. On Hwy QQ in King (south of Waupaca off Hwy 22); phone 715-258-9912

Tourist Information

Waupaca Area Chamber of Commerce
221 S. Main St.
Waupaca, WI 54981
715-258-7343

10

The Northwoods

Including Minocqua, Woodruff, Sayner, Star Lake, St. Germain, Boulder Junction, Lac du Flambeau, Eagle River, Rhinelander, Laona, Langlade, Tomahawk, Merrill, Athelstane, Crivitz, and the beautiful lakes and forests in between

Northwoods vacations have been sought for more than a century by visitors who want to relax and take life a little more slowly. The key to a successful Northwoods family vacation is to find the perfect lakeside accommodation and enjoy the woods, waters, and wildlife, the clear air, the sparkling winter snow. Bring your bird, tree and mammal identification guides.

This year-round vacation land encompasses an area with thousands of glacial lakes and hundreds of thousands of acres of county, state, and federal parks and forests. Vacations here focus on the outdoors—hiking, boating, fishing, swimming, skiing, snowmobiling, and just loafing. But museums and historic sites, amusement parks, shopping areas, and cultural events are increasingly available to visitors.

The communities in the Northwoods developed to serve the logging industry in the late 1800s. Logging is still important, but papermaking, farming, manufacturing and tourism now dominate the Northwoods economy.

Visitors to the area can arrive via scheduled airline to Rhinelander. The vast majority, though, come by car on Hwys 51, 45, and 41, which run north-south, and Hwys 8, 54, and 70, which run east-west through the area.

Minocqua and Woodruff

This area has become the tourism capital of the Northwoods, with more amusements, attractions, shops, and restaurants devoted to pleasing visitors than in any other Northwoods communities. Hwy 51 brings hundreds of thousands of travelers from Illinois and southern Wisconsin every summer, and, increasingly, in fall and winter. Woodruff is the headquarters for the Northern Highland-American Legion State Forest, which stretches over 200,000 acres in Iron, Vilas, and Oneida counties. Scattered throughout the state forest are private holdings with resorts, restaurants and visitor attractions.

Things to Do

Northern Highland-American Legion State Forest encompasses literally thousands of lakes, hundreds of miles of rivers and streams, and, of course, thousands of acres of forest. All of which means there's plenty to do here. The forest has 18 campgrounds, canoe trails and 100 canoe campsites, boat launch ramps, picnic areas, and swimming beaches. Naturalists give lectures and lead forest walks at the Crystal Lake campground from Memorial Day through Labor Day. There are also hiking, cross-country ski, and snowmobile trails. Abundant wildlife includes deer, black bear, loons, ducks, herons, bald eagles, and osprey.

Forest superintendent, 8770 Hwy J, Woodruff, WI 54568; phone 715-356-5211. Forest headquarters at Department of Natural Resources Woodruff office, east of Woodruff off Hwy 47. Handicap accessible camping and picnic facilities. $ for camping and for some developed use areas.

The **Woodruff State Fish Hatchery** is a world leader in musky production. The hatchery annually produces some 45,000 muskies and 1.2 million walleyes for stocking. The hatchery operation includes egg hatching and fish rearing facilities as well as ponds to rear forage fish for the young muskies to eat. A show pond of native Wisconsin fish, aquaria with native fish, and record-size mounted fish are on display.

On County Hwy J east of Woodruff; phone 715-356-5211. Open 8-4:30 Monday-Friday. Guided tours 11 a.m. Monday-Friday from Memorial Day through Labor Day. A self-guiding brochure is also available. Free.

The **Bearskin State Trail** runs on an abandoned rail corridor 18 miles from downtown Minocqua south to the tiny community of Harshaw. The trail winds through lovely woods and over picturesque streams. It crosses Bearskin Creek nine times, runs along the shore of South Blue Lake, and crosses Lake Minocqua on a long trestle. There's a rest area with picnic tables, grills, drinking water, and rest rooms at South Blue Lake, about nine miles from Minocqua. Hiking and snowmobiling are also allowed in the trail.

Trail begins at the end of Front St., two blocks west of Oneida St. (Hwy 51) in downtown Minocqua. Trail superintendent address: Trout Lake Headquarters, Route 1, Box 45, Boulder Junction, WI 54512. Phone 715-385-2727. $ for bicyclists.

Jim Peck's Wildwood Wildlife Park gives kids a chance to pet porcupines, baby rabbits, and other domestic and wild animals and to feed deer, goats, trout, and a variety of hungry critters. Kids enjoy the fawn yard, where they can feed and pet spotted fawns. Educational programs daily. You can also rent an electric boat for a ride on the park's lagoon.

On Hwy 70 two miles west of intersection with Hwy 51, Minocqua; phone 715-356-5588. Open 9-5:30 daily early May through mid-October. $.

Circle M Corral Family Fun Park has a little of everything—water slide, go-karts, bumper boats, mini-train, miniature golf, kiddie go-karts, wading pools, batting cages, shooting gallery, video games, and horse and pony rides. The park also has a snack bar and picnic area.

On Hwy 70 two and one-half miles west of intersection with Hwy 51, Minocqua; phone 715-356-4441. Open 10-dusk daily early May through mid-October. $.

Serious miniature golf enthusiasts will want to play at **Settler's Mill**, the largest and most difficult miniature golf course in the Northwoods. Eighteen holes of challenging fun, plus a video game room.

On Hwy 51 just south of Minocqua; phone 715-356-9797. Open 10-10 daily Memorial Day weekend through Labor Day, 10-dark September weekends. $.

Adjoining Settler's Mill is **Holiday Acres**, offering go-karts, bumper cars, and horseback rides.

On Hwy 51 just south of Minocqua; phone 715-356-4400. Horseback rides hourly 9-5, karts and cars 9 a.m.-11 p.m. daily, Memorial Day through Labor Day. $.

Wilderness Cruises takes visitors on tours of the Willow Flowage on the 76-foot Wilderness Queen. Cruises take you along wooded shoreline and past islands where osprey and eagles nest. Meals are served on some cruises.

Dock is on Willow Dam Rd. (south of Minocqua on Hwy 51, west on County Hwy Y); phone 715-453-3310 or 800-472-1516. Cruises weekends in May, daily Memorial Day weekend through early October. Reservations required for all cruises. $.

The **Northwoods Wildlife Center** is a hospital for sick and injured wildlife. Guided tours of the facility give visitors a chance to learn about Northwoods animals and see how injured animals are healed to return to the wild.

On Hwy 70 just west of intersection with Hwy 51, Minocqua; phone 715-356-7400. Open for tours 10-2 Monday-Saturday. Call for an appointment. Free.

The **Northern Lights Playhouse** presents musicals and comedies in summer stock. The company also offers weekly children's theater performances.

On Hwy 51, ten miles south of Minocqua; phone 715-356-7173. Performances daily late May through September. Children's theater 11 a.m. Wednesday and Saturday, early June through August. $.

Warbonnet Zoo presents both wild and domestic animals that kids can feed and pet. There are deer, wild turkeys, peacocks, miniature horses, baby goats, a tiger, and much more. The zoo has a picnic area, cafe, and gift shop.

On Hwy 51, ten miles south of Minocqua; phone 715-356-5093. Open daily 9-7 early May through September. Call for winter hours. $.

Scheer's Lumberjack Shows feature lumberjacks competing in such northwoods sports as logrolling, speed-climbing, cross-cut sawing, canoe jousting, and log chopping. In addition, the camp cook provides music and comedic commentary.

In Woodruff on Hwy 47 just east of Hwy 51 intersection; phone 715-356-4050. Wheelchair accessible. Seventy-five minute shows rain or shine (covered grandstand) at 7:30 Tuesday, Thursday, Saturday, and 2 Wednesday and Friday late June through late August. Call to be sure—they sometimes cancel shows in July because the lumberjacks are at competitions elsewhere. $.

The **Min-Aqua Bats** perform amazing water ski acrobatics three times weekly all summer.

At the Aqua Bowl on Park St., two blocks west of downtown Minocqua. No phone. Shows at 7 Sunday, Wednesday, and Friday from mid-June through late August. Free, donation requested.

Torpy Park, two blocks north of downtown Minocqua on Hwy 51, has an excellent swimming beach with lifeguard, playground, shaded picnic area, and tennis courts. Evening band concerts throughout the summer. Free.

Winter Fun

Minocqua is a snowmobiling and cross-country skiing center. Enthusiasts use the hundreds of miles of state and county snowmobile trails and the many miles of ski trails in **Northern Highland-American Legion State Forest**. For information on ski and snowmobile trails, contact the Minocqua Chamber of Commerce (see Tourist Information below) or the forest superintendent (see Things to Do above)

Minocqua Winter Park is a cross-country ski center with more than 35 miles of groomed trails for all skill levels, plus lessons, rentals, ski shop, warming house, and snack bar. This facility is one of the best in the Midwest, and is excellent for family skiing. Some lighted trails for night skiing. The park sponsors a number of races and other special events throughout the winter.

Ten miles west of Minocqua on Hwy 70 to Squirrel Lake Rd., follow signs to Winter Park. Mailing address Box 558, Minocqua, WI 54548; phone 715-356-3309. Open daily early December though mid-March, weather permitting. Trail fee.

Shopping

Downtown Minocqua is the place for serious shopping. Souvenir shops, candy stores, boutiques and variety stores are all within a few blocks. Oneida Street (Hwy 51) is the main thoroughfare and heart of the shopping district.

Book World has the area's largest selection of magazines, novels, nonfiction and Midwest regional books. It also carries children's books and games. 522 Oneida St.; phone 715-356-7071. Open 9-9 Monday-Saturday, 9-5 Sunday in summer, 9-8 Monday-Saturday and 9-5 Sunday in winter.

Treats

Minocqua has several candy and fudge shops, but the best is **Bosacki's Soda Fountain**, which creates heavenly fudge and chocolates. Not in the mood for candy? Their malts, shakes, and sundaes are pretty darn good, too. In the lower level of Bosacki's Boat House Restaurant at the Hwy 51 bridge in downtown Minocqua; phone 715-356-5292. Open daily 11 a.m-midnight in summer.

Rentals

BJ's Sportshop rents bicycles as well as sailboards and motorboats on Lake Minocqua. They also rent cross-country skis. On Hwy 51 one-half mile north of downtown Minocqua; phone 715-356-3900.

Minocqua Sport Rentals supplies fishing and ski boats, jet skis, paddle boats, sailboats, and bicycles in the summer and rents snowmobiles in the winter. On Hwy 70 three blocks west of intersection with Hwy 51; phone 715-356-4661.

Fun Rentals rents motorboats, jet skis, pontoon boats, and snowmobiles. At the 7855 Leary Road (east of Minocqua off Hwy 51); phone 715-356-1050 or 800-358-7101.

Where to Stay

The Minocqua area has many fine resorts and motels. Depending on your vacation plans, you can stay in a motel, a luxury condo, or a rustic housekeeping cottage.

Pointe Resort and Hotel, at the bridge on Hwy 51 just south of Minocqua. Mailing address Box 880, Minocqua, WI 54548. Phone 715-356-4431. This condo development offers waterside accommodations in a modern facility with plenty of amenities. This is the place to stay in Minocqua if you want pampering. The all-suite facility has a fully furnished living room with cable TV and a fully equipped kitchen in every unit. There's an indoor pool, tennis courts, boats, organized hikes and other activities for kids. Short walk to restaurants and shopping.

Best Western Lakeview Motor Lodge, in town on Hwy 51 at the bridge; mailing address Box 575, Minocqua, WI 54548; phone 715-356-5208 or 800-852-1021. On Lake Minocqua, swiming beach, fishing pier, cable TV, suites available, short walk to restaurants and shopping.

Minocqua Shores, Box 313, Minocqua, WI 54548; phone 715-356-5101. Across Lake Minocqua from downtown. An old-fashioned housekeeping cottage resort with newer condo units added. Only 13 units total, so it's a small, friendly resort. All units fully furnished. Lovely grounds, beach, boats available, boat launch ramp and dock, playground, cable TV. Baby furniture available.

The Beacons, 8250 Northern Rd., Minocqua 54548; phone 715-356-5515 or 800-236-3225. A lakeside resort on beautifully landscaped grounds with condo units that sleep four to six. Each has a kitchen and is fully furnished, including a fireplace and cable TV. Game room, playground, beach, indoor pool, exercise room, whirlpool, sauna, boats, hiking trails. Handicap accessible unit available. Across Lake Minocqua from town.

Campers can choose from among the 18 campgrounds in the **Northern Highland-American Legion State Forest** (see Things to Do above).

Where to Eat

Bosacki's Boat House is a Minocqua landmark, a spot where local residents and visitors mingle. The large lunch menu features sandwiches, soup, and a salad bar. The dinner menu is heavy on beef, chicken, and seafood. Children's menu. The dining room overlooks Lake Minocqua. On Hwy 51 at the bridge; phone 715-356-5292. Open daily for lunch and dinner; soda fountain (see Treats above) open summer only.

The **Island Cafe** has great food and is usually uncrowded. The Greek owner regularly produces Greek specials in addition to the large menu of full breakfasts, sandwiches, soups, plate lunches, and dinner specials. Excellent homemade muffins and pies. Children's menu.

314 Oneida St., Minocqua; phone 715-356-6977. Open daily for breakfast, lunch, and dinner.

Polecat and Lace features very good sandwiches, steaks, veal, and seafood dishes. Children's menu and heart-healthy selections. On Oneida St. in Island City Square, downtown Minocqua. Phone 715-356-3335. Open Monday-Saturday for lunch and dinner.

Cross Trails Restaurant features homemade soups, sweet rolls, and pies. One sweet roll is a more than adequate, and very tasty, breakfast. Full breakfasts, sandwiches, full dinners in typical hearty Wisconsin cafe style, featuring beef, chicken, seafood. Children's menu. Save room for pie. On Hwy 51 between Minocqua and Woodruff; phone 715-356-5202. Open daily for breakfast, lunch, and dinner.

Lula's Deli pumps out terrific pancakes, waffles, omelettes, and homemade bakery items for breakfast, then goes on to produce a wide variety of deli sandwiches along with homemade soups and great salads for lunch. For dessert there's ice cream or homemade brownies or cookies. Take-outs available for that picnic you've been planning. On Hwy 51 North at the north end of Woodruff; phone 715-358-2200. Open daily for breakfast and lunch.

Extended Hours Grocery Store

Trig's Food and Drug
Hwy 70 West Center
(just west of Hwys 70-51 intersection)
Minocqua
715-356-9456

Emergency

For fire, police, or ambulance, dial 911.

Tourist Information

Greater Minocqua Chamber of Commerce
Information center
8216 Hwy 51 South
Minocqua, WI 54548
715-356-5266
800-446-6784

Sayner, Star Lake, St. Germain, and Boulder Junction

Once logging towns, these small Vilas County communities are the center of one of the oldest resort areas in Wisconsin. Visitors have been coming to this area to enjoy the lakes, the cool summer weather, and the clear air for more than a century.

This area is off the beaten path. Visitors arrive via Hwy 51, then take County Hwys M, N, or K to Sayner, Boulder Junction, and Star Lake; or they come via Hwys 70 and 155 to St. Germain and Sayner, then take County Hwys N and K to Star Lake and Boulder Junction.

Things to Do

These communities are at the heart of the **Northern Highland-American Legion State Forest** (see Things to Do-Minocqua). Hiking, ski, and snowmobile trails crisscross the land, and canoe trails wind along the streams and lakeshores. Campgrounds, beaches, picnic areas, and boat launch ramps are easy to find. One of the most interesting areas in the forest is **Crystal Lake**, a clear, entirely sand-bottom, spring-fed lake with the best beach in the north. There's also a picnic area and campground on the shores of this delightful little lake. It's worth a side trip. On County Hwy N three miles west of Sayner. $ for camping and some recreational facilities.

The **Vilas County Historical Museum** has exhibits of life in early pioneer Vilas County. On display are boats, antique outboard motors, household implements such as washing machines, stoves, and spinning wheels, plus player pianos and a host of other everyday items. In addition, there's a large display of snowmobiles from the first machine (invented in 1924 by a Sayner native) to the latest Arctic Cat. A Sayner resident also donated a large collection of mounted animals, both native and exotics. All in all, this eclectic little museum is a good place to while away a rainy afternoon.

On Hwy 155 at south end of Sayner; phone 715-542-3388. Open daily 10-4 Memorial Day weekend through last weekend in September. Free, donation requested.

Elmer's Fun Park has two go-kart tracks, bumper boats, and guided horseback rides.

On Hwy 70 two and one-half miles east of St. Germain; phone 715-479-7311. Open 9 a.m.-10 p.m. daily late May through early September. Last trail ride leaves at 6.

The **Plum Ski-ters** present their water ski show—pyramids, ballet, barefooting, jumping, trick skiing, and clowning around—three times a week in summer from their show site on Razorback Road, off County Hwy N two miles west of Sayner. No phone. Shows at 7 p.m. Sunday, Tuesday, and Thursday mid-June through late August. Free, donation requested.

Bicycling has become a popular Northwoods activity. In addition to the **Bearskin State Trail** (see Things to Do-Minocqua, above) there are several popular off-road bike trails that the entire family can enjoy. **Razorback Ridges**, on Hwy N two miles west of Sayner (look for McKay's Corner Store), has 30 miles of wooded off-road bike trails for all skill levels. And there's an ice cream parlor at the trailhead. Best of all, they're open daily, and they're free (donation requested). Phone 715-542-3019 for information. The **Boulder Area Trails** begin behind the Boulder Junction Chamber of Commerce Office (see below for address and phone) just south of town on Hwy M. There's a paved 3.5-mile trail to a picnic area on the shores of Trout Lake, plus over 10 miles of dirt trails winding through the woods and past several lakes. These trails are also open daily and are free.

Winter Fun

For information about cross-country ski and snowmobile trails in the **Northern Highland-American Legion State Forest**, contact the forest superintendent (see Things to Do-Minocqua above).

In winter **Razorback Ridges** becomes a cross-country ski area with more than 12 miles of excellent groomed trails for skiers of all skill levels. There's a warming house and refreshment area at the trailhead.

On County Hwy N two miles west of Sayner at McKay's Corner Store. Open daily during winter as snow conditions permit. For information, contact the Sayner-Star Lake Lions Club, Box 120, Sayner, WI 54560; phone 715-542-3019. Trail use free, donation requested.

Shopping

The Bookworm has an excellent selection of children's books, games, and puzzles plus plenty of regional books and national bestsellers. 5433 County Hwy M two blocks south of downtown Boulder Junction; phone 715-385-2191. Open daily year-round.

Treats

When the hungries grab you in Boulder Junction, head for the **Crusts and Crocks Bakery** for wonderful bread plus great pies and cheesecake and other tasty things they felt like baking that day. On Hwy K just east of downtown; phone 715-385-0204.

Rentals

Schauss Woodwork, on Main Street (Hwy K) in Boulder Junction, rents canoes, fishing boats, and paddleboats on area lakes. Phone 715-385-2434.

St. Germain Marine, on Hwy 70 in St. Germain, rents water-ski boats, fishing boats, jet skis, and outboard motors, as well as snowmobiles. Phone 715-479-4930.

Where to Stay

Hintz's North Star Lodge, Hwy K, Star Lake, WI 54561; phone 715-542-3600 or 800-788-5215. This rustic resort began as a retreat for lumber and railroad barons who came north to see the progress of logging operations and to fish Star Lake and enjoy the cool summer air. The main lodge is the original, built in 1894. The fully furnished lakeside cottages have been updated, as has the restaurant. A beautiful setting on a lovely lake with a beach, game room, boats. Resort open early May through mid-October.

Deer Run Condominium Resort, Box 356, St. Germain, WI 54558; phone 715-479-6884. This turn-of-the-century resort has been modernized. All cottages are fully furnished, including microwave and color TV. Cribs and high chairs available. The lovely wooded grounds on Big St. Germain Lake have a playground, beach, and boat dock. There's a video game room in the restaurant.

Clearview Rentals, 8617 Big St. Germain Dr., St. Germain 54558, phone 715-542-3546 or 715-542-3865. Furnished vacation cottages on the shore of Big St. Germain Lake. All cottages have TV and VCR and microwave (in addition to the full kitchen). Some have fireplaces. Rowboat included with each cottage. Beach and play area. Motorboat rental available. Restaurant on the grounds if you don't feel like cooking dinner. Quiet, wooded, on the lake.

White Birch Village, Box 284, Boulder Junction 54512; phone 715-385-2182. Modern housekeeping homes on White Birch Lake east of Boulder Junction off Hwy K. Wooded grounds, quiet and secluded. A family resort with beach, paddleboats and motorboats, playground, hiking trails, game room. Open May through October.

Evergreen Lodge, Box 560, Boulder Junction 54512; phone 715-385-2132. Small resort with cabins on wooded grounds on Little Crooked Lake (south of Boulder Junction off Hwy K). Choose a light housekeeping (microwave and refrigerator only) or deluxe housekeeping (full kitchen) cabin. No matter which type of cabin you choose, daily breakfast is included in your rental, as is Sunday dinner. Playground, beach, paddleboat, hiking, game room, movies, picnic area, whirlpool, sauna. Rustic and secluded.

State forest campgrounds in the area are on Plum Lake, Crystal Lake, Razorback Lake, Firefly Lake, Big Muskellunge Lake, and Star Lake. Contact the forest superintendent for information (see Things to Do-Minocqua above).

Where to Eat

Glenbrook Station serves bountiful and very good breakfasts, sandwiches and soups, and a variety of dinner entrees, all at reasonable prices. Homemade desserts. In Sayner on Hwy 155; phone 715-542-3906. Open daily for breakfast, lunch, and dinner.

Worthen's Sayner Pub is a homey place with good homemade pizza, spaghetti, burgers and sandwiches, and a game room with a pool table and video games to occupy the kids while dinner is being prepared. On Hwy 155 in Sayner; phone 715-542-3647. Open daily for breakfast, lunch, and dinner.

The **Whitetail Inn** is in a building made from huge pine logs. Inside the modern, open dining area serves excellent meals ranging from soups, salads, and sandwiches to supper club seafood, chicken, and beef dishes. There's also an amazing Sunday brunch. At the junction of Hwy 70 and Hwy C three miles west of St. Germain; phone 715-542-2541. Open daily for lunch and dinner.

The **Clearview Supper Club** does indeed have a wonderful view of Big St. Germain Lake. Excellent dinners from a large traditional supper club menu plus nightly specials and Friday fish fry. 8599 Big St. Germain Dr., between Hwy 155 and Hwy C north of St. Germain; phone 715-542-3474. Open daily for dinner.

Hintz's North Star Lodge serves excellent food—great salad bar, wonderful beef, chicken, and seafood, terrific Friday night fish fry, and wonderful homemade pie. Reserve a piece of pie when you arrive so you won't be disappointed. On Hwy K in Star Lake; phone 715-542-3600. Open Tuesday-Saturday for dinner early May through mid-October.

The **Guides Inn** has a menu that's a cut above the traditional northwoods supper club with entrees such as beef Wellington. But there's plenty for kids to eat, too. Everything is made fresh daily, including bread, soups, and desserts. On Hwy M just south of downtown Boulder Junction; phone 715-385-2233. Open daily for dinner.

Big Bear Eatery is in a cluster of new log buildings that also house gift shops and a bakery. Big Bear features wonderful sandwiches, pizza, salads and soups, and their soon-to-be-famous "Big Bear Butt Bar-B-Q." And there's always those terrific desserts. Great place for casual dining. On Hyw K just west of Boulder Junction; phone 715-385-0203. Open daily for lunch and dinner.

Emergency

For fire, police or ambulance, call 479-4441 in Sayner, Star Lake or St. Germain. In Boulder Junction, call 356-3311 for fire or ambulance, or 800-472-7290 for police.

Tourist Information

Sayner-Star Lake Chamber of Commerce
Box 191
Sayner, WI 54560
715-542-3789

St. Germain Chamber of Commerce
Hwy 70 & 155
Box 155
St. Germain, WI 54558
715-542-3423
800-727-7203

Boulder Junction Chamber of Commerce
Information center on Hwy M just south of town
Box 286
Boulder Junction, WI 54512
715-385-2400

Lac du Flambeau

This Chippewa Indian community is at the center of the Lac du Flambeau reservation. Easiest access is Hwy 47 north from Woodruff.

Things to Do

The Chippewa hold a weekly **Pow-wow** throughout the summer, with dancing, drumming, and authentic tribal costumes. An excellent opportunity to introduce your children to Native American culture.Adjoining the Pow-wow site is the **Chippewa Museum & Cultural Center**. This well-designed small museum has exhibits of a fur trader cabin, dugout and birchbark canoes, arrowheads, beadwork and crafts, and tribal dress.

Pow-wow site and Cultural Center adjoining on County Hwy D, just off Hwy 47. Pow-wows Tuesdays at 7 p.m. July through mid-August. Cultural Center phone 715-588-3333. Cultural Center open 10-4 daily May through October, 10-2 Tuesday, Wednesday, Thursday November through April, or by appointment. $ for both Cultural Center and Pow-wow.

The **Chippewa Tribal Fish Hatchery** raises fish to release in lakes on the reservation. Tours are offered Wednesdays 1-3:30 May through August. There's also a trout pond at the hatchery where you and the kids can catch fish instead of just looking at them.

On Hwy 47 just north of town; phone 715-588-3303. Open daily May through August. Hatchery tours free, $ for trout fishing.

Where to Stay

Dillman's Sand Bay Properties, Lac du Flambeau, WI 54538; phone 715-588-3143. Off County Hwy D on Sand Lake Lodge Rd. This modern resort rents fully furnished cabins on the shore of White Sand Lake. Cook your own meals or eat in the excellent restaurant. The resort has tennis courts, beach, playground, boats, bikes, water skiing, hiking trails and supervised activities for kids. Open mid-May through mid-October.

Fence Lake Lodge, 12919 Frying Pan Camp Lane (off Hwy 47 between Woodruff and Lac du Flambeau), Lac du Flambeau 54538; phone 715-588-3255. This beautiful resort complex on the shore of (you guessed it) Fence Lake features luxurious log buildings with views of the lake. Lodging options include standard motel rooms or suites with whirlpool and fireplace. The resort offers all the amenities—a large beach, boat rentals, playground, game room, TVs and VCRs, picnic areas, hiking trails on the 300-acre wooded grounds, restaurant and snack bar.

Lac du Flambeau Tribal Campground and Marina, just north of town on Hwy 47; mailing address Box 284, Lac du Flambeau, WI 54538; phone 715-588-7479. Lakeside campground with 72 units on open and wooded sites, offering full hookups, showers, store, laundry, game room, boat rentals, separate tent and RV sites. Good location on a peninsula jutting out into Flambeau Lake. Some sites have piers.

Where to Eat

Dillman's Sand Bay Properties dining room provides lakeside dining with good food, great views. Off County Hwy D on Sand Lake Lodge Rd.; phone 715-588-3143. Open daily mid-May through mid-October for breakfast and dinner. Dinner reservations advised.

Fence Lake Lodge offers lakeside dining (outdoors in good weather). Full breakfast menu, excellent sandwiches and soups, large dinner menu featuring seafood, chicken, steaks, and specialties such as veal Oscar. There's also a large dessert menu. Children's menu. In Fence Lake Lodge, 12919 Frying Pan Camp Lane, off Hwy 47 between Woodruff and Lac du Flambeau; phone 715-588-3255. Open daily for breakfast, lunch, and dinner. Dinner reservations suggested.

Emergency

For fire, police, or ambulance, call 588-3335

Tourist Information

Lac du Flambeau Chamber of Commerce
Lac du Flambeau, WI 54538
715-588-3346

Eagle River

One of the major commercial centers of northern Wisconsin, Eagle River began as a logging town in the late 1800s. The area is noted for the Eagle River Chain of Lakes, a chain of 28 connected lakes that is the longest in the world. Most visitors arrive on either Hwy 45, which runs north-south, or Hwy 70, which runs east-west.

Things to Do

Eagle River is just outside the boundary of the **Nicolet National Forest**, which encompasses more than 650,000 acres to the east and south of Eagle River. Trails for hiking, horseback riding, cross-country skiing, and snowmobiling run through the forest. Rustic campgrounds (no hookups), picnic areas, beaches, and boat launch ramps are also provided by the Forest Service. Trail maps and locations of boat launch ramps, picnic areas, and campgrounds are available at the Eagle River ranger station.

The district ranger station is on Hwy 45 at the edge of Eagle River. Mailing address Nicolet National Forest, Eagle River District, Box 1809, Eagle River, WI 54521; phone 715-479-2827. Most facilities free, camping $.

Carl's Wood Art Museum can only be called unusual. Carl and his cronies have carved everything from 12-foot-tall grizzly bears to small wooden bowls using only a chain saw. The sheer size of most of the creations will impress the kids.

1230 Sundstein Rd., just off Hwy 70 on west side of Eagle River; phone 715-479-1883. Open 10-5 Monday-Saturday Memorial Day weekend through mid-October. $.

Kartway and **Little Falls Miniature Golf** offer adjoining amusement opportunities. Kartway, as you might guess, has several go-kart tracks of varying difficulty, plus bumper boats and a shooting gallery. Little Falls has 18 challenging holes with water and mechanical hazards. They also offer horse and pony rides.

Both on Pleasure Island Rd. one mile north of town on Hwy 45. Kartway phone 715-479-4450. Both open daily Memorial Day through September. $.

Riverview Park, a city park on the shore of the Wisconsin River, has tennis courts, playground, picnic area, and boat dock. Located on Railroad Street at the bridge three blocks from downtown, it's a good place to rest or romp after shopping or dining.

Silver Lake Park is a city park with a lovely picnic area and swimming beach with lifeguard and bath house. Take Silver Lake Road north from Wall Street, then right on Lakeshore Drive. Open Memorial Day weekend through Labor Day.

Winter Fun

Nicolet National Forest has hundreds of miles of cross-country ski and snowmobile trails. Contact the Eagle River District Office (see Things to Do above) for maps and other information.

Eagle River Nordic has 30 miles of groomed cross-country ski trails in the Nicolet National Forest for all skill levels. There's a warming house with snacks, sales, and rentals. Lessons and guided tours in the forest also offered. On Crossover Rd., off Hwy 70 east of Eagle River (call for directions); phone 714-479-7285. Trail fee.

Decker's Snow-Venture Tours offers guided snowmobile tours in northern Wisconsin and elsewhere. Equipment, accommodations, and meals provided. No previous snowmobile experience needed. Contact them at Box 1447, Eagle River, WI 54521; phone 715-479-2764.

For indoor fun, try bowling at the **Eagle Lanes**, on Hwy 70 just west of town. Call 715-479-4555 for open bowling hours.

Events

JANUARY. The **World Championship Snowmobile Derby** attracts top snowmobile racers to Eagle River every winter for world championship racing. Thrilling and noisy—just the thing for kids. Held in mid-January at the Eagle River Derby Track, on Hwy 45 just north of town. Contact the Derby office at Box 1447, Eagle River, WI 54521; phone 715-479-4424 during weekday business hours.

FEBRUARY. **Klondike Days** focuses on slower-paced but no less thrilling winter activities. Dogsled racing, lumberjack contests, horse pulling contests, Native American cultural exhibits, chainsaw carving demonstrations, craft shows, plus food and entertainment. Lots of activities for everyone in the family. Held the last weekend in February in locations throughout Eagle River. Contact the Eagle River Information Bureau (see below) for information.

OCTOBER. There are thousands of acres of cranberry bogs in the north, and Eagle River offers homage to the red berry at its annual **Cranberry Festival**. Activities include an arts and crafts fair, antiques market, fun runs, chainsaw carving demonstrations, a petting zoo, horse-drawn wagon rides, bog and winery tours, plus lots of family entertainment, and an incredible amount of cooking with cranberries. The first weekend in October throughout Eagle River. Contact the Eagle River Information Bureau (see below) for details.

Shopping

Souvenirs, fudge shops, clothing, and variety stores are concentrated along Wall Street, the main thoroughfare.

Book World has a good selection of children's books, games and puzzles, plus adult selections including best sellers and regional books. 114 E. Wall St.; phone 715-479-7094. Open 9-6 Monday-Friday, 9-5 Saturday and Sunday.

The Children's Boutique has a complete selection of clothing for infants through size 14, plus blankets and comforters, stuffed animals and gifts. 107 E. Wall St.; phone 715-479-3347. Open 10-5 Monday-Saturday.

Rentals

Heckel's Eagle River Marina rents pontoon boats, fishing boats, ski boats, and jet skis. And in the winter, they rent snowmobiles. At 437 W. Division St., Eagle River; phone 715-479-4471.

Boat S'Port rents ski boats, fishing boats, canoes, paddleboats, sailboats and motors. Off Hwy 70 east of Eagle River; phone 715-479-8000.

Holiday Harbor Marina rents fishing boats and pontoon boats. Off Hwy 45 north of Eagle River; phone 715-479-7788.

Pine-Aire Marina rents fishing boats and ski boats, outboard motors, canoes, pontoon boats, aqua cycles, and jet skis. On Chain O'Lakes Rd. off Hwy 45 north of Eagle River; phone 715-479-9208, or 800-597-6777.

Where to Stay

Eagle River Inn, 5260 Hwy 70 West, Eagle River, WI 54521; phone 715-479-2000. A modern resort hotel on the Wisconsin River just west of Eagle River. Boat dock, game room, TV, playground, indoor pool, exercise room, tennis courts. Suites and kitchens available. Restaurant on premises. Children free with parents.

Chanticleer Inn, 1458 E. Dollar Lake Rd. (off Hwy 70 east), Eagle River, WI 54521; phone 715-479-4486. A charming lakeside resort with fully furnished villas and townhouses. Beach, rental boats, water skiing, tennis courts, playground, snowmobile trails. Excellent restaurant.

Pine-Aire Resort and Campground, 4443 Chain O'Lakes Rd., Eagle River; phone 715-479-9208 or 800-597-6777, offers both fully furnished lakefront cottages and 136 campsites. Campground provides electrical and water hookups, showers, laundry, store, dump station. Each cottage has a fireplace, TV, full kitchen, and a boat and pier. Cottages and campers can both enjoy the resort's 1800 feet of lakefront, the restaurant, tennis and basketball courts, playgrounds, swimming area, family recreation program and marina with boat rentals. Winter visitors can use the resort's groomed cross-country ski trail. The resort also has direct access to more than 500 miles of groomed snowmobile trails. The resort also has a restaurant which serves breakfast and dinner daily May through October.

Where to Eat

The **Chanticleer Inn** offers a variety of daily specials and old standards such as chicken and seafood. Everything is tasty. Children's menu. 1458 E. Dollar Lake Rd., off Hwy 70 east of Eagle River; phone 715-479-4486. Open daily for breakfast and dinner.

The **Colonial House** is the place for desserts. The sandwiches, pizza, and breakfasts are good, but the ice cream and pies are wonderful. Old fashioned ice cream parlor decor—dark wood booths, pressed tin ceiling, marble topped tables. Children's menu. 125 S. Railroad St.; phone 715-479-9424. Open daily for breakfast, lunch, and dinner.

The **Copper Kettle Restaurant** is an Eagle River favorite. And no wonder. They offer great breakfasts (try one of the pancakes from the Pancake Hall of Fame), wonderful homemade soups and chili, excellent sandwiches, and a traditional dinner menu. 207 E. Wall St.; phone 715-479-4049. Open daily for breakfast, lunch, and dinner.

Extended Hours Grocery Store

Trig's Food and Drug
Wall Street east of downtown
715-479-6411.

Emergency

Police 479-4343
Fire 479-4321
Ambulance 479-4441

Tourist Information

Eagle River Information Bureau
Railroad St.
Eagle River, WI 54521
715-479-8575
800-359-6315

Rhinelander

This city of 8,000 is the economic and commercial center of the Northwoods. Most visitors arrive by car on either Hwy 17, which runs north-south, or on Hwy 8, which runs east-west. Some arrive by scheduled airline at the Rhinelander-Oneida County Airport, where car rental is available.

Things to Do

Rhinelander Logging Museum exhibits include a reproduction of a 19th-century logging camp, complete with blacksmith shop, bunkhouse and kitchen, as well as an old schoolhouse, CCC camp, train depot, firehouse, and miniature sawmill. There are also displays of logging equipment and several narrow-gauge rail cars used for hauling logs, lumberjacks, and provisions to and from the camps. The museum is located in **Pioneer Park**, a city

park that contains a picnic area, tennis courts, and a large playground.

Pioneer Park is on Oneida St. just south of downtown; museum phone 715-369-5004. Museum open daily 10-5 from mid-May through Labor Day. Both museum and park are free.

White Pines Family Fun Center offers go-karts, an 18-hole miniature golf course, an arcade, and a snack bar. Everything you need to keep the kids occupied for a couple of hours.

On Hwy 17 north of Rhinelander; phone 715-362-4653. Open daily Memorial Day weekend through Labor Day. $.

Hodag Park has a picnic area, playgrounds, tennis courts, and beach as well as water ski shows.

On Boom Lake in Rhinelander; for water ski show information, phone 715-362-7464. Park open year-round, water ski shows 7:30 p.m. Thursday and Sunday mid-June through late August. Free.

Winter Fun

Fort Wilderness has 20 miles of groomed cross-country ski trails. The facility offers ski rental and a warming shelter, ski shop, and snack bar as well as tubing, snowshoeing, and sleigh rides.

On Hwy 47 ten miles north of Rhinelander, then east on Bridge Rd.; mailing address 6180 Wilderness Trail, McNaughton, WI 54543; phone 715-277-2587. Closed Monday and Tuesday. Trail fee.

Shopping

DeByle's is the Northwoods' largest department store with a good selection of clothing and accessories for everyone in the family. They have some terrific sales and a discount room. On the corner of Brown and Davenport in downtown Rhinelander; phone 715-362-4406. Open 9-5 Monday-Thursday and Saturday, 9-8 Friday.

Book World has a good selection of children's books, puzzles, and games, as well as adult fiction and non-fiction plus regional books, magazines, and newspapers. 58 N. Brown St.; phone 715-369-2627. Open 7 a.m.-8 p.m. Monday-Friday, 8-5 Saturday, 7:30-4 Sunday.

Rentals

Bikes-N-Boards rents mountain bikes. 913 River St., Rhinelander; phone 715-369-1999.

The Sled Shop rents snowmobiles in the winter and pontoon boats and jet skis in the summer. 4211 Birchwood Dr., Rhinelander; phone 715-362-9200.

Where to Stay

Best Western Claridge Motor Inn, 70 N. Stevens St.; phone 715-362-7100 or 800-528-1234. An excellent downtown motel with a resident Labrador retriever as well as an indoor pool, exercise room, video games, cable TV, coin laundry and a restaurant. Suites available.

Holiday Inn, on Hwy 8 just west of town; mailing address Box 675, Rhinelander, WI 54501; phone 715-369-3600. Typical Holiday Inn, with indoor pool, exercise room, video games, coin laundry. Next to snowmobile trails. Suites available.

Shady Rest Lodge, 8440 Shady Rest Rd., Rhinelander 54501; phone 715-282-5231. This full service resort on a peninsula on Manson Lake offers guests a modified American Plan (breakfast and dinner) in summer and a European Plan (no meals) in spring and fall. Guests rent a room in the lodge or fully furnished lakeside cottages, each of which has a boat. In addition, the resort has sailboats, canoes, paddleboats, bicycles, fishing equipment, a tennis court, and playground for guests to use. And, of course, there's a beach. From late June through late August the resort also offers activities mornings and each evening. Babysitting available. Open May through October.

Holiday Acres, Box 460, Rhinelander 54501; phone 715-369-1500. This large resort on Lake Thompson has everything you need for a great vacation. Choose a room in the main lodge or a fully furnished cottage (most with a fireplace) on the spacious grounds. The resort has a beach and an indoor pool, boats for guests, tennis courts, picnic areas, playground, and plenty of room to roam on the resort's 1000 acres of woods. In winter the wooded hiking trails become groomed cross-country ski trails. The resort also has a restaurant if you don't feel like cooking.

West Bay Camping Resort, 4330 South Shore Dr., just east of Rhinelander, Hwy 8 to Faust Rd. to South Shore

Dr.; mailing address Box 338, Rhinelander, WI 54501; phone 715-362-3481. On Lake Thompson. Full hookups, showers, store, playground, beach, outdoor pool, canoes and paddleboats for guests, boat dock, boat rentals. They also have fully furnished cabins for rent.

Where to Eat

Local residents congregate at the **Rhinelander Cafe & Pub**. Extensive menu featuring a variety of sandwiches, soup, salads, and typical Wisconsin cafe dinners—beef, chicken, seafood. Downtown at 33 N. Brown St.; phone 715-362-2918. Open daily for breakfast, lunch, and dinner.

The **White Stag Inn** specializes in steaks, pork chops, chicken, and seafood, all excellently prepared. Not for vegetarians. Kids can get burgers. 7141 Hwy 17 north, Sugar Camp (12 miles north of Rhinelander); phone 715-272-1057. Open daily for dinner.

The **Claridge Motor Inn's Cavalier Room** serves some of the best meals in town. Extensive menu, everything's good. At 70 N. Stevens St.; phone 715-362-7100. Open daily for breakfast, lunch and dinner.

Extended Hours Grocery Stores

Trig's Food and Drug
Oneida Mall, 232 Courtney (just north of downtown)
715-369-1470

Cirilli's Super Valu Discount Foods
1631 N. Stevens
715-362-4944

Emergency

For fire, police or ambulance, dial 911

Tourist Information

Rhinelander Area Chamber of Commerce
450 Kemp St.
Box 795
Rhinelander, WI 54501
715-365-7464
800-236-4386

Laona

This small community 40 miles east of Rhinelander on Hwy 8 is the home of the Northwoods' best logging museum.

Things to Do

A visitor to the **Lumberjack Special & Camp 5** begins with a ride on the Lumberjack Special, an operational steam train that everyone must ride to and from Camp 5. The camp includes a working blacksmith shop, logging museum, nature center, a forest tram tour that explains forest management and timber cutting practices, a petting zoo, and a pontoon boat ride, plus a gift shop and snack bar. The Lumberjack Special & Camp 5 complex is an excellent combination of fun and education for adults and children.

On Hwy 8 in Laona; phone 715-674-3414 or 800-774-3414. Train departs Laona depot 11 a.m., noon, 1 p.m., 2 p.m. daily from mid-June through last weekend in August. $.

Tomahawk and Merrill

These Wisconsin River towns are 20 miles apart on Hwy 51. For a very scenic but slightly longer drive, make the trip between the two communities on Hwy 107, which runs right along the Wisconsin River.

Things to Do

Tenneco Packaging makes corrugated packaging materials. Tours of the mill are offered mid-June through mid-August.

N9090 County Hwy E, Tomahawk; phone 715-453-2131. Call for tour times. CHILDREN UNDER 12 NOT ALLOWED. Free.

Kwahamot Water Ski Shows provide water ski thrills with jumping, trick skiing, clowns, and large boats making noise and going very fast.

Memorial Park at the Business Hwy 51 bridge in Tomahawk. No phone. Shows at 8 p.m. Tuesday, Thursday, Sunday Memorial Day weekend through Labor Day. Free, donation requested.

Sara Park is Tomahawk's largest, with a beach on the Wisconsin River, bath house, and playing fields. It is also the trailhead for the Hiawatha Trail, a six-mile long bike-hike trail on an abandoned railroad bed. The trail begins behind the activity center in the park. On W. Somo Avenue. Park open daily. Free.

Council Grounds State Park is a lovely park in the woods along the Wisconsin River near Merrill. The park has a great beach, a boat launch ramp, canoe rental, hiking trails, picnic areas, campground, and cross-country ski trails. Naturalists lead hikes and present evening programs during the summer.

Two miles north of Merrill off Hwy 107; phone 715-536-8773. Handicap-accessible fishing pier, picnic area, and camping facilities. Open with services April through October; open for skiing in winter, but no services. $.

Winter Fun

The **Lincoln County Forests** have a number of excellent ski trails. **Underdown** has 25 miles of groomed cross-country ski trails for intermediate and advanced skiers. Off Hwy K north of Merrill, east on Hwy H to Copper Lake Road then three miles east. **Otter Run** also has 15 miles of groomed trails designed for beginner and intermediate skiers. Off Hwy 51 north of Merrill to County Hwy S. Both ski areas have toilets, water, and parking lots.

For information, contact the Forestry, Land & Parks Department, Lincoln County Courthouse Annex, Merrill, WI 54452; phone 715-536-0327 during business hours. The Forestry, Land and Parks Department also has information about snowmobile trails in the Tomahawk-Merrill area.

When the weather outside is frightful, local residents go bowling. **Lincoln Lanes**, on Business Hwy 51 in Merrill, has open bowling all winter. Phone 715-536-9405. The **Tomahawk Bowl**, at 309 W. Wisconsin Ave. in Tomahawk, also has open bowling. Phone 715-453-2386.

Rentals

Midwest Sports rents cross-country skis at their store at 416 W. Main St., Merrill; phone 715-536-3288.

Tomahawk Sports Center rents ski boats, personal watercraft, and pontoon boats in summer, and snowmobiles in winter. 693 N. 4th St., Tomahawk; phone 715-453-5373.

Where to Stay

Best Western Lake Aire Motel, five miles north of Tomahawk on Business 51; mailing address 11925 Business 51N, Tomahawk, WI 54487; phone 715-453-5189 or 800-528-1234. This small motel on Lake Nakomis is exceptionally well maintained and is on beautiful wooded grounds. The motel has a beach, cable TV, and is on snowmobile trails.

Bit-O-the-North Resort, W7250 Loop Rd., Tomahawk 54487; phone 715-453-2069 or 888-277-5000. This small but well-maintained resort features modern log housekeeping cottages on the shore of Lake Mohawksin south of Tomahawk. Cottages are fully furnished, including microwave, dishwasher, grill, and TV. Amenities include a beach, boat for each cottage, playground, and wooded grounds on the lake. Children 14 and under stay free with parents.

Where to Eat

La Nou's has the area's best hamburgers, sandwiches, soup, and homemade rolls and pies. Large sandwich menu, salads, full dinners, plate lunch specials. The desserts are worth going out of your way for. 204 W. Wisconsin, downtown Tomahawk; phone 715-453-4707. Open daily for breakfast, lunch, and dinner if you eat early—it's usually closed by 6 p.m.

Tourist Information

Tomahawk Chamber of Commerce
208 N. 4th St.
Tomahawk, WI 54487
715-453-5334
800-569-2160

Merrill Area Chamber of Commerce
720 E. 2nd St.
Merrill, WI 54452
715-536-9474

Langlade

This small community is at the heart of the Wolf River recreation area. Reach it via Hwy 64 east from Antigo or on Hwy 55 north from Shawano.

Things to Do

Several outfitters serve those who want to **raft the Wolf River** whitewater. This river is usually the easiest of Wisconsin's whitewater rafting rivers, and is a good river to try rafting for the first time. NOTE: Most companies have a minimum age for participants; usually children must be at least 10 or 12 years old. Check with the outfitter.

Buettner's Wild Wolf Inn provides rafts, shuttles, showers, and a changing area for after the ride. Trips from one and one-half to eight hours. On Hwy 55 just south of Langlade; phone 715-882-8612. Trips are offered from April through mid-October, weather permitting. $.

River Forest Rafts provides rafts, shuttles, changing area, and picnic areas. Trips from two and one-half to eight hours. Just off Hwy 55 six miles south of Langlade; phone 715-882-3351. Trips offered from April through mid-October, weather permitting. $.

The **Nicolet National Forest** stretches east and north from Langlade, with hiking, skiing, snowmobiling, camping, and picnic areas. For information, contact the Forest Supervisor, Nicolet National Forest, Rhinelander, WI 54501. Phone 715-362-1300.

Athelstane and Crivitz

These small communities are at the heart of a resort and outdoor recreation area centered on the Peshtigo River. Most visitors reach the area via Hwy 141, which runs north-south through Crivitz.

Things to Do

Peshtigo River rafting. A number of outfitters provide rafts, shuttles, and other services. The five-mile stretch of the river known as Roaring Rapids is the longest continuous stretch of whitewater in the Midwest. Trips are exciting, fun, and not particularly dangerous if you follow a few safety precautions. NOTE: Most outfitters have a minimum age for participants. They generally require that children be at least 10 or 12 years old. Also, rafting during the high water of spring run-off in April is more dangerous than the regular summer trips run May through September.

Kosir's Rapid Rafts runs three trips daily on the Peshtigo from mid-May through September. HCR 1, Box 172A, Athelstane, WI 54104; phone 715-757-3431. $.

Thornton's Whitewater Raft Company provides rafts and a shuttle for one trip at 12:30 Monday-Friday and three trips at 9, 12 and 3 Saturday and Sunday mid-May through September. Two trips at 9 and 1 are offered Saturday and Sunday April through mid-May. Box 216, Athelstane, WI 54104; phone 715-757-3311. $.

If rafting isn't your idea of a good time, **Peshtigo River Tours** lets you see the beautiful and undeveloped High Falls Flowage downstream from all that whitewater. The 50-passenger, flat-bottom boat gets close to shore for a look at eagle nests, osprey, and other wildlife.

Tours leave from the Peshtigo River Resort near Athelstane; phone 715-757-3769 or 715-757-3151. Tours Tuesday, Wednesday, Thursday, and Saturday, early June through mid-August, and Saturdays late August through early October. $.

Where to Stay

Popp's Resort, W11581 Hwy X, Crivitz, WI 54114; phone 715-757-3511 or 715-757-3491. On the High Falls Flowage northwest of Crivitz (take County Hwy A to County Hwy X). Resort with two-bedroom apartments and fully furnished cottages. TV, restaurant, boat rentals, cross-country ski trails and snowmobile trails adjacent.

Shaffer Park Motel, N7217 Shaffer Rd., Crivitz, WI 54114; phone 715-854-2186. Five miles west of Crivitz on County Hwy W. Small motel on lovely grounds on the shore of the Peshtigo River. TV, playground, outdoor pool, boats for guests, cross-country ski trails, and snowmobile trails. Restaurant serves good food, open daily for dinner only, open for brunch and dinner on Sunday.

Where to Eat

The Baker's Kitchen serves great food—homemade desserts, soups, sandwiches, full dinners. Children's menu. On Hwy 141 in Crivitz; phone 715-854-2933. Open daily for breakfast, lunch and dinner.

Emergency

For fire, police or ambulance, dial 911.

Tourist Information

Crivitz Recreation Association
N9661 Parkway Rd.
Crivitz, WI 54114
715-757-3253

11

The Great Northwest

Including Superior, Ashland, Bayfield, Madeline Island, Hurley, Mellen, Park Falls, Cable, Hayward, Spooner, St. Croix Falls, Grantsburg, and all the wild places in between

This land was made for good times together. The Northwest is Wisconsin's version of the wide open spaces, beckoning with hundreds of thousands of acres of federal and state park and forest lands, with free-flowing rivers, meandering streams, waterfalls and lakes, and with abundant wildlife. The air is clear. The scenery is tremendous. The cities are small, the folks friendly.

Family adventures—canoeing a wild river, strolling a driftwood-scattered Lake Superior beach, riding a horse through towering pines, touring a Great Lakes freighter, and just relaxing together—are easy to come by in the Northwest. There are fewer video games and amusement parks in this area, but there are brilliant sunsets, water-falls, and quiet beaches.

It was into the Northwest that early French fur traders and missionaries came, establishing settlements on Madeline Island, and developing trading routes from Lake Superior to the Mississippi River via the rivers and lakes of the Northwest. The resident Chippewa tribes signed treaties turning over much of their land to the Europeans, who proceeded to clear the forests, fish Lake Superior, build cities and homes, and develop farms.

Today, the Northwest is an area of farming, lumbering, small factories, Great Lakes shipping, and tourism. Major north-south highways are Hwys 53 and 13. Major east-west routes are Hwys 2 and 8, and Hwys 70 and 77. Hwy 63 cuts diagonally across the region from southwest to northeast. Scheduled air service to Superior (via the airport in neighboring Duluth, Minnesota) is available.

Superior and Vicinity

One of the finest inland shipping ports in the world, Superior was for many years a tough and brawny town where millions of tons of iron ore, coal, and grain passed through the port annually. Today the port is still busy, but this city of 28,000 is also known for the University of Wisconsin-Superior campus, as a regional commercial center and, increasingly, as a stop for travelers. Most travelers come to the area via Hwy 53 from the south or on Hwy 2 from east or west.

Things to Do

Tour the port. The huge ore docks are truly impressive, and seeing Great Lake freighters being loaded and unloaded is pretty amazing. They use some very large equipment. You can wander around on your own, up to a point, or take a harbor tour on the *Vista Star* or *Vista King*, owned by **Duluth-Superior Excursions**. The narrated tours last one and one-half to two and one-half hours and let you see the harbor and other sights, including the huge grain elevators, an interesting aerial lift bridge that rises horizontally above the harbor to let boats pass under, and some of the Lake Superior shoreline. Some tours include a meal.

Boarding at Barker's Island dock in Superior and at Duluth Entertainment and Convention Center dock in Duluth; phone 218-722-6218; for meal reservations, 218-722-1728. Cruises daily mid-May through mid-October. $.

For a closer look at an old Great Lakes freighter, tour the **S.S. Meteor Maritime Museum**. The *Meteor* is the only surviving example of an early 20th-century freighter called a whaleback. After your tours of the *Meteor* you can look around the museum, with its hundreds of maritime artifacts that are reminders of the heyday of Great Lakes shipping. Also on the grounds are a miniature golf course, a playground, and a number of souvenir and food shops.

At Whaleback Wharf on Barker's Island (off Hwy 2); phone 715-394-7716. Open 10-5 daily Memorial Day weekend through Labor Day, 10-5 weekends after Labor Day through mid-October. $.

Lock your kids up at the **Old Firehouse and Police Museum**. The restored firehouse houses a number of pieces of antique fire fighting equipment, and an example of a turn-of-the-century jail cell.

Hwy 2 east, Superior; phone 715-394-7716. Open 10-5 daily early June through August. $.

The **Superior Speedway** provides plenty of stock car racing excitement every Friday night at 8 from late May through mid-September. Car racing is fast, noisy, and action-packed. Kids love it. The speedway is at the Head of the Lake Fairgrounds, Hwy 35 at 47th St.; phone 715-394-7848. $.

Lake Superior offers some of the best **lake trout fishing** in the world, and local charter operators will take you to where the big ones are. Try E. Fish N. Sea Charters, 218-879-5111 or 800-980-4814; or First Mate Charters, 715-392-3177 or 800-824-6466; or KDK Charter Service, 218-724-1264 or 888-724-1264. Any of these guys will take you out for a full or half day, will provide all the equipment, and will clean your catch.

Pattison State Park protects Big Manitou Falls, a 165-foot cataract that crashes through a narrow gorge of the Black River. Big Manitou is the highest waterfall in Wisconsin. Two other waterfalls are also in the park, along with a small man-made lake with a beach, hiking trails, picnic areas, and a campground. In summer, naturalists provide interpretive programs. A beautiful park.

Thirteen miles south of Superior on Hwy 35; mailing address Rt. 2, Box 435, Superior; phone 715-399-8073 or 715-399-3111. Handicap-accessible camping and picnic facilities. Open daily year-round. $.

Amnicon Falls State Park is one of the most scenic in the state. The park's centerpiece is the Amnicon River as it crashes through four waterfalls inside the park. A rustic covered footbridge lets visitors walk above the roaring falls. This is one of those spots where your kids can drive you nuts by leaning over the railing to get a better look at the swirling water below. The park has riverside picnic, swimming, and play areas, a nature trail, and a campground.

Ten miles east of Superior on Hwy 2, then north one quarter mile on County Hwy U; mailing address same as Pattison State Park (see above). Phone 715-398-3000 or 715-399-3111. Open daily first weekend in May through first weekend in October. $.

The **Brule River State Forest** is a narrow ribbon protecting the beautiful Brule River, one of the nation's top trout fishing and canoeing streams. The forest also includes eight miles of Lake Superior shoreline. The river contains stretches of wild whitewater for experienced canoeists and kayakers only, but there are also stretches of quiet, slow-moving water perfect for family paddling. Along the river are canoe launching sites (motorboats are prohibited), picnic areas, and campgrounds. In addition to canoeing, family activities in the forest include hiking, climbing over the rocks along the river, and beachcombing on the Superior shore.

Twenty-five miles east of Superior, access by either Hwy 2 or Hwy 13. Forest headquarters one mile south of Hwy 2 near the village of Brule; mailing address Brule River State Forest, Box 125, Brule, WI 54820; phone 715-372-4866. Open daily year-round. $ for some developed areas.

Winter Fun

Superior has a 4,500-acre **municipal forest** within the city boundaries. In the forest are more than 15 miles of groomed cross-country ski trails for beginner, intermediate, and expert skiers, plus separate trails for snowmobilers. Trail access from the west end of 28th St. For information, contact the Superior Parks and Recreation Department, 715-394-0270.

Pattison State Park offers challenging cross-country ski trails, as well as outdoor ice skating and snowmobile trails.

There are more than four miles of groomed beginner-intermediate cross-country ski trails in the **Brule River State Forest**. Parking is on Hwy 2 west of the village of Brule.

Many Wisconsin downhill skiers step over the border to ski at Duluth's **Spirit Mountain**. With a 710-foot vertical drop, and runs up to a mile, it's a challenging, and large, ski area. The facility also has nearly 25 miles of groomed cross-country ski trails. Off I-35 in Minnesota south of Duluth; phone 218-628-2891.

Events

JULY. **Head of the Lakes Fair** activities include grand-stand shows, stock car races, demolition derby, a midway with rides, and of course the animals. Held the last week-end in July at Head of the Lakes Fairgrounds, Hwy 35 and 47th St. in Superior. Phone 715-394-7848. $.

Shopping

Mariner Mall has more than 40 stores ranging from specialty boutiques to full-service department stores. There are four movie theaters, an arcade, candy stores, clothing, drug, and book stores. At 28th St. and Hill Ave. in downtown Superior; phone 715-392-7117. Open 10-9 Monday-Friday, 10-6 Saturday, 11-5 Sunday.

Rentals

Brule River Canoe Rental provides canoes, kayaks, and shuttle service for trips lasting from one and one-half hours to three days. They also rent sea kayaks for paddling on Lake Superior. On Hwy 2 in Brule; phone 715-372-4983 or 715-392-3132. Season is early May to late October.

Where to Stay

Best Western Bridgeview Motor Inn, 415 Hammond Ave., Superior; phone 715-392-8174 or 800-777-5572. Downtown, near docks and attractions. Indoor pool, whirlpool, sauna, game room, cable TV and free movies, coin laundry, refrigerators available, free conti-nental breakfast.

Days Inn Bayfront, 110 Harbor View Parkway, Superior; phone 715-392-4783 or 800-325-2525. Indoor pool, whirlpool, sauna, game room, cable TV, restaurant.

Where to Eat

Town Crier Steak, Cake & Seafood House really does serve good steak, cake, and seafood. Be sure to order homemade muffins, a house specialty. This friendly family restaurant also serves skillet meals, steaks, shrimp, ribs, chicken, and fish as well as sandwiches, chili, soups, and casseroles. Children's menu. 4927 E. Second St., Superior; phone 715-398-7521. Open daily for breakfast, lunch, and dinner.

Extended Hours Grocery Store

Super One Foods
1515 Oakes Ave.
715-392-6218

Emergency

For fire, police or ambulance, dial 911.

Tourist Information

Chamber of Commerce
Tourist Information Center
Harbor View Parkway at Barker's Island
Superior, WI 54880
715-392-2773
800-942-5313

Ashland, Bayfield, and Madeline Island

These former lumber, fishing, and Great Lakes shipping communities nowadays welcome tourists to enjoy the brisk waters of Lake Superior, the beautiful islands of Chequamegon Bay, and the historic sites of one of the earliest European settlements in Wisconsin. Visitors arrive via Hwy 2, which runs east-west through Ashland, a city of 9,000 and the commercial and economic center of the area, and on Hwy 13, which loops along the shore of Lake Superior and the Bayfield Peninsula, winding through the small communities of Washburn and Bayfield, the Red Cliff Chippewa Reservation, and along the wild shore between the city of Superior and the peninsula. A drive along Hwy 13 from Superior to Bayfield is wonderfully scenic. There are many places to stop and romp in the sand. The tiny communities of Port Wing, Herbster, and Cornucopia are good places to stop for a snack.

Things to Do

The **Northern Wisconsin History Center** is a good place to start your tour of this area. An excellent half-hour multi-media production and a series of exhibits explain the history of the area, focusing on the fur trade, the coming of the railroads, Lake Superior shipping, and the immigrants who attempted to farm this harsh land.

The center is settling in to a new downtown location; phone 715-682-6600 for address and hours. Wheelchair accessible. Open daily June through August. $ for movie.

The **Chequamegon National Forest** stretches into the Bayfield Peninsula, with hiking, skiing, and snowmobile trails, camping, and other facilities.

There's a district ranger station on Hwy 13 in Washburn; mailing address U.S. Forest Service, Box 578, Washburn, WI 54891; phone 715-373-2667. Open regular business hours. $ for camping.

Apostle Islands National Lakeshore encompasses 21 islands and 12 miles of unspoiled peninsula shoreline, saving them for wildlife, recreation, and historic preservation. There's a visitor center in Bayfield, where displays and films explain the flora, fauna, and history of the islands, and where you can get information about boat trips to the islands. Visitors can take tours ranging from a few hours on a cruise ship to a week's primitive camping. Kayaking among the islands is also popular. In summer, two islands have naturalists who guide visitors on nature walks to the remaining lighthouses and to a restored commercial fishing camp. The islands are beautiful, rugged, and uncrowded. For a preview, check out their Web site at http://www.nps.gov/apis.

Visitor Center in the old Bayfield County Courthouse, 415 Washington Ave., Bayfield; phone 715-779-3397. Open daily 8-6 Memorial Day weekend through Labor Day, daily 8-4:30 early September through October, 8-4:30 Monday-Friday November through April, 8-4:30 daily May 1 until Memorial Day weekend. Visitor center and islands free. Private transportation to the islands $.

Apostle Islands Cruise Service provides boat tours of the islands. At the dock at the end of Rittenhouse Ave.; mailing address Box 691, Bayfield, WI 54814; phone 715-779-3925 or 800-323-7619. Tours Memorial

Day weekend through second week in October. Variety of daily cruises, plus water taxi service to the islands. Reservations recommended. $.

Fishing for that trophy trout or salmon is a thrill on beautiful Lake Superior. **Charter fishing** boats are available for half and full day trips, and they provide all equipment and supplies. For a list of charter captains, contact the Bayfield Chamber of Commerce (see below).

Lake Superior breezes beckon. Your family can learn to **sail**, charter a sailboat, or just go for a sailboat ride for a few hours. Bayfield sailboat companies include Sailboats, Inc., 117 S. First St., phone 715-779-3269; Catchun-Sun Charter Co., Box 955, phone 715-779-3111; Apostle Islands Cruise Service (they have a schooner as well as tour boats), phone 715-779-3925 or 800-323-7619; and Trek and Trail, Rittenhouse Ave., phone 715-779-3595 or 800-354-8735.

The **Booth Cooperage Museum** shows kids how food was processed and shipped in the days before refrigeration. The museum has exhibits and a slideshow explaining how coopers made barrels that were used to ship salted fish from Bayfield to Chicago and other far-away places. The only museum of its kind in Wisconsin.

One Washington Ave., Bayfield; phone 715-779-3400. Open 9:30–5:30 daily Memorial Day weekend through first weekend in October. Free.

There's lively entertainment for the family all summer at **Big Top Chautauqua**, an old-fashioned tent show based on the 19th-century Chautauqua idea of music, theater, and generally uplifting and wholesome presentations that are both educational and entertaining. The Lake Superior Big Top Chautauqua presents a summer-long schedule of musical shows, storytellers, plays, lectures, slide shows, and whatever else they can find. Great fun, mostly with a regional slant. Get there early and enjoy a picnic on the grounds.

South of Bayfield on Hwy 13 at Mt. Ashwabay ski hill; mailing address Box 455, Washburn, WI 54891; box office phone 715-373-5552; tickets sales 9-4 Monday-Saturday. Shows regularly mid-June through early September, rain or shine. $.

Bayfield is famous for its **apple orchards**. If you're visiting in spring, drive out among them to see the apple blossoms. If you're there in fall, go out to buy fresh-from-the-tree apples. Many orchards also raise strawberries, raspberries, and other fruits and vegetables, so grab your kids and head out for a pick-your-own extravaganza. Many orchards have direct sales stores at the site. Drive out Washington Avenue to County Hwy J and follow it in a loop among the orchards. It will take you back to Hwy 13 north of Bayfield.

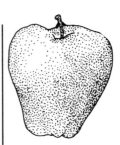

Bayfield has an excellent **community recreation center** with an indoor pool, whirlpool, racquetball courts, exercise rooms, and a lounge. Visitors are welcome to use the pool, exercise room, and courts if they're not occupied by school groups.

Corner of Broad St. and Wilson Ave.; phone 715-779-5408. Call for open swim hours. $.

While you're in the neighborhood, stroll a few blocks past the recreation center to the **commercial fishing docks** to see the remainder of a once huge industry. Try some smoked lake trout. It's excellent.

For a 20-minute, fun boat ride, take the **Madeline Island Ferry** from Bayfield to LaPointe. Madeline Island is the largest of the Apostles, the only one that is not part of the national lakeshore, and the only one that is inhabited year-round. In winter the ferry gives way to an ice sled.

Leaves from the dock at foot of Washington Ave.; phone 715-747-2051. Ferry runs from ice-out to freeze-up, with trips about every half hour during the height of the summer tourist season. The ferry takes cars and other vehicles and pedestrians. $.

Just a block from the ferry dock in LaPointe is the **Madeline Island Historical Museum**. French fur traders built a fort on the island in the late 17th century, and Madeline Island became an important fur trading and missionary center. The museum combines four pioneer log structures and is surrounded by a log stockade of the type built by French fur traders. Exhibits focus on daily life of traders, missionaries, settlers, loggers, fishermen and the Chippewa who lived here when the Europeans arrived. The museum is a fun jumble of items, kids are allowed to touch some things, and there's a display of a working lighthouse beacon that's very impressive.

One block from the ferry dock in LaPointe; phone 715-747-2415. Open 9-5 daily late May through mid-September, call for hours after September 15. Closes for the season after first weekend in October. $

Big Bay State Park on Madeline Island has a gorgeous mile-long sand beach, wave-and-ice-sculpted sandstone formations, plus picnic areas, hiking trails through green and mossy forest, and a campground. Lovely.

On County Hwy H five miles from LaPointe; mailing address Box 589, Bayfield; phone 715-747-6425 in summer, 715-779-4020 off-season. Open daily year-round. $.

Winter Fun

Mt. Ashwabay ski hill has 13 downhill runs, on a vertical drop of 317 feet. The hill offers rentals, lessons and a chalet with ski shop and restaurant. The area also has 25 miles of groomed cross-country ski trails for beginner through expert. Rentals and lessons for both downhill and cross-country are available. Three miles south of Bayfield on Hwy 13; mailing address Rt. 1, Box 222, Bayfield; phone 715-779-3227 or 715-779-5494.

Events

OCTOBER. The **Bayfield Apple Festival** honors the apple with plenty of apple food—cakes, cider, caramel apples, applesauce, apple fritters, and so on—plus a parade, an apple queen, street entertainers, costume and hat contests, apple peeling contests, and, of course, pie tasting. Wholesome fun. Held all over Bayfield the first weekend in October. Contact the Chamber of Commerce (see Tourist Information below) for information.

Rentals

Trek and Trail rents bicycles and sea kayaks, gives kayak lessons, and offers guided kayak tours of the islands. In winter, they offer guided showshoe tours through the forest on the peninsula. On Rittenhouse Ave., Bayfield; phone 715-779-3595 or 800-354-8735.

Madeline Island Bike Rentals has bicycles and mopeds for rent at the ferry dock in LaPointe. Phone 715-747-6872.

Bodin's on the Lake rents mountain bikes, kayaks, cross-country skis, and snowshoes. Lakeshore Dr., Ashland, phone 715-682-6441.

Where to Stay

Bayfield on the Lake, 10 South First St. on the lakefront; mailing address Box 70, Bayfield; phone 715-779-3621 or 800-842-1199. Very well furnished one- to four-bedroom suites with fully equipped kitchen, fireplace, deck, cable TV, washer and dryer. Park with play area adjoining, two blocks to city indoor pool, next to restaurants.

Reiten Boatyard, 320 Wilson Ave., Bayfield; phone 715-779-3621 or 800-842-1199. Modern condos with fireplace, galley kitchen, cable TV, lake view, adjacent beach. Across the street from city indoor pool, easy walk to restaurants.

Port Superior Village, on Hwy 13 three miles south of Bayfield; mailing address Box 800, Bayfield 54814; phone 715-779-5123. Two-bedroom condos with fireplace, fully equipped kitchen. On the lake, indoor pool, tennis courts, TV and VCR, boat slips, marina, restaurant.

Best Western Holiday House, on Hwy 2 just west of Ashland; mailing address Rt. 3, Box 24, Ashland 54806; phone 715-682-5235, or 800-528-1234. Well-maintained motel on Lake Superior shore with indoor pool, whirlpool, sauna, cable TV, restaurant.

Hotel Chequamegon, 101 Lakeshore Drive West (Hwy 2), Ashland 54806; phone 715-682-9095. A reconstruction of a turn-of-the-century hotel. Very well done with beautiful furnishings. Indoor pool, suites available, restaurant, view of the Ashland lakefront and ore docks, easy walk to downtown. Overall, the hotel is a bit formal, especially the restaurants, but the accommodations are excellent.

Campers should head for the **Red Cliff Campground**, a well-designed lakeshore facility with full hookups, laundry, showers, and adjoining marina. Tent and RV sites. On Hwy 13 in village of Red Cliff, four miles north of Bayfield; phone 715-779-3743 or 715-779-5717. Open early May through October.

Where to Eat

Pier Plaza serves great breakfasts with homemade rolls and pastries, and they do a fine job with burgers, fish fries, and other standards. Not fancy, but moderately priced and good, plus it's right on the water, so the kids can watch the boats. On the Bayfield City Dock; phone 715-779-3330. Open daily for breakfast, lunch, and dinner.

Greunke's is a Bayfield tradition famous for its whitefish livers. But if that's not for you, they have a variety of less exotic taste treats. Wonderful and bountiful breakfasts, sandwiches, burgers, homemade soups, and salads, and full dinner menu with lots of offerings besides whitefish livers—try a steak or chicken dish. Excellent homemade desserts. 17 Rittenhouse Ave. near the city dock; phone 715-779-5480. Open daily in summer for breakfast, lunch, and dinner. Call for winter hours.

Emergency

In Ashland, for fire, police, or ambulance, dial 911
In Bayfield, for fire, police, or ambulance, call 373-6120

Tourist Information

Ashland Chamber of Commerce
320 Fourth Avenue West
Ashland, WI 54806
715-682-2500
800-284-9484

Bayfield Chamber of Commerce
Box 138
Bayfield, WI 54814
715-779-3335
800-447-4094

Madeline Island Chamber of Commerce
Box 274
LaPointe, WI 54850
715-747-2801

Red Cliff Chamber of Commerce
Box 1350
Bayfield, WI 54814
715-779-5225

Hurley

Hurley has quite a past as a mining and logging town that was famous for its bars and red-light district. Today this community of 2,000 offers more sedate and family-centered pleasures. Hwys 2, 77, and 51 funnel visitors into the area for winter sports, waterfall watching, and resort vacations. Hurley is also a gateway to the upper Michigan ski areas at Powderhorn, Indianhead, and in the Porcupine Mountains.

Winter Fun

Whitecap Mountain downhill ski area has some of the longest runs in the state—more than 5,000 feet with a vertical drop of 400 feet. This large ski facility has 33 runs for skiers of all skill levels, and offers rentals, lessons, ski shop, chalet with restaurant, and child care. Snowmobile trails are also nearby. West of Hurley on Hwy 77; mailing address Whitecap Mountain, Montreal, WI 54550; phone 715-561-2227 or 800-933-SNOW.

Rentals

A-1 Snowmobile Rentals rents the machines along with all the accessories such as snowmobile suits and helmets. They also offer guided snowmobile tours through the area. On Hwy 77 West; phone 715-561-4300 or 800-483-3838.

Where to Stay

Holiday Inn, 1000 Tenth Ave., Hurley; phone 715-561-3030 or 800-HOLIDAY. Standard Holiday Inn with good facilities—indoor pool, whirlpool, game room, cable TV, coin laundry, restaurant. Suites available.

Where to Eat

Fontecchio's Liberty Bell Chalet, a Hurley tradition, serves excellent Italian and American food in an informal setting. Pizza, spaghetti, and other dishes for the kids, and a variety of entrees for you, plus a great salad bar. Children's portions available. 109 Fifth Ave., at the west end of Silver St., Hurley; phone 715-561-3753. Open daily for dinner, and Monday-Thursday for lunch.

Tourist Information

Hurley Area Chamber of Commerce
207 Silver St.
Hurley, WI 54534
715-561-4334
24-hour recreation line 715-561-FUNN

Mellen

This city of 1,000 on Hwy 13 twenty-six miles south of Ashland is a good base for outdoor activities.

Things to Do

Mellen adjoins a large area of the **Chequamegon National Forest**, with hiking, boating, camping, picnic areas, skiing, and snowmobiling, plus waterfalls. Contact the Forest Superintendent (see Things to Do-Park Falls, below) for maps and information.

Copper Falls State Park is one of the most scenic state parks, with its ancient lava flows cut by flowing water to form deep gorges punctuated by spectacular waterfalls. Brownstone Falls and Copper Falls are the park's largest falls. In addition to hiking trails to the falls, the park has a playground, picnic areas, beach, and campground. A naturalist conducts guided hikes and evening interpretive programs during the summer. The park also has 14 miles of groomed cross-country ski trails.

Two miles northeast of Mellen on Hwy 169; mailing address RR 1, Box 17AA, Mellen, WI 54546; phone 715-274-5123. Handicap-accessible camping and picnic facilities. Open daily year-round. $.

Park Falls and Vicinity

This community of 3,300 is the center of a vast outdoor recreation area encompassing Price County and parts of neighboring Sawyer, Iron, and Ashland counties. Hwy 13 runs north-south through Park Falls and is the main route for visitors to the area. Hwy 70 runs east-west through a large resort area to the south of Park Falls.

Things to Do

Park Falls is headquarters of the **Chequamegon National Forest**, an 840,000-acre expanse of public lands stretching over six north central and northwest Wisconsin counties. The forest offers hundreds of lakes, miles of streams and rivers, trails for hiking, cross-country skiing, snowmobiling, horseback riding, and even motorcycles and ATVs, plus picnic areas and campgrounds. There are launch sites for canoes and motorboats and plenty of places to swim and fish.

Chequamegon National Forest Headquarters, 1170 Fourth Ave. South, Park Falls, WI 54552; phone 715-762-2461. Headquarters open 7:30-4:30 Monday-Friday. $ for camping.

The **Flambeau River State Forest** protects the banks of the North and South forks of the Flambeau River, preserving more than 60 miles of river for recreation. Canoeing is extremely popular on the Flambeau. However, some rapids are difficult and you should canoe some stretches of the river only if you and your children are experienced paddlers. Contact the forest superintendent for maps and information. There are canoe campsites along the North Fork of the river. Also provided in the forest are hiking, skiing, and snowmobile trails, and campgrounds and beaches on Connors Lake and Lake of the Pines (both in Sawyer County). The forest is 20 miles west of Park Falls on Hwy 70.

Flambeau State Forest Superintendent, W1613 County Road W, Winter, WI 54896; phone 715-332-5271. Handicap-accessible camping and picnic facilities. $ for camping.

Timm's Hill County Park is the place to go if you and your kids want to stand atop the highest point in Wisconsin. The park has hiking trails and a picnic area, but the reason everyone goes there is to climb Timm's Hill, elevation 1,951.5 feet above sea level, then climb the observation tower for spectacular views of the wooded hills rolling off for miles to the horizon.

Thirty-eight miles south of Park Falls on Hwy 13, then east on Hwy 86. Open year-round. Free.

One of the most unusual attractions in the state is the **Wisconsin Concrete Park**. This county park is dedicated to the work of self-taught concrete artist Fred Smith, who over the course of 15 years created some 200 sculptures. The figures are heavily decorated with broken glass, whole beer bottles, bits of ceramic tile, and other bright items. Mr. Smith's work includes an eight-horse hitch pulling a wagon, Paul Bunyan with Babe the Blue Ox, dogs, deer, and other animals and human figures, all at least life size. The figures are charming and whimsical. The park has no facilities except rest rooms.

On Hwy 13 twenty miles south of Park Falls just outside Phillips. Open year-round. Free.

Winter Fun

There are many miles of **Chequamegon National Forest** cross-country ski trails in the Park Falls area. The Newman Springs Ski Trails are 12 miles east of Park Falls on Hwy 182. The Wintergreen Trail system is south on Hwy 13, then east on Hwy 70. Both are usable by beginner and intermediate skiers. The Oxbo Trail, south on Hwy 13, then west on Hwy 70, in the **Flambeau State Forest** has eight miles of trail loops for all skill levels.

For maps and information, contact the National Forest Superintendent and the State Forest Superintendent (see Things to Do above), or the Park Falls Chamber of Commerce (see Tourist Information below).

For indoor winter sports, Park Falls residents choose bowling. **Flambeau Lanes** has open bowling, a video arcade, and a lounge with both a sandwich menu and live entertainment. Stay all winter. On Hwy 13 at south edge of Park Falls; phone 715-762-3237.

Rentals

9 Mile Tavern/Canoe Rentals rents canoes and provides shuttle service for Flambeau River trips. Rt. 1, Park Falls; phone 715-762-3174.

The **Oxbo Resort** rents canoes and provides shuttle service for Flambeau River trips. They also rent fishing boats, mountain bikes, and cross-country skis. Rt. 1, Box 251, Park Falls; phone 715-762-4786.

Flambeau Sports and General Store rents canoes and provides shuttle service for trips on the Flambeau River. On County Hwy F west of Phillips; phone 715-339-2012.

Where to Stay

Palmquists The Farm, N5136 River Road, Brantwood, WI 54513; phone 715-564-2558 or 800-519-2558. This working 800-acre beef and tree farm houses guests in rustic but very comfortable lodges and provides wonderful home-cooked meals. Guests enjoy bicycling, hay rides, cross-country skiing on 25 miles of private trails, sleigh rides, bonfires, and lots of fun. A real break from routine and a chance to get the kids away from the TV and video games.

Northway Motor Lodge, Hwy 13 south, Park Falls; phone 715-762-2406. Modern motel with indoor pool, exercise room, cable TV with free movies, video games, near restaurants and next door to Flambeau Lanes for bowling.

Idle Hour Resort, N14516 Shady Knoll Road, Park Falls (east off Hwy 70); phone 715-762-3872. Lakeside resort in the Chequamegon National Forest. Housekeeping cabins on wooded grounds, beach, boats, playground, and planned activities for kids. Lodge with restaurant.

Emergency

Fire 762-3333
Sheriff 339-3011
Ambulance 762-3150

Tourist Information

Park Falls Area Chamber of Commerce
400 Fourth Ave. S., Suite 8
Park Falls, WI 54552
715-762-2703
800-762-2709

Cable

Hwy 63 provides easy access to this tiny community at the center of a major resort and recreation area.

Things to Do

Cable is smack in the middle of a large section of the **Chequamegon National Forest**, with its plethora of winter and summer trails, lakes and rivers, picnic areas and campgrounds. For information and maps, contact the Forest Superintendent (see Things to Do-Park Falls, above).

Blue Moon Pottery makes and sells a variety of unique clay pieces. Visitors to the pottery shop can watch pots, plates, vases and other items being made.

Two miles north of Cable on Hwy 63, then west three miles on Blue Moon Rd.; mailing address Rt. 1, Box 67, Drummond, WI 54809; phone 715-798-3509. Potters working 9-4 Monday-Friday.

Off-road biking is becoming increasingly popular, and Cable has become a center for the sport. In addition to trails in the Chequamegon National Forest, Telemark Lodge (see Where to Stay below) has miles of beautiful trails, and bikers can ride on the route used for the famous Birkebeiner cross-country ski race from Hayward to Telemark.

Winter Fun

Telemark Resort has both downhill and cross-country skiing. The downhill facility has 10 runs on a hill with a vertical drop of 370 feet. The downhill area has ski rentals, lessons, including special kids lessons, chalet, restaurant, and child care. The resort has more than 20 miles of beautiful groomed cross-country ski trails, with the same amenities available to downhill skiers, including rentals and lessons. Telemark also offers an outdoor ice skating rink and horsedrawn sleigh rides. Rental skates available. Three miles east of Cable on County Hwy M; mailing address Box 277, Cable; phone 715-798-3811 or 800-472-3001 (Wisconsin and adjoining states).

Rentals

New Moon Ski & Sport rents off-road bikes at Telemark Resort, and also conducts full and half day guided rides for bicyclists of all skill levels. On County Hwy M three miles east of Cable; phone 715-798-3811, ext. 576.

Where to Stay

Telemark Resort, three miles east of Cable on County Hwy M; mailing address Box 277, Cable; phone

715-798-3811 or 800-472-3001. A complete family resort
built around a downhill ski area. In addition to downhill
and cross-country skiing, the year-round facility offers
indoor and outdoor pools, game rooms, bicycling, horseback riding, indoor tennis, basketball, volleyball, playgrounds, golf course, free movies in a theater, TV in
rooms, child care and organized children's activities,
restaurants, shops, and a choice of accommodations from
a lodge room to a four-bedroom townhouse. The resort is
not on a lake, but owns lakeshore property ten miles
away for fishing, swimming, and boating.

Lakewoods, on County Hwy M eight miles east of
Cable; phone 715-794-2561. A large family resort on Lake
Namekagon. Lots of watersports including swimming,
fishing, canoeing, sailing, and waterskiing. Tennis and
volleyball courts, indoor and outdoor pools, golf course,
video games, TV, restaurant. Scheduled children's activities in summer. Snowmobile and cross-country ski rentals
for use on the adjoining trails. Accommodations range
from a lodge room to four-bedroom cottages and condos.

Mogasheen Resort, east from Cable on County Hwy M,
then north on County Hwy D; mailing address HC73,
Box 418, Cable 54821; phone 715-794-2113. A low-key
resort with housekeeping cottages in the heart of the
Chequamegon National Forest on Lake Namekagon.
Amenities include a beach, paddleboats, canoes, and rowboats, playground, bicycles, game rooms, tennis and
volleyball courts, hiking trails, indoor pool, TV, cross-
country ski trails, snowmobile trails, snack bar.

Emergency

Sheriff 373-6120
Ambulance 798-3200
Fire 798-4444

Tourist Information

Cable Area Chamber of Commerce
Box 217
Cable, WI 54821
715-798-3833
800-533-7454
Web site http://cable4fun.com

Hayward

This formerly wild and rowdy lumber town is today the center of a resort and outdoor recreation area. Hundreds of lakes and the Chequamegon National Forest provide opportunities for recreation and for solitude. With a population of 2,000-plus, Hayward is also the commercial center of a multi-county area. Routes 63, 77, and 27 converge on Hayward, funneling visitors to the city for summer fishing, boating, hiking and loafing, and winter skiing, snowmobiling, and relaxing.

Things to Do

Even if you don't like fishing, visit the **National Fresh Water Fishing Hall of Fame**. It will be your kids' only chance to get inside a 45-foot-high, 200-foot-long fiberglass muskie. The view from the creature's toothy open mouth is actually quite nice. Other giant fish dot the seven-acre Hall of Fame grounds, and inside the buildings are antique boats and motors, hundreds of mounted fish, rods, reels, lures, and other fishing equipment, and the actual hall of fame itself, which displays pictures of famous anglers. There's a miniature golf course next door and a snack bar and gift shop on the grounds.

Hall of Fame Dr., Hayward; phone 715-634-4440. Everything except the big muskie is wheelchair accessible. Open 10-5 daily mid-April through October. $.

Wilderness Walk recreational park lets kids pet and feed domestic and wild animals. Other animals are displayed in natural surroundings. There's also an Old West town, picnic areas, and a snack bar.

Three miles south of Hayward on Hwy 27; phone 715-634-2893. Open 10-4:30 daily mid-May through Labor Day. $.

Scheers Lumberjack Shows provide action-packed entertainment as lumberjacks compete in sports such as canoe jousting, speed climbing, chopping, sawing and log rolling. Clowns offer a lively interlude between events.

On County Hwy B off Hwy 27 just east of Hayward; phone 715-634-5010. Shows at 7:30 p.m. Wednesday and Friday and 2 Tuesday, Thursday, and Saturday mid-June through early September. $.

The **Namekagon River** is part of the St. Croix National Scenic Riverway. It is slow moving, with only a few small rapids, perfect for family canoeing. There are a number of canoe landings on the river in the Hayward area. At Trego, on Hwy 63 twenty miles southwest of Hayward, is the Trego Information Station (open summer only, phone 715-635-8346), with displays explaining the natural and cultural history of the river, and with information about canoeing, camping, and picnic sites along the river. Summertime river levels vary, so call for information before planning your canoe trip.

For maps and information, contact the Riverway Superintendent, Box 708, St. Croix Falls, WI 54024; phone 715-483-3284. Free.

The **Chequamegon National Forest** surrounds Hayward with pristine areas for hiking, boating, camping, and picnicking. For specifics, contact the Great Divide Ranger District, 604 Nyman Ave., mailing address Box 896, Hayward 54843; phone 715-634-4821. Free. $ for camping.

The **Chippewa Flowage** is one of the largest lakes in Wisconsin, and most of its shoreline is state and federal land, so it is quite wild. **Chippewa Queen Tours** takes visitors on two-hour narrated cruises around the flowage, offering a history of the flowage and surrounding area and a chance to see wildlife and to enjoy the beautiful shore. There's also a three-hour dinner cruise for sunsets and wildlife viewing.

At Treeland Resort, on the Chippewa Flowage east of Hayward, mailing address Rt 4, Box 4288, Hayward 54843; phone 715-462-3874. Cruises offered Monday, Wednesday, Friday, Saturday, and Sunday Memorial Day weekend through the first weekend in October. Dinner cruises Wednesday and Saturday only. Reservations recommended for two-hour tour, required for dinner tour. $

Stables in the area offer **horseback riding**. They have both horses and ponies and give riding lessons as well as providing guided trail rides.

Mrotek's Stables has trail rides of 35 minutes to two hours; ten miles east of Hayward on Hwy 77; phone 715-462-3674; open Memorial Day weekend through November. Appa-Lolly Ranch has trail rides and overnight camping trips; four miles east of Hayward on Hwy 77; phone 715-634-5059; open year-round.

Events

JULY. The **Honor the Earth Pow-wow** attracts hundreds of Native Americans who join in dances, drumming and arts-and-crafts displays as well as selling traditional foods. Visitors by the thousands also join in the fun. One of the largest pow-wows in the nation. Held the third weekend in July at the Lac Court Oreilles Tribal Park at County Hwys K and E, eleven miles southeast of Hayward. Call the Hayward Chamber of Commerce (see below) for information.

JULY. The **World Lumberjack Championships** bring more than 200 competitors for chopping, sawing, logrolling, tree climbing, and other lumberjack sports. There's also entertainment, food, and lots of people in plaid flannel shirts. Good fun. In Hayward the last weekend in July. Call the Hayward Chamber of Commerce (see below) for information.

Rentals

New Moon Ski & Sport rents mountain bikes and cross-country skis. Hwy 63 just north of Hayward; phone 715-634-8685.

Hayward Marine rents ski boats and fishing boats. Hwy 77 east of Hayward; phone 715-634-4373.

Where to Stay

Ross' Teal Lake Lodge, Rt. 7, Hayward; phone 715-462-3631. A low-key lakeside resort that has managed to provide great amenities while maintaining that homey feeling. The resort has 24 housekeeping cottages along a half mile of shoreline on a quiet lake where waterskiing is not permitted. Canoes, pontoon boats, sailboats, and water bikes are available for guests to rent. The resort has a golf course (kids can ride along on the cart or play if they want), tennis court, a beach, a heated outdoor pool, a playground, nature trails, bicycles, evening programs and movies, recreation room with video games, groomed cross-country ski trails, a coin laundry, and a main lodge and restaurant. Cook your meals or eat at the restaurant. Fishing on Teal Lake is excellent.

Treeland Resort, Rt 4, Box 4288, Hayward 54843; phone 715-462-3874. A large resort on the Chippewa Flowage that has been in operation since the 1920s. It's been upgraded and modernized and expanded along the way. Choose a motel unit or a fully funished cottage. Guests have a game room, outdoor pool, beach, boats, playground, tennis courts, and hiking and bike trails available. In winter, cross-country skiing and snowmobiling are just outside the door. The resort also has a restaurant and offers cruises on the Chippewa Flowage.

Where to Eat

The **Moose Cafe** is famous for its humorous "Road Kill Menu," but they really serve edible, and very good, food. Especially their fresh-baked bread, cinnamon rolls, and pies. Their chicken, ribs, fish, and pasta dishes won't leave you hungry, either. A Hayward institution. 106 N. Dakota Ave.; phone 715-634-8449. Open daily for breakfast, lunch, and dinner.

Extended Hours Grocery Store

Marketplace IGA
Hwy 63 North
715-634-8996

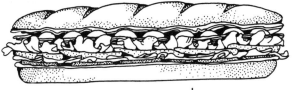

Emergency

Fire and police 634-4858
Ambulance 634-4322

Tourist Information

Hayward Chamber of Commerce
101 W. First St.
Hayward, WI 54843
715-634-8662
800-724-2992
Web site http://www.haywardlakes.com

Spooner

This city of 2,800 at the junction of Hwys 53 and 63 is the center of a summer resort area.

Events

JULY. **Heart of the North Rodeo** has all the professional rodeo action events—bull riding, calf roping,

saddle bronc riding, steer wrestling, bareback bronc riding, plus clowns, barrel racing, and other fun. One of the top rodeos in the Midwest. Plenty of excitement led by top rodeo cowboys and cowgirls. Special entertainment for kids. Held in mid-July. For tickets and information write Rodeo, Box 406, Spooner, WI 54801; phone 800-367-3306. $.

Grantsburg

This village of 1,200 is reached by Hwy 70 from the east or west, or on Hwy 48 from the south.

Things to Do

St. Croix National Scenic Riverway facilities nearby include the Marshland Visitor Center, just west and across the river in Minnesota (phone 320-629-2148). The station, which is open in the summer only, has displays about the river and its history, and information about boating and other activities on the river. There's a picnic area on the Wisconsin side of the river opposite the information station. (See Things to Do-St. Croix Falls below for address and phone for the main riverway headquarters.)

The **Governor Knowles State Forest** stretches in a narrow band for 55 miles along the St. Croix River both north and south from Grantsburg. Within the forest are 38 miles of hiking trails, a 35-mile horseback riding trail, snowmobile trails, cross-country ski trails, and canoe landings and canoe campsites along the St. Croix. Wildlife including deer, bear, hawks, bald eagles, heron, ducks, and geese are abundant in the forest.

Governor Knowles State Forest, Box 367, Hwy 70, Grantsburg, WI 54840; phone 715-463-2898. Handicap accessible picnic facilities. $ for some developed areas.

Crex Meadows Wildlife Area has 31,000 acres of marsh, lake, and prairie land. It is a paradise for wildlife, with more the 245 species found there. An extensive road and trail system, with strategically placed observation areas, gives visitors a chance to see sharp-tailed grouse, sandhill cranes, eagles, herons, blackbirds, geese, and other birds as well as badgers, deer, and other wildlife.

Popular visiting times are during the spring and fall waterfowl migration, though summer and winter visitors also have a chance to see many species of wild animals. A picnic area with restroom facilities is located in the heart of the wildlife area.

Headquarters at intersection of County Hwys F and D one-half mile north of Grantsburg; mailing address Ranger Station, Box 367, Grantsburg; phone 715-463-2896. Open daily year-round. Free.

Winter Fun

Governor Knowles State Forest has 10 miles of groomed cross-country ski trails running through gentle, wooded terrain and along the St. Croix River. Ask the Forest Superintendent (see Things to Do above) for information about the Brandt Pines Ski Trail.

Rentals

Wild River Outfitters rents canoes and provides shuttle service on both the upper St. Croix and Namekagon rivers. They also rent solo kayaks for the St. Croix. 15177 Hwy 70, Grantsburg; phone 715-463-2254.

Tourist Information

Grantsburg Chamber of Commerce
416 South Pine St.
Grantsburg, WI 54840
715-463-2405

St. Croix Falls

This historic community of 1,700 on the St. Croix River is the center for many outdoor activities. Hwy 8 (east-west) and Hwy 87 (north-south) bring most visitors to the area.

Things to Do

The **St. Croix National Scenic Riverway** protects 252 miles of the St. Croix and its tributary the Namekagon as they flow through Wisconsin and Minnesota. St. Croix Falls is the headquarters of the riverway. The St. Croix River in this area offers canoeing, motorboating, fishing, camping, picnic areas, beaches, and parks. The

Visitor Center houses exhibits about the river and the logging history of the area, and personnel at the center can give you advice about canoe trips and other activities on the river.

Superintendent, St. Croix National Riverway, Box 708, St. Croix Falls, WI 54024. Visitor Center at Massachusetts & Hamilton Streets; phone 715-483-3284. Visitor Center open 8:30-5 Monday-Thursday and 8:30-6 Friday-Sunday Memorial Day through Labor Day, open 8:30-4:30 Monday-Friday the rest of the year. Free.

Canoeing on the St. Croix is a fun family activity. The river below St. Croix Falls is calm, slow, and scenic. Quest Canoe Rental offers three-hour to two-day trips on the river, including canoes and shuttle. At Hwys 8 and 35 just south of St. Croix Falls; phone 715-483-1091.

Interstate State Park occupies one of the most beautiful stretches of the St. Croix River, as it flows through a narrow gorge of sheer rock walls called the Dalles of the St. Croix. The park is known for the rock formations carved millions of years ago by the swirling waters of glacial Lake Duluth as that huge prehistoric lake drained into what is now the Mississippi River, leaving behind the St. Croix River in its present bed. The park has hiking and ski trails, a beach, picnic areas, campgrounds, and the Ice Age Interpretive Center, which offers a variety of summer programs, many especially for children.

Park on Hwy 35 one and one-quarter miles south of St. Croix Falls; mailing address Box 703, St. Croix Falls, WI 54024; phone 715-483-3747. Handicap-accessible picnic, fishing pier, and camping facilities. Open daily year-round. $.

Across the river in Taylors Falls, MN, Scenic Boat Tours offers daily cruises through the Dalles from Memorial Day weekend through Labor Day, and weekend cruises in May, September, and October. At the Hwy 8 bridge; phone 612-465-6315. $.

Fawn Doe Rosa animal park has an excellent display of wildlife such as mountain lions and grizzly bears as well as approachable fauna such as deer, ponies, and other wild and domestic animals. Kids can feed and pet a variety of baby animals. Pony rides are offered. Picnic area and snack bar.

Two miles east of St. Croix Falls on Hwy 8; phone 715-483-3772. Open 10-6 daily May through September, weekends in October. $.

Just up the river in nearby Osceola, the **Osceola & St. Croix Valley Railway** operates antique steam engines and newer diesels that pull trains on 45-minute and 90-minute excursions through the St. Croix valley. A wonderful slow-paced way to see the scenery.

Trains depart from the station just off Hwy 35 in Osceloa; phone 612-228-0263 or 800-711-2591. Trains run weekends and holidays from Memorial Day weekend through the last weekend in October. Call for schedules and routes. $.

Winter Fun

Interstate Park offers 11 miles of groomed cross-country ski trails. The park office provides a warming shelter, toilets, water, and parking.

Downhill skiers will find plenty of action at **Trollhaugen**, with its 22 runs and 260-foot vertical drop. The hill offers rentals, ski lessons, a ski shop, snack bar, and lounge with live entertainment. The hill has a special SKIWEE instructional program for children. On County Hwy F, one mile east of Dresser, which is five miles south of St. Croix Falls. Phone 715-755-2955 or 800-826-7166 (Minnesota only).

Where to Stay

Dalles House, junction Hwys 8 and 35, St. Croix Falls, WI 54024; phone 715-483-3206 or 800-341-8000. Fifty-room motel with indoor pool, sauna, cable TV with HBO, restaurant, coin laundry, adjacent to snowmobile trails and near the entrance to Interstate State Park.

Where to Eat

Dalles House Restaurant offers a coffee shop and a dining room for a light snack or a full meal. On Hwy 35 just south of St. Croix Falls; phone 715-483-3246. Open daily for breakfast, lunch, and dinner.

The **Valley Family Restaurant** has a large breakfast menu plus lunch and dinner specials featuring steaks, seafood, homemade soups, and salad bar. On Washington Street in downtown St. Croix Falls; phone 715-483-9902. Open daily for breakfast, lunch, and dinner.

Tourist Information

Polk County Information Center
710 Hwy 35 South
St. Croix Falls, WI 54024
715-483-1410
800-222-POLK

Waterfall Hunting

Wisconsin's northwestern tier of counties has hundreds of waterfalls of all shapes and sizes, thanks to geologic forces that have been at work for somewhere in the neighborhood of a billion years. Waterfalls are scattered throughout Iron, Ashland, Bayfield, and Douglas counties. They range from gushing torrents foaming through steep gorges to delicate ribbons trickling down small crevices. Some are easy to find and can be seen from the car. Others require a good map and a hike through the woods. Look along the Montreal River between Hurley and Saxon Harbor. Look in the Chequamegon National Forest. Look in Copper Falls, Amnicon, and Pattison state parks. Waterfall hunting is a terrific reason to explore back roads and stroll down wooded trails. Waterfall maps and information are available from:

Superintendent, Chequamegon National Forest
1170 Fourth Avenue South
Park Falls, WI 54552
715-762-2461

Iron County Extension Office
Courthouse
Hurley, WI 54534
715-561-2695

Ashland Chamber of Commerce
320 Fourth Avenue West
Ashland, WI 54806
715-682-2500
800-284-9484

12

West Wisconsin River Country

Including Eau Claire, Chippewa Falls, Menomonie, Spring Valley, Downsville, Somerset, Hudson, River Falls, Black River Falls, and the Great River Road from Pepin south to Alma, Fountain City, and Trempealeau

Family activities in this area center around the rivers—riding an inner tube down a splashing rapids, watching egrets standing still and majestic in river shallows, seeing huge barges pass through Mississippi locks, bicycling on a riverside path, or exploring the islands on a houseboat.

This beautiful and largely undiscovered land is defined and shaped by rivers—the St. Croix, the Apple, the Chippewa, the Red Cedar, the Black, and, of course, the stately Mississippi.

The rivers were highways for exploration and settlement, and they brought commerce and prosperity to the region. French fur traders followed the Mississippi and its tributaries into the heart of the continent. Loggers floated billions of board feet of lumber down the rivers to the sawmills. Settlers cleared farms and built cities in the river valleys.

The region is framed by I-94 as it loops east then north, by I-90 to the south, and by Hwy 35, the Great River Road, on the west.

Eau Claire

Founded as a sawmill and logging town at the confluence of the Eau Claire and Chippewa rivers, this city of

55,000 is today a regional industrial, commercial, and higher education center. Reach the city via I-94 or on Hwy 53.

Things to Do

Carson Park is a lovely 134-acre park with picnic areas, a beach, tennis courts, hiking trails, playgrounds, rides on an antique steam train, and two museums. The **Paul Bunyan Logging Camp** is a recreated 1890s logging camp, complete with bunkhouse, cook shanty, blacksmith shop, and antique logging equipment. Displays and exhibits include films showing how the lumberjacks felled and transported trees. The **Chippewa Valley Museum** exhibits depict the history of the area, with a log cabin, a one-room school, and furnishings and daily household items from 19th-century Eau Claire. There are some hand-on exhibits, and the operating turn-of-the-century ice cream parlor is a favorite with visitors.

Carson Park is accessible from Menomonie St. or Lake St. Open daily. Free.

Paul Bunyan Logging Camp phone 715-835-6200. Open 10-4:30 daily mid-April through Labor Day, 1-4:30 Tuesday-Friday and 10-4:30 Saturday and Sunday in September after Labor Day. $.

Chippewa Valley Museum phone 715-834-7871. Open 1-5 Tuesday-Sunday. Extended summer hours. $.

The **Ski Sprites** entertain with water ski shows on Half Moon Lake in Carson Park. Show site is at the corner of Charles and Randall streets. Call the Convention and Visitors Bureau, 715-831-2345, for information. Shows at 6:30 p.m. Wednesday and Sunday June through Labor Day. Free.

The **L.E. Phillips Planetarium** of the University of Wisconsin-Eau Claire gives tours of our solar system and the entire universe. All in a few hours. The Planetarium is in Phillips Science Hall, on Roosevelt Avenue on the UW-Eau Claire campus. Evening shows throughout the school year. For show times, call 715-836-4833. $.

The **Chippewa River State Trail** runs through Eau Claire and goes west. It will eventually link up with the Red Cedar Trail but currently it ends west of town. That's

OK, though because the trail offers plenty of family biking and hiking right now. The 2.2-mile segment of the trail in the city is paved and runs along the shore of the Chippewa River. Perfect for a ride and a picnic. Outside of town the trail continues for 13 miles on an abandoned railroad right-of-way. It's flat and there's no car traffic.

For information and a map, contact the Department of Natural Resources, phone 715-839-3700, or the Eau Claire Area Convention and Visitors Bureau, 715-831-2345. Trail use is free in the city, $ for the segment outside the city.

Triple Play Sports Park has a challenging multi-level 18-hole miniature golf course built into a hillside. Weave your way around waterfalls, water traps, and other hazards. There's also an arcade, batting cage, and a netted golf driving range.

1250 W. Clairemont Ave.; phone 715-834-3100. Open daily in warm weather. Call for hours. $.

Mini Putter Miniature Golf offers 18 holes of indoor fun, plus video games, pool, foosball, air hockey, and other activities. At 3178 London Rd. (south off Clairemont Ave., near London Square Mall); phone 715-835-8043. Call for hours. $.

Winter Fun

Glide through the winter with public skating at the **Hobbs Municipal Indoor Ice Center**. At 915 Menomonie St.; phone 715-839-5040. $.

You can cross-country ski right in **Carson Park** on a groomed one-mile trail that's easy enough for beginners. For information, contact the Eau Claire City Parks Department, 715-839-5032.

Eau Claire takes bowling seriously. Open bowling is offered at **Wagner's 66 1/2 Lanes**, one of the largest alleys in Wisconsin, on Hwy 53; phone 715-832-9298. **Wagner's West** has a mere 24 lanes, but you'll only need one lane anyway. At 1616 N. Clairemont; phone 715-833-6717.

Events

JUNE. **Sawdust Days** celebrates Eau Claire's past as a logging town with carnival rides, a parade, an art fair, entertainers, food, and fun runs. Held in late June in Pioneer Park. Phone 715-831-2345 or 800-344-3866 for details. $.

Shopping

Eau Claire has several large malls. **Oakwood Mall**, at Golf Road and Hwy 53, is the city's largest mall, with nearly 100 stores, specialty shops, restaurants and movie theaters. **London Square Mall**, on Mall Drive (off Clairemont Ave. to London Rd.), has more than 50 stores, including several large department stores and a large food court. Both malls open daily.

Rentals

Riverside Bike and Skate rents bicycles, ice skates, roller blades, and canoes. They also provide shuttle service for canoe trips on the Eau Claire and Chippewa rivers and offer Paddle and Peddle trips, on which you paddle downstream, then bicycle back to the starting point. 902 Menomonie St.; phone 715-835-0088.

Where to Stay

Holiday Inn Convention Center, 205 S. Barstow St.; phone 715-835-6121 or 800-950-6121. Downtown hotel with easy access to UW-Eau Claire campus, parks. Amenities include indoor pool, cable TV, restaurant.

Ramada Inn, 1202 W. Clairemont Ave. (Hwy 12); phone 715-834-3181 or 800-482-7829. Large motel with indoor and outdoor pools, whirlpool, exercise room, playground, game room, cable TV, restaurant.

Best Western Midway Motel, 2851 Hendrickson Dr. (off Hwy 37 just north of I-94); phone 715-835-2242 or 800-528-1234. Comfortable motel with indoor pool and games area, whirlpool, cable TV, restaurant.

Extended Hours Grocery Store

Randall Foods
2615 London Rd.
715-834-2081

Emergency

For fire, police, or ambulance, dial 911

Tourist Information

Eau Claire Area Convention & Visitors Bureau
3625 Gateway Dr.
Eau Claire, WI 54701
715-831-2345
800-344-3866

Chippewa Falls

A former logging town, this charming city of 13,000 is just ten miles north of Eau Claire on Hwys 53 and 178. The city is best known as the home of Leinenkugel Beer.

Things to Do

Irvine Park and Zoo is a beautiful 300-acre park with playgrounds, picnic areas, a campground, tennis courts, a swimming pool, ice skating rink, and miles of hiking trails. The small zoo features animals that are native to Wisconsin, many of which are in large enclosures. The Little Red Barn houses farm animals and a petting zoo. A few blocks down the street from the park entrance is the **Leinenkugel brewery**, with tours and a gift shop with tasting room.

Main park entrance on Bridgewater Rd.; phone 715-723-3890. Open daily. Free. Brewery at Bridgewater Rd. and Jefferson Ave. (Hwy 124); phone 715-723-5557. Brewery tours, Monday-Saturday June through August, less frequent the rest of the year. Call for tour times. Gift shop and tasting room open 9-5 Monday-Friday and 9-4 Saturday year-round. Free.

Lake Wissota State Park, 6,300 acres on the shores of a man-made lake, has hiking and ski trails, beach and bath house, horseback riding trails, picnic areas, and a campground. From Memorial Day weekend through Labor Day a naturalist is on hand to give lectures and lead nature hikes. There's also a self-guiding nature trail that winds along the edge of a beaver pond.

On County Hwy O, six miles north of Chippewa Falls on Hwy 124, then east on Hwy S; mailing address 18127 County Hwy O, Chippewa Falls 54729; phone 715-382-4574. Handicap-accessible picnic and camping facilities and fishing pier. Open daily. $.

Winter Fun

Each December, **Irvine Park** becomes a Christmas Village festooned with more than 35,000 lights. Life-size Christmas scenes, both Biblical and secular, are placed throughout the park. Walk or drive through, 7 a.m. to 9:30 p.m. daily from early December through New Year's Day. For information, contact the Chippewa Falls Parks, Recreation, and Forestry Department, 715-723-3890.

Throughout the winter, ice skate at an outdoor rink at **Irvine Park**, or cross-country ski on more than seven miles of groomed trails at **Lake Wissota State Park**.

Events

JULY. The **Northern Wisconsin State Fair** is a large regional fair featuring animal shows and animal judging, exhibits, entertainment, a midway, and lots of other great fair activities. Held the second week in July at the fair grounds in Chippewa Falls. Call the Chamber of Commerce (see below) for dates and information.

Tourist Information

Chamber of Commerce
811 North Bridge St.
Chippewa Falls, WI 54729
715-723-0331

Menomonie and Vicinity

Home of the University of Wisconsin-Stout campus, Menomonie straddles the Red Cedar River. I-94 passes north of this city of 14,000, and Hwys 25 (north-south) and 29 (east-west) run through the community.

Things to Do

Wakanda Park and the **Lion's Club Game Park** are perfect for an afternoon outing. The Game Park houses elk, buffalo, deer, and other native animals in large fenced enclosures. Across the road, wooded Wakanda Park has a beach on Lake Menomin, picnic areas, playgrounds, and a nature trail. This park is close to I-94, and is a good spot for a travel break.

On Pine St., exit I-94 on Hwy 25 toward Menomonie, then left (east) on Pine. Contact Chamber of Commerce (see below) for information. Open daily. Free.

The **Red Cedar State Trail** stretches for 14.5 miles south from Menomonie on a converted railroad right-of-way along the Red Cedar River. The trail is scenic and wooded. Riverside Park, a city park with picnic and playground areas and a canoe launch site, is adjacent to the trailhead in Menomonie.

Trailhead in Menomonie on Hwy 29 where it crosses the Red Cedar River; mailing address Rt. 6, Box 1, Menomonie 54751; phone 715-232-1242. Open daily for hiking and biking and for cross-country skiing. $ for bicycling.

The **Mabel Tainter Theater** is a so-ugly-it's-handsome melange of late 19th-century architecture with a restored main stage that hosts both local and traveling performers. Many events are for children and families. Tours are available most afternoons.

Mabel Tainter Box Office, 205 Main St., Menomonie; phone 715-235-9726. Performances year-round. $.

Eighteen miles west of Menomonie in tiny Spring Valley is **Crystal Cave**, and it is well worth the side trip. The cave, discovered by local farm boys in 1881, has three levels and some 30 different rooms. The hour-long tours are exceptionally well done, with lots of information presented in a fun way by knowledgeable guides.

On Hwy 29 one mile west of Spring Valley; mailing address W2465 Hwy 29, Spring Valley, WI 54767; phone 715-778-4414 or 800-236-CAVE. Open 9-6 daily Memorial Day weekend through Labor Day, 9-5 weekends in April, May, September, October. Tours leave every half hour. $.

Rentals

Red Cedar Outfitters rents bicycles, inner tubes, canoes, ice skates, and cross-country skis. They provide a shuttle service for those who want to bicycle or canoe one-way on the Red Cedar River or on the Red Cedar Trail. On Hwy 29 at the head of the Red Cedar Trail in Menomonie; phone 715-235-5431.

Where to Stay

Holiday Manor Motor Lodge, 1815 N. Broadway (Hwy 25); phone 715-235-9651 or 800-528-1234. A Best Western motel with an indoor pool, games, cable TV and free movies, refrigerators available, close to restaurants.

Where to Eat

The Creamery is seven miles down the Red Cedar Trail (or Hwy 25) in Downsville, and you'd be well advised to make the trip by bike, canoe, or car. The food in this renovated creamery is outstanding. The ever-changing menu focuses on salads, pasta, fresh vegetables, sandwiches, fresh fish, beef, and chicken, plus homemade breads, pastries, pies, and cakes. While the restaurant is great for adults, it's not too stuffy to take kids, and in fact has a good children's menu. The restaurant is a favorite with bicyclists, so you can be sure the atmosphere is informal. Off County Hwy C in Downsville; phone 715-664-8354. Open Tuesday-Sunday for lunch and dinner; closed January-March.

Emergency

For fire, police or ambulance, dial 911

Tourist Information

Menomonie Area Chamber of Commerce
P.O. Box 246
700 Wolske Bay Rd., suite 200
Menomonie, WI 54751
715-235-9087
800-283-1862

Somerset

This community on Hwy 35 north of Hudson is famous for Apple River tubing.

Things to Do

Tubing the Apple River is one of the hottest warm weather sports in Wisconsin. Tubers bounce downstream along the shallow Apple, with extra thrills provided by a few small rapids. Popular and easy. Many adults make the trip equipped with a few cans of beer or other snacks. There are many Apple River tube rental outfitters that provide a tube and shuttle service. A few of the largest are:

- **Terrace Tubes**, on Hwy 35 in Somerset; phone 715-247-3535
- **Somerset Camp Tube Rentals**, on Hwy 35 in Somerset; phone 715-247-3728
- **Float-Rite Park**, on Spring St. in Somerset; phone 715-247-3453 or 800-826-7096
- **River's Edge Tubing and Waterslides**, on Hwy 64 in Somerset; phone 715-247-3305
- **Apple River Campground**, off Hwy 35 in Somerset; phone 715-247-3378 or 800-637-8936.

For those tired of tubing, **Wild Waters Water Park** offers a change of pace—waterslides. The park has three, all long. It's also got an 18-hole miniature golf course if you want to dry out. There's also a small kiddie pool and activity area for younger children. The park has a picnic area and concessions, as well as changing rooms for when the kids are finally done with the waterslides.

South of Somerset on Hwy 35/64; phone 715-247-3363. Open daily 10-8 Memorial Day weekend through Labor Day. $.

Tourist Information

Somerset Area Chamber of Commerce
Box 357
Somerset, WI 54025
715-247-3366

Hudson

The gateway to Wisconsin (or to Minnesota if you're going west), Hudson is an historic St. Croix River community easily accessible via I-94.

Things to Do

Willow River State Park is built around two man-made lakes on the Willow River. The park has hiking and cross-country ski trails, a beach, picnic areas, and a lovely wooded lakeside campground. There's a summer naturalist program with lectures and guided nature hikes.

1034 County Hwy A (six miles northeast of Hudson); phone 715-386-5931. Handicap-accessible picnic and camping facilities. Open daily. $.

While away an afternoon in **Lakefront Park**, a city park on the St. Croix that has a beach with lifeguards, playground, picnic areas, and lots of room for the kids to run off excess energy while you relax and watch the boat traffic on the river or read a book. On First Street in downtown Hudson. For information, call the Hudson Parks and Recreation Department, 715-386-4774. Open daily. Free.

Winter Fun

Willow River State Park has more than eight miles of groomed cross-country ski trails. Most are designed for beginner and intermediate skiers.

Where to Stay

Best Western Hudson House, 1616 Crestview Dr. (exit 2 off I-94); phone 715-386-2394 or 800-528-1234. Modern, well-maintained motel with indoor pool, whirlpool, exercise room, games, cable TV, restaurant, lounge, miniature golf.

Where to Eat

Mamma Maria's is where you find the locals. And with good reason. It's got great Italian food. The menu features a wide range of pasta dishes, chicken, seafood, steaks, and pizza. Maria also makes excellent soups, salads, and desserts. For lunch try a sandwich or pizza. Carry-outs available. 708 Sixth St. (Hwy 35) north of Hudson; phone 715-386-7949. Open Tuesday-Sunday for lunch and dinner.

Tourist Information

Hudson Chamber of Commerce and Tourism Bureau
502 Second St.
Hudson, WI 54016
715-386-8411
800-657-6775

River Falls

This small city on the Kinnickinnic River is the home of a University of Wisconsin campus.

Things to Do

Wisconsin has become a magnet for big-time football teams looking for a place to practice. Four NFL teams—the Kansas City Chiefs, the New Orleans Saints, the Chicago Bears, and the Green Bay Packers—hold their summer training camps in Wisconsin. The **Kansas City Chiefs summer training camp** uses the athletic facilities of the River Falls UW campus.

Training camp runs from mid-July through mid-August. Practices are held on the Ramer Field Sports Complex on South Main Street. The daily morning and afternoon practices are open to the public. There are also autographing sessions and special full-contact practice sessions. For details, call the Chiefs hotline at 800-522-5222 (July and August only) or try the River Falls Chamber of Commerce, 715-425-2533.

Kinnickinnic State Park protects the delta where the Kinnickinnic River flows into the St. Croix. The 1,200-acre park features a large beach on the river, seven miles of hiking and cross-country ski trails with overlooks into the St. Croix Valley, and picnic areas. A good choice for an afternoon romp.

W11983 820th Ave., River Falls 54022; phone 715-425-1129. Handicap-accessible picnic area. Open daily. $.

The Great River Road south from Pepin, with stops in Nelson, Alma, Fountain City, and Trempealeau

Hwy 35, the Great River Road, runs along the Wisconsin side of the Mississippi River. For Great River Road listings for La Crosse and communities to the south, see Southwest Wisconsin, page 241.

Things to Do—Pepin

Laura Ingalls Wilder Park is a city playground and picnic area that honors Wilder, who was born a few miles from Pepin (see Children's Classics, page 239). In the park is the Old Depot Museum, which actually is the old Pepin railroad depot, moved to this spot. The museum displays local railroad memorabilia and has two rail maintenance cars on display.

On Hwy 35. No phone. Park open daily. Depot museum open 8-5 daily May through October. Both free.

Pepin Historical Museum focuses on Laura Ingalls Wilder, with displays about her life. The museum also has displays depicting Pepin pioneer homestead life (see Children's Classics, p. 239).

On Hwy 35; phone 715-442-3161. Open 9-noon and 1-5 daily, mid-May through mid-October. Free.

The Pepin **municipal beach** has lifeguards and a bath house. It is adjacent to the marina at the end of Lake Street. Open daily in summer. Free.

Events—Pepin

SEPTEMBER. **Laura Ingalls Wilder Days** celebrates Pepin's most famous native. The 19th-century-style celebration includes readings from Wilder's books, displays about the author, a Wilder look-alike contest, plays derived from her stories, hay rides, a petting zoo, storytellers, and lots of other family-oriented events. Held the third weekend in September throughout Pepin. Phone 715-442-3011.

Where to Eat—Pepin

The Pickle Factory serves dynamite sandwiches, burgers, and other light entrees in a great location on the river next to the Pepin marina. Eat outdoors on the deck and watch the river traffic. Phone 715-442-4400. Open daily for lunch and dinner in summer and fall; call for winter hours.

Treats—Nelson

The **Nelson Cheese Factory** is famous for its many varieties of cheese, all of which are on sale, and some of which you can watch being made. They also sell wonderful crackers and other snack items to eat with the cheese, or you can walk away with excellent ice cream or candy. Don't pass this place without stopping. On Hwy 35 at the south end of town; phone 715-673-4725. Open 9-7 daily.

Things to Do—Alma

Lock & Dam #4 is one of many operated by the U.S. Army Corps of Engineers to move boat traffic on the Mississippi River. Number 4 has a very good observation tower where you can watch everything from barges to small fishing boats going through the locks. Just off Hwy 35. Great fun, and free.

Alma Beach has a large sand beach with bath house, picnic area, tennis courts, volleyball nets, basketball hoops, plus a boat launch area. On Beach-Harbor Road off Hwy 35 one mile north of Alma; phone 608-685-3330. Open daily in summer, park facilities free.

Buena Vista Park has awesome panoramic views of the Mississippi from atop a 500-foot bluff. The park has a picnic area, but the bluff edge is not fenced, so watch kids closely, especially the small ones. The views are worth the ten-minute drive to the park from Hwy 35. On County Hwy E off Hwy 35. Open daily. Free.

Rentals—Alma

Great River Harbor rents flat-bottom fishing boats, canoes, kayaks, paddleboats, and water bikes for poking around the Mississippi and the Chippewa, Buffalo, and Zumbro rivers. Hwy 35 South; phone 608-248-2454.

Northport Marine rents houseboats for Mississippi River vacations. At the Alma Marina one mile north of town off Hwy 35; phone 608-685-3333.

Things to Do—Fountain City

Merrick State Park stretches along the shore of the Mississippi, offering hiking, swimming, picnicking, canoeing, camping, and a boat launch ramp. Walking along the shore and canoeing among the backwater sloughs in the park give you the opportunity to see wildlife and to enjoy the solitude and quiet of the river. The campground has waterside sites.

On Hwy 35 just north of Fountain City; mailing address S2965 Hwy 35, Fountain City 54629; phone 608-687-4936. Handicap-accessible camping and picnic facilities. Open daily year-round. $.

The **Fountain City municipal park** has a swimming pool, tennis courts, and a picnic area. On Hwy 35 at south end of town. No phone. Open daily weather permitting. $ for swimming.

Where to Stay—Fountain City

Fountain Motel, 810 S. Main St., Fountain City, WI 54629; phone 608-687-3111. A small, neat, basic motel, like most in the small towns along the Great River Road. Adjacent to city swimming pool and park, cable TV, restaurant across the street.

Things to Do—Trempealeau

Trempealeau National Wildlife Refuge is a 5,600-acre wonderland of egrets, herons, grouse, geese, eagles, deer, muskrats, and hundreds of other animals. A five-mile wildlife drive, a river viewing platform, a one-mile nature trail, and miles of informal hiking trails provide many chances to see wildlife. Bicycling on refuge roads is allowed, and the Great River State Trail runs through the refuge. The Prairie View Trail is handicap accessible. This is a magical place, teeming with wildlife, and is well worth a visit. Best viewing times are early morning and around sunset. Spring and fall during the migrations are prime birdwatching periods.

Off Hwy 35 north of Trempealeau; mailing address Rt. 1, Box 1602, Trempealeau, WI 54661; phone 608-539-2311. Open daily during daylight hours. Free.

The **Great River State Trail** lets bicyclists, hikers, cross-country skiers, and snowmobilers make the 22-mile trip from Onalaska north to the Trempealeau National Wildlife Refuge on a refurbished railroad right-of-way. Along the way are marshes, bluffs, and river views.

Trail headquarters at Perrot State Park, Rt. 1, Box 407, Trempealeau, WI 54661; phone 608-534-6409. Open daily. $ for bicycling.

Perrot State Park is simply beautiful. The 1,434-acre park encompasses bluffs, sloughs, and lowlands at the confluence of the Mississippi and Trempealeau rivers. With wonderful views, beautiful woods, and terrific topography, this is a not-to-be-missed park. Park offerings include hiking and cross-country ski trails, bicycling, canoeing among the many islands in the two rivers, picnic areas, and campgrounds. Spring through fall there's a naturalist to lead hikes and give lectures. Be sure to hike to the top of the 520-foot Brady's Bluff for a great view of the Mississippi River.

On Hwy 93 one mile north of Trempealeau; mailing address Rt. 1, Box 407, Trempealeau, WI 54661; phone 608-534-6409. Handicap accessible picnic and camping facilities. Open daily. $.

Lock & Dam #6 has a very good viewing area with an observation platform, toilets, and picnic area. Boats are so close you can almost touch them as they are raised and lowered in the lock. At the end of Fremont St, off Hwy 93 at south edge of town. No phone. Open daily. Free.

Winter Fun—Trempealeau

Perrot State Park has more than eight miles of groomed cross-country ski trails, some of which are relatively flat for beginning skiers.

Rentals—Trempealeau

Trempealeau Hotel Trading Post rents bicycles and canoes. At 150 Main St., Trempealeau; phone 608-534-6898.

Where to Stay—Trempealeau

Pleasant Knoll Motel, 11451 Main St., Trempeleau; phone 608-534-6615. A small, basic motel with wonderful river views. Cable TV with free movies, whirlpool for guests, handicap accessible rooms available, kitchen facilities available.

Where to Eat—Trempealeau

The **Trempealeau Hotel**, when not engaged in other business such as renting out rooms and outdoor equipment, puts out some terrific food. The full menu includes plenty of sandwiches and kid items, plus vegetarian specials. It's homemade, it's good, it's moderately priced. 150 Main St., Trempealeau; phone 608-534-6898. Open Saturday and Sunday for breakfast, daily for lunch and dinner.

Black River Falls

This city of 3,800 began as a mill town harnessing the power of the Black River. I-94 provides easy access for visitors.

Things to Do

The **Black River State Forest** covers 66,000 acres of pine and oak forests clustered around high sandstone outcroppings. The Black River and the East Fork of the Black River flow through the area, and there are many marshes. Visitors will find miles of hiking, off-road biking, ski, snowmobile, and ATV trails, plus picnic areas and campgrounds. There's swimming, canoeing, and self-guided nature trails. The 25 miles of groomed cross-country ski trails are considered some of the best in Wisconsin, and because this area is a hidden treasure, the trails are uncrowded. The ski trails are designed mainly for intermediate and expert skiers, though beginners can find suitable trails.

On Hwy 54 east of Black River Falls; mailing address 910 Hwy 54 East, Black River Falls, WI 54615; phone 715-284-1400 or 715-284-4103. Handicap accessible picnic facilities. Open daily. $ for camping and some developed areas.

Rentals

Black River Canoe Rentals does indeed rent canoes and provide shuttle service for trips of two hours to four days on the calm and scenic Black River. At N5885 Hwy 54W, Black River Falls; phone 715-284-5181.

Where to Stay

Best Western Arrowhead Lodge, at I-94 and Hwy 54; mailing address 600 Oasis Road, Black River Falls, WI 56415; phone 715-284-9471 or 800-528-1234. A very good motel with two-room suites, an indoor pool, games, cable TV with free movies, a nature trail, ski trails, and snowmobile trails adjacent. The motel has a restaurant that serves good food.

Tourist Information

Black River Falls Chamber of Commerce
336 N. Water St.
Black River Falls, WI 54615
715-284-4658

Stops Along I-94

Sometimes the kids need to get out and run around. Sometimes you all need some decent food. Sometimes you just need to get out of the car. But where? Try these:

Wakanda Park and the **Lions Club Game Park**, Menomonie. This large park has a beach and bath house, playground, picnic areas, and lots of room to run around. The Game Park houses large beasts such as buffalo, elk, and reindeer. You can stroll between the large enclosures that house them. Take the Hwy 25 exit toward Menomonie, go to Pine Street then go east. Wakanda Park is at the end of Pine Street. It's a two mile drive from the exit. There are restaurants and fast food places on Hwy 25 near the Interstate.

The **Norske Nook**, Osseo. This local cafe is nationally famous for its pies, and rightly so. They also have good, small town cafe food, including burgers, salads, plate lunches, and dinner specials. But be sure to leave room for pie. Exit I-94 at Hwy 10, then go west a half mile into Osseo. Turn left (south) at the water tower, then right onto West 7th Street. The Norske Nook is on West 7th. It's open for breakfast, lunch, and dinner every day except Sunday in winter. The Nook's phone number is 715-597-3069. There's a grassy village park surrounding the water tower, so you can turn the kids loose to run off that excess energy. Osseo is 25 miles south of Eau Claire on I-94.

Mill Bluff State Park is a small state park that protects spectacular rock formations that rise out of the surrounding flat plain. The park has hiking trails, including trails to the top of Mill Bluff, where there are great views of the surrounding countryside. There's also a small lake with a swimming beach, and a wooded picnic area with water and toilets. The park is on Hwy 12 between the communities of Camp Douglas to the south and Oakdale to the north. Exit I-90/94 at either of these exits and follow the signs to the park. Phone 608-427-6692. The park is open Memorial Day weekend through Labor Day. Admission fee.

Children's Classics

West Wisconsin River Country is the birthplace of two great classics of children's literature, *Caddie Woodlawn*, by Carol Ryrie Brink, and *Little House in the Big Woods*, by Laura Ingalls Wilder.

Caddie Woodlawn and its sequel, *Magical Melons*, tell the story of Ms Brink's grandmother, Caroline Augusta Woodhouse, as she grew up in the tiny community of Downsville in the 1850s, 1860s, and 1870s. The Caddie Woodlawn Home is located on the old Woodhouse homestead, 14 miles south of Menomonie on Hwy 25 (just south of the present community of Downsville). The park contains the original house where Caroline Woodhouse lived, as well as other buildings from the homestead. There's also a picnic area. The park is open daily during warm weather and is closed during the winter. Admission is free. A brochure detailing the sites described in the novels is available from the Dunn County Historical Society, Box 437, Menomonie, WI 54751. Ask for the Caddie Woodlawn Country brochure.

Roughly 35 miles from Downsville, as the crow flies, another little girl was growing up on the Wisconsin frontier of the 1860s and 1870s. Laura Ingalls Wilder's Little House series is perhaps the most famous chronicle ever written of childhood on the frontier. *Little House in the Big Woods*, the first in the series, is the story of Laura's early years on the Wisconsin homestead. Wilder was born on a farm in the hills seven miles from the Mississippi River community of Pepin. The Laura Ingalls Wilder Memorial Society maintains a replica of the Ingalls log cabin on County Hwy CC, across the road from the original Ingalls homestead. In Pepin, the Pepin Historical Museum collection is largely devoted to Wilder, both her time in Wisconsin and her entire career. The museum sells all the Little House books. It's on Hwy 35, phone 715-442-3161. The museum is open 9-noon and 1-5 daily mid-May through mid-October. Admission is free.

13

Southwest
Coulee Country

**Including La Crosse, Sparta,
Ontario, Westby, Prairie du Chien,
Cassville, Potosi, Platteville,
Shullsburg, Mineral Point,
Dodgeville, Spring Green, Monroe,
and New Glarus**

A family vacation in southwest Wisconsin is a happy mix of historic and cultural activities with outdoor fun amid some of the most spectacular scenery in the Midwest. The area offers such family vacation activities as a rendezvous with 19th-century fur traders, a houseboat vacation on the Mississippi, eagle watching, and touring a lead mine.

The Coulee Country was shaped by rivers—the Mississippi, the Wisconsin, the Kickapoo, the Sugar, the Pecatonica, and a host of smaller streams. The glaciers mysteriously left it untouched, leaving the Southwest with a rugged topography different from the rest of Wisconsin. The region was also shaped by metals, especially the lead and zinc that attracted the miners who founded some of the first communities in the Wisconsin Territory.

The Southwest is a land of river valleys and ridges interspersed with winding back roads that lead to small communities founded by English, Norwegian, German, Swiss, and French immigrants. Here is a quiet and uncrowded place to relax and slow down.

Most visitors to Coulee Country take I-90 to Sparta or La Crosse, Hwy 35 or Hwy 60 to Prairie du Chien, Hwy 151 to Dodgeville or Platteville, or Hwy 14 to Spring Green. La Crosse has scheduled air service. The Great River Road continues its trip along the Mississippi, on Hwy 35 from La Crosse to south of Prairie du

Chien, switching to Hwy 133, then to Hwy 151 as it exits Wisconsin.

La Crosse

This city of 50,000 is the commercial and economic capital of Southwest Wisconsin. The city lies on lowlands along the Mississippi with dramatic bluffs at its back. La Crosse boasts a University of Wisconsin campus, regional health care facilities, major industries, an excellent park system, and a spectacular setting. The city frequently appears on lists of "most livable" cities.

Things to Do

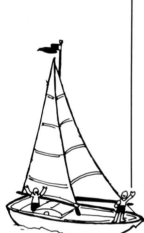

Cruising the Mississippi means beautiful scenery, a chance to see wildlife, and the sight of giant river barges. There are two ways to enjoy the river. You can rent a houseboat for a weekend or a week (see Rentals below), or you can take a shorter trip on either the *Island Girl*, a 150-passenger motor yacht, or on the *La Crosse Queen*, a 150-passenger paddlewheeler. Both offer narrated tours, including lunch, brunch, and dinner cruises. Trips are one and one-half to four hours long.

Island Girl docked at Port of America's Bikini Yacht Club across the river from downtown on Hwy 14; mailing address 621 Park Plaza Dr.; phone 608-784-0556. Cruises offered daily early May through late October. $.

La Crosse Queen docked at Riverside Park at the west end of State St. in downtown La Crosse; mailing address Box 1805, La Crosse 54602; phone 608-784-8523. Cruises offered daily early May through late October. $.

The **Museum at the La Crosse Visitors Center** is well worth a stop. Not only can you get information about the La Crosse area, you can find out about the history, geology, and biology of the region. The museum has a number of excellent hands-on exhibits, including a chance to try on 19th-century clothing and a film about the area. **Riverside Park**, where the Visitor Center is located, has picnic areas, ducks to feed, and plenty of room to run off excess energy.

Riverside Park is at the foot of State St. in downtown La Crosse; phone 608-782-2366. Wheelchair accessible. Visitor Center open 10-5 daily Memorial Day through Labor Day, closed weekends rest of the year. Free.

Myrick Park and Zoo has picnic areas, a major playground, tennis courts, a wading pool, carnival rides for young children, and a small zoo that includes a farm animals and a petting zoo. The park adjoins the Myrick Marsh Trail system, with hike-bike trails.

2000 La Crosse St. (Hwy 16); phone 608-789-7190. Wheelchair accessible. Open 8-8 daily May through October, 9-3 daily November through April. Free.

For a panoramic view of La Crosse and the river, take the kids to **Grandad Bluff**, the highest point in La Crosse County. You can see three states (Wisconsin, Minnesota, and Iowa) from 530 feet above the city. The bluff rim is fenced and there's a picnic area and rest rooms. From the east end of Main Street, follow Bliss Road. It's open daily, and it's free.

Hixon Forest is a nature preserve that encompasses both lowland and bluff. The forest has seven miles of hiking and ski trails and a nature center. You can hike to the top of a bluff or stay on flatter terrain. The nature center has a continuing series of programs and events especially for children.

2702 Quarry Rd. (off Hwy 16); phone 608-784-0303. Hiking trails open daily. Nature center open 11-4 Monday-Saturday, noon-4 Sunday. Free.

The **Pump House Regional Center for the Arts** offers a changing program of performances by musicians, storytellers, dancers, mimes, and other entertainers, as well as art exhibits. Many performances are for kids and families.

119 King St.; phone 608-785-1434. Call for hours and schedule of events. Free, donation requested.

The **La Crosse River State Trail** runs for 21.5 miles along a refurbished railroad right-of-way from the La Crosse suburb of Medary to Sparta, where it connects with the Elroy–Sparta State Trail (see Things to Do–Sparta, page 248). Along its route the trail passes through several small towns where food, lodging, and supplies are available. The trail is open for bicycling, hiking, and snowmobiling.

Trailhead near intersection of County Hwy B and Hwy 16 in Medary; mailing address c/o Wildcat Mountain State Park, Box 98, Ontario, WI 54651; phone 608-337-4775. Or contact the La Crosse Convention and Visitors Bureau (see Tourist Information below). Open daily. $ for bicycling.

The **Great River State Trail** begins in Onalaska, just north of La Crosse, and runs on a refurbished rail corridor 22.5 miles along the Mississippi River through Perrot State Park to the Trempealeau National Wildlife Refuge (see Things to Do-Trempealeau, page 234). This beautiful trail is open for bicycling, hiking, snowmobiling (on some sections), and cross-country skiing.

Trailhead near intersection of Hwy 35 and 157 in Onalaska; mailing address c/o Perrot State Park, Rt. 1, Box 407, Trempealeau, WI 54661; phone 608-534-6409. Open daily. $ for bicycling.

Goose Island County Park offers a variety of recreational opportunities in a beautiful Mississippi River setting. The park has picnic areas, playgrounds, game room, hiking and ski trails, a beach, canoe rental, bicycling on park roads, wildlife everywhere, and even a store. A great place to spend an afternoon or a weekend, which you can do because the park has a large full-service campground with sites right on the shore.

Off Hwy 35 five miles south of La Crosse; mailing address La Crosse County Parks & Recreation Department, Courthouse, La Crosse; phone 608-785-9770. Campground phone 608-788-7018. Open daily. $ for camping.

Riverside Amusement Park will keep the kids occupied with go-karts, batting cages, arcade games, and miniature golf. At 1304 Interchange Place (take George St. off Hwy 53 to North George St.); phone 608-781-7529. Open 11-11 daily (Fridays until midnight) May through October. $.

The **New Orleans Saints** professional football team comes to La Crosse for their **summer training camp**, held on the UW-LaCrosse athletic fields. Visitors can watch twice-daily practices and scrimmages and see the players up close.

At the UW-La Crosse athletic fields at Pine St. and East Ave. Call the Saints Hotline, 608-789-4550 (in service July and August only) for exact schedules. Practices held mid-July through mid-August. Free.

Winter Fun

Mt. La Crosse has taken advantage of the steep topography of the area to develop one of the state's best downhill, snowboard, and cross-country ski areas. The 17 downhill runs on a vertical drop of 516 feet include the longest run in the state—nearly a mile. There's also a snowboard area and three miles of groomed cross-country ski trails for all skill levels. The chalet offers downhill, cross-country, and snowboard rental, plus lessons for cross-country, snowboard, and downhill. There's a special downhill ski school for kids ages 5 to 10. On Hwy 35 six miles south of La Crosse; mailing address Box 9, La Crosse 54602; phone 608-788-0044 or 800-426-3665.

Treats

Whatever you do, DO NOT MISS the **Sweet Shop**. This neighborhood confectionery does just two things—handmade chocolates and homemade ice cream. And it does them to perfection. They don't mind if you bring your lunch and eat at their tables, then order dessert. North of downtown at 1113 Caledonia St. (parallels Hwy 53 one block east); phone 608-784-7724. Open 9-6 daily.

Downtown La Crosse is blessed with the **Elite Candy Shop**, which in addition to wonderful chocolates also puts out great bakery, and even serves breakfast and lunch. Go there. 412 Main St.; phone 608-784-9115. Open 8:30-3 Monday-Saturday.

Rentals

Fun 'N the Sun Houseboat Vacations rents delux houseboats for three days or longer. The boats are fully furnished, complete with a full kitchen, microwave, color TV, VCR, air conditioning, and a grill. You need no nautical experience. They show you how to do everything before you cast off. 1312 Herman Court, Onalaska 54650; phone 608-783-7326.

Great River Cruises rents houseboats that sleep from two to ten, for three days or longer. The boats come fully equipped, and no nautical experience is required. They teach you everything. 2700 Del Ray, La Crosse 54601; phone 608-783-3879.

Houseboating Adventures rents fully equipped houseboats that sleep four to twelve, for three days or longer.

No boating experience needed. Box 2094, La Crosse 54602; phone 608-784-6711 day or 608-689-2650 evening.

Where to Stay

Roadstar Inn, 2622 Rose St. (Hwy 53); phone 608-781-3070. Basic motel with cable TV and free movies, refrigerators available, adjacent to miniature golf and go-kart track, restaurants nearby.

Hampton Inn, 2110 Rose St. (Hwy 53); phone 608-781-5100 or 800-HAMPTON. A moderate-priced motel with indoor pool, whirlpool, fitness area, cable TV with free movies, restaurants nearby. Kids under 18 stay free with parents.

Best Western Midway Motor Lodge, 1835 Rose St.; phone 608-781-7000 or 800-528-1234. On the Black River, with boat dock facilities and private beach. There's also an indoor pool, whirlpool, sauna, exercise room, games area, cable TV, and a restaurant, plus available refrigerators. Kids under 12 stay free with parents.

Radisson Hotel La Crosse, 200 Harborview Plaza; phone 608-784-6680 or 800-333-3333. Luxury hotel on a terrific Mississippi River location adjoining Riverside Park within an easy stroll of downtown. Amenities include an indoor pool, whirlpool, exercise room, cable TV and free movies, game room, restaurants, and the chance to watch river traffic from your room. Kids under 17 stay free with parents.

Marriott Courtyard, 500 Front St.; phone 608-782-1000 or 800-321-2211. La Crosse's newest riverside hotel in a great location near Riverside Park and within walking distance of downtown. Amenities include an indoor pool, whirlpool, fitness area, cable TV, game room, and restaurant. Kitchenettes available. Kids under 18 stay free with parents.

Campers should head for the **Goose Island Campground**, with more than 400 sites (many on the Mississippi River), a store, showers, electricity, dump station, plus many amenities such as playgrounds, beach, hiking trails, and canoe rental. Five miles south of La Crosse off Hwy 35; phone 608-788-7018. Operated by the La Crosse County Parks and Recreation Department, Courthouse, La Crosse; phone 608-785-9770.

Where to Eat

Ardie's Restaurant is a La Crosse tradition. You may well be greeted by Ardie herself, who keeps watch over the entire operation. That's why the food is so good. In addition to full breakfasts and a large sandwich menu, Ardie is especially proud of her fish and chicken dishes. Children's menu. 514 Lang Dr. (Hwy 35); phone 608-784-2242. Open daily for breakfast, lunch, and dinner.

Piggy's is a must for anyone who's not a vegetarian. One of the most popular and famous restaurants in La Crosse, the menu is heavy on—naturally—pork. But they also serve chicken, seafood, and beef dishes, all well prepared and carefully served. Lunches feature a large sandwich menu. Dinner reservations recommended. 328 S. Front St. (near Riverside Park downtown); phone 608-784-4877. Open daily for lunch and dinner.

Mr. D's Donut Shop and Restaurant goes heavy on D's famous homemade doughnuts, which are available practically any time of day, since they make them all night. But Mr. D isn't in business just to give his customers a sugar high. He also serves 15 types of omelettes, plus pancakes and other breakfast specials, as well as 52 kinds of sandwiches. 1146 State St., at the intersection with West Ave. (Hwy 35); phone 608-784-6737. Open daily for breakfast and lunch. Fresh doughnuts on sale from 9 p.m. through the night.

Rudy's is the place to go for roller-skating carhops. This family-owned drive-in has been at this location since 1966, but the family has been in the business since the 1930s. They know what they're doing. And what they're doing is serving great hot dogs, fries, burgers, chicken baskets, fish sandwiches, and all the traditional drive-in items. And, of course, they've got great ice cream, root beer floats, and shakes. It's an experience. Kids' menu. At the corner of 10th and La Crosse streets;

phone 608-782-2200. Open daily March through October for lunch and dinner.

Extended Hours Grocery Stores

Cub Foods
9344 Hwy 16
Onalaska
608-781-4200

Emergency

For fire, police or ambulance, dial 911.

Tourist Information

La Crosse Area Convention & Visitor Bureau
410 E. Veterans Memorial Drive, Riverside Park
La Crosse, WI 54601
608-782-2366
800-658-9424

Sparta

Easily reached by I-90, this city of 8,000 is best known to tourists as the western terminus of the famous Elroy-Sparta State Trail.

Things to Do

Sparta is the meeting place for two state trails—the **La Crosse River State Trail** (see Things to Do-La Crosse, above), and the **Elroy-Sparta State Trail**. The Elroy-Sparta was the nation's first railroad-grade-to-bike trail, and it's been a huge success. The 32-mile trail offers spectacular views and three tunnels carved out of solid rock as it passes through a number of small towns, where camping, food, picnic areas, rest rooms, bike rental, and shuttle service are offered. The trail is also open for hiking and snowmobiling.

Trailhead off Johns St. just south of I-90 (take Hwy 16 exit), Sparta; mailing address Kendall Depot, Box 297, Kendall 54638; phone 608-463-7109. Open daily. $ for bicycling.

M&M Ranch claims to have the largest collection of exotic animals in the Midwest. And they've got a bunch. Llamas, miniature horses and donkeys, parrots, African pigmy hedgehogs, pot-bellied pigs, a camel, and lots of other species you won't see in the Wisconsin woods. The ranch offers a 90-minute tour that includes up-close looks at the animals, a parrot show, other trained animals, and a petting zoo. Just the place for the animal lover in your family. The ranch has a gift shop, snack bar, and picnic area.

On Dalton Rd. (go west from Sparta on Hwy 16, then south on Hwy J, then east on Dalton Rd.); mailing address Rt. 1, Box 318, Sparta 54656; phone 608-486-2709. Open 10-3 Tuesday, Thursday, Saturday, Sunday Memorial Day weekend through Labor Day, Saturday and Sunday in September and October, weather permitting. $.

Where to Stay

Just-N-Trails Bed and Breakfast Vacation Farm, 7452 Kathryn Ave on Hwy J, Sparta 54556; phone 608-269-4522. Try a farm vacation for a day or a week on this 213-acre, third-generation dairy farm. A wonderful family place where you and the kids can pet a calf, watch cows being milked, stroll in the woods, or try cross-country skiing on the farm's trails or snow tubing on the nearby hill. Families rent a cabin just steps away from the house and barn. Amenities include all the outdoor activities you want, as well as a fireplace, whirlpool, kitchenette, and breakfast.

Country Hospitality Inn, 737 Avon Rd.; phone 608-269-3110 or 800-456-4000. A modern motel with tidy rooms and an indoor pool, whirlpool, cable TV with free movies, coin laundry, free cribs. Handicap accessible rooms and suites with kitchenettes available. Restaurants nearby. Children stay free with parents.

Tourist Information

Sparta Area Chamber of Commerce
111 Milwaukee St.
Sparta, WI 54656
608-269-4123

Ontario

This small farm community in the hills of Vernon County is the center for recreation in the Kickapoo River valley. Reach Ontario on either Hwy 131 (north-south) or Hwy 33 (east-west).

Things to Do

Wildcat Mountain State Park encompasses 3,470 acres of Kickapoo River valley and ridges. The park offers horseback riding trails and a special campground for riders and their mounts, plus hiking and ski trails, picnic areas, panoramic views of the valley, a canoe launch site, and a campground for those without horses. During the summer a naturalist leads hikes and gives lectures.

On Hwy 33 one and one-half miles east of Ontario; mailing address Box 90, Ontario 54651; phone 608-337-4775. Handicap-accessible camping and picnic facilities. Open daily. $.

Canoeing the Kickapoo is a perfect way to introduce your children to the fun of river paddling. The Kickapoo is narrow and winding but placid. Sheer sandstone bluffs line the river in some areas. In other places, cows graze along the banks. The stretch from Ontario south to LaFarge is the most popular for canoeing, though you could certainly go all the way to the confluence of the Kickapoo and the Wisconsin River, 125 river miles from Ontario. Most paddlers spend only a few hours on the river, however.

Rentals

Kickapoo Paddle Inn rents canoes and provides shuttle service. Box 80, Ontario 54651; phone 608-337-4726 or 800-947-3630.

Mr. Duck Canoe Rental rents canoes and provides shuttle service. Box 56, Ontario 54651; phone 608-337-4711.

Where to Stay

Trillium, Rt 2 E10596 Salem Ridge Rd., La Farge 54639; phone 608-625-4492. This 85-acre working farm in the hills of the Kickapoo Valley south of Ontario rents two guest cottages for a day or two or a week. There's a small and cozy one-bedroom cottage with a living room sofabed, and a three-bedroom house with wonderful views. Both have stone fireplaces and a covered porch complete with a swing. Paths lead through the woods on the farm. A lovely location for a few days of relaxing with no TV and no distractions. Breakfast included in the price of the cottage. No credit cards.

Westby

This small community on Hwy 14 twenty-five miles east of La Crosse was settled by Norwegians. It shows.

Events

FEBRUARY. The **Snowflake International 90 Meter Ski Jumping Tournament** asks the question "Can man fly?" Some of the contestants, from as far away as Japan and Norway, come pretty close to doing just that. A spectacular spectator sport to which TV cannot do justice. Held in mid-February at the Snowflake Ski Club, four miles north on County Hwy T. Phone 608-634-4000 for information.

Where to Eat

Borgen's Cafe & Bakery is so good, many people time their trip on Hwy 14 to fit in a meal or snack break in Westby. In addition to Norwegian bakery specialties, Borgen's turns out wonderful pies, cookies, sweet rolls, and a Friday night smorgasbord that will have you waddling back to your car. On Main St. (Hwy 14); phone 608-634-3516. Open daily for breakfast, lunch, and dinner.

Prairie du Chien

The second oldest city in Wisconsin (after Green Bay), Prairie du Chien began as a French fur trading post, and for 200 years was a key stop on the trade routes. Today the city thrives on Mississippi River commerce, recreation, and industry.

Family activities in this community of 6,000 focus on outdoor recreation and the area's long and interesting history. You'll likely arrive on either Hwy 35, the Great River Road, which runs north-south, or on Hwy 18, which runs east-west and crosses into Iowa.

Things to Do

Villa Louis is the restored mansion of Hercules Dousman, Wisconsin's first millionaire, who made his fortune in the fur trade. Costumed guides provide tours of the house and outbuildings, explaining how a rich 19th century Wisconsin family lived. There's also an excellent fur trade exhibit in the adjoining Astor Warehouse. The spacious grounds have plenty of room for kids to romp. Villa Louis hosts a number of special events during the year. In mid-June the Fur Trade Rendezvous brings costumed participants to a weekend of 1820s revelry. In early September the Villa Louis Carriage Classic attracts top carriage drivers to compete in a variety of events on the Villa Louis grounds. If your kids like horses, this is a not-to-be-missed event.

On Villa Louis Rd. (take Washington St. toward the river); mailing address Box 65, Prairie du Chien; phone 608-326-2721. Open 9-5 daily May through October. $.

Fort Crawford Medical Museum is the only Wisconsin museum which focuses on the progress of medicine through the ages. Exhibits include dioramas, reconstructed turn-of-the-century doctor's and dentists's offices, and modern anatomical models in the adjoining Hall of Health, which also has a section on gadgets of medical quackery, including a tapeworm trap and several cures for baldness. The exhibits are excellent, but there are no hands-on exhibits. The educational displays are interesting without being too detailed for kids to understand. This museum is best for kids over six. The museum is housed in the reconstructed 1830s Fort Crawford Hospital. A picnic area is on the museum grounds.

717 S. Beaumont St. (off Main St. at south end of town); phone 608-326-6960. Open 10-5 Wednesday-Sunday May 1 through October. $.

You can also **rent a houseboat** for a Mississippi River vacation (see Rentals below).

Wyalusing State Park is at the confluence of the Wisconsin and Mississippi rivers. There's a magnificent view from atop the 500-foot bluffs. The park, one of the state's most scenic, has hiking, off-road bike, and ski trails, small caves, picnic areas, marked canoe trails along the Mississippi shore, canoe rentals, and campgrounds. A naturalist leads hikes and nature programs throughout the summer. A spectacular park. Worth a special trip.

Six miles south of Prairie du Chien, take Hwy 35 to County Hwy C, then west; mailing address 13342 County Hwy C, Bagley, WI 53801; phone 608-996-2261. Handicap accessible picnic and camping facilities. Open daily. $.

The **Kickapoo Indian Caverns** are the largest cave system in Wisconsin. They were used by local Indian tribes, then were mined by early European settlers, and now are open for tours. The 45-minute tour includes several impressive rooms, plus information about cave geology. Facilities above ground include a gift shop, picnic area with pit toilets, and water. Bring your own picnic supplies and snacks.

On Rhein Hollow Rd. off Hwy 60 in Wauzeka, which is 15 miles southeast of Prairie du Chien; mailing address Wauzeka, WI 53826; phone 608-875-7723. Tours daily 9-5 (last tour 4:15) mid-May through October.

Rentals

Willy & Nellie's Canoes rents canoes and paddleboats and provides shuttle service for trips on the Mississippi, Wisconsin and Kickapoo rivers. They also rent bicycles. Two locations—at the Bait Shanty at the end of Hwy 60 (across from the Tourist Information Center) in Prairie du Chien, and in Wyalusing State Park; phone for both locations 608-326-8602.

Boatels rents fully equipped houseboats for Mississippi River cruising for a weekend or longer. No boating experience needed. You have to cross the river to McGregor, Iowa; phone 319-873-3718.

Where to Stay

Brisbois Motor Inn, Hwy 35N, Prairie du Chien; phone 608-326-8404 or 800-356-5850. Modern motel with indoor pool, cable TV with free movies, suites available. Restaurant adjacent.

Best Western Quiet House, Hwy 18-35-60 South, Prairie du Chien; phone 608-326-4777 or 800-528-1234. Very nice rooms with cable TV and free movies, indoor pool, exercise room. Restaurant adjacent.

Campers should head to **Wyalusing State Park** (see Things to Do above), or if you want a full service luxury resort campground, go to **Jellystone Park** in Bagley, just down County Hwy X from Wyalusing. Jellystone has 200 campsites with full hookups available. Of course it has showers. It also has an 18-hole miniature golf course, a swimming pool, playground, a YOGI cartoon theater, special activities for kids, and it's just across the road from the Mississippi River. Mailing address 11354 Hwy X, Bagley, WI 53801; phone 608-996-2201.

Emergency

Police 326-2421
Fire 326-8411
Ambulance 326-8414

Tourist Information

Prairie du Chien Chamber of Commerce
211 S. Main St.
Prairie du Chien, WI 53821
608-326-8555
800-PDC-1673

Wisconsin Information Center
Hwy 18 at the bridge
Open 8-6 daily Memorial Day to Labor Day, 9-5 daily April, May, September, October
608-326-2241

Cassville

Take County Hwys X, VV, and A from Wyalusing State Park south to the small river town of Cassville. The drive follows the Mississippi River and takes you through some of the most dramatic scenery in Wisconsin.

Things to Do

Stonefield Village is a recreated turn-of-the-century Wisconsin village. Visitors can watch brooms being made, see blacksmiths at the forge, enjoy penny candy, and check out the milliner, the pharmacist, the photographer's studio, and other village shops. Costumed guides explain life in turn-of-the-century Wisconsin communities. Adjacent to Stonefield is the State Farm Museum, with antique farm equipment on display, plus frequent demonstrations. You may tour the entire complex in a horse-drawn wagon. The Stonefield saloon sells snacks and drinks. There are a number of special events throughout the season.

On County Hwy VV just north of Cassville; mailing address Box 125, Cassville 53806; phone 608-725-5210. Open 9-4 daily May, June, September, October, open 9-5 daily July and August (last tickets sold one hour before closing). $.

Nelson Dewey State Park occupies a site directly across the road from Stonefield Village. The park includes the restored home of Nelson Dewey, Wisconsin's first governor. Tours of the house are offered. The best part of the park for kids, though, are the bluffs and uplands behind the Dewey home. The view from the 400-foot-high bluffs is terrific, and bald eagles, hawks, and other birds are often seen floating on air currents over the Mississippi. The park has picnic areas, hiking trails, and a campground. Beautiful and uncrowded.

On County Hwy VV just north of Cassville; mailing address Box 658 Cassville 53806; phone 608-725-5274. Handicap accessible picnic facilities. Open daily. $.

The **Cassville Ferry** takes autos, bikes, and pedestrians to Iowa on a 20-minute ride across one of the narrowest spots on the Mississippi. A good way to get in a short but scenic river trip. The ferry dock adjoins Riverside Park, a large city facility with playgrounds, picnic areas, toilets, and room to run around.

Ferry leaves from Prime Street car ferry landing; phone 608-725-5180. The ferry runs 9-9 daily Memorial Day weekend through Labor Day, and 9-9 Saturdays and Sundays in May, September, and October. $.

Potosi

This Mississippi River village on Hwy 133 is famous for its three-mile-long Main Street.

Things to Do

The **St. John Mine** is a hand-dug lead mine that was in use by the local Indians when French fur traders arrived in 1690. Later, miners expanded the mine and between 1828 and 1870 produced thousands of tons of lead ore. The 40-minute tour takes visitors through the winding mine as guides explain 19th-century mining methods. The mine owners also rent canoes and provide shuttle service for trips on the Mississippi and other nearby rivers.

On Hwy 133; mailing address St. John Mine, Potosi 53820; phone 608-763-2121. Open 9-5 daily May through October. $.

Platteville

This city of 9,600 began as a lead and zinc mining center. Today it is the commercial, industrial, and educational center of southwest Wisconsin. Most visitors arrive in Platteville on Hwy 151.

Things to Do

The **Platteville Mining Museum** tour includes a ride in ore cars (above ground), and a trip through a restored 1845 lead mine. Above ground exhibits explain the history of lead and zinc mining in the area and display old mining equipment. Anyone with mobility problems will be confined to visiting the exhibits area, as the mine tour includes a long flight of stairs. The museum is well worth a visit. On the grounds are a playground and picnic area.

405 E. Main St.; phone 608-348-3301. Open 9-5 daily May through October. $.

Adjoining the Mining Museum is the **Rollo Jamison Museum**, an eclectic collection consisting of things Mr. Jamison collected during his long life. And he collected a lot, all of which he donated to the city. The displays are arranged to show daily life in the 19th and early 20th centuries. Included are farm implements, cameras, mechanical music boxes, washing machines, and thousands of other items. Many of the items are in working condition and tour guides, with audience help, demonstrate their use. Kids find many of the items on display interesting and fun.

405 E. Main St.; phone 608-348-3301. Open 9-5 daily May through October. $.

The **Chicago Bears Summer Training Camp** is held every year from mid-July through mid-August on the campus of the University of Wisconsin-Platteville. The public can view the morning and afternoon practices during the the training camp. The city goes all out to welcome the Bears with events such as ice cream socials, concerts, brat fries, and a chance to get a Bear autograph. Call the Bears hotline, 608-342-1496, or contact the Platteville Chamber of Commerce (see Tourist Information below) for exact dates, practice times, and other information.

Grizzly Flats is an indoor amusement area with a train theme. Roller skatiing is the focus here, but kids can also play video games and skill games, or have a pizza or burger in the malt shop. At 500 E. Highway 151; phone 348-7246. Open daily afternoons and evenings. $.

For an outdoor play break, try **Pool Park**, which has the city swimming pool, or **Legion Field Park**, which has picnic areas, rest rooms, playing fields, and a playground. The parks are near each other. Take Second Street north from downtown about a mile to Sylvia Street and turn left to reach Pool Park. Or take Second Street north and turn right on Pitt Street to reach Legion Field Park. For detailed park information, contact the Platteville Parks Department, 75 N. Bonson; phone 608-348-9741.

Where to Stay

Best Western Governor Dodge Inn, just south of town on Hwy 151; mailing address Box 658; phone 608-348-2301 or 800-528-1234. Basic motel with indoor pool, whirlpool, sauna, cable TV with free movies, and a restaurant.

Where to Eat

The **Timbers Supper Club** serves very good meals from a large menu, including many heart healthy items. Children's menu. 970 Ellen St., at the junction of Hwys 151, 80, and 81; phone 608-348-2406. Open daily for lunch and dinner, brunch served on Sunday.

Emergency

For fire, police or ambulance, dial 911.

Tourist Information

Platteville Chamber of Commerce
275 West 151
Platteville, WI 53818
608-348-8888

Shullsburg

This community of 1,500 on Hwy 11 was named for Jesse Shull, one of the area's early and most successful lead miners.

Things to Do

Badger Mine & Museum provides guided tours of an 1827 lead mine and has exhibits of mining tools, farm equipment from 1850-1950, a 19th-century kitchen, carpenter shop, blacksmith shop, and recreated general store and drug store of early Shullsburg. The adjoining city park has picnic areas, tennis courts, a playground, and a swimming pool.

279 Estey St., Shullsburg, WI 53586; phone 608-965-4860. Open 10-4 daily Memorial Day weekend through Labor Day. $.

Mineral Point

Wisconsin's best preserved example of a 19th-century mining town, this community of 2,300 is today known as a center for arts and crafts, antiques, and bed and breakfast inns. There are limited activities for children here if they don't enjoy gallery hopping.

Things to Do

Pendarvis includes restored homes of the Cornish miners who came to Mineral Point in the 1830s and 1840s to work in the lead mines. Costumed guides lead tours of the log and stone structures, explaining life in early Mineral Point.

114 Shake Rag St.; phone 608-987-2122. One-hour tours conducted 9-5 daily May through October. $.

Soldiers Memorial Park is located directly across Shake Rag Street from Pendarvis. This large city park has tennis courts, a swimming pool, toilets, picnic area, and playground. $ for swimming, everything else free.

Where to Stay

Redwood Motel, Hwy 151; phone 608-987-2317. Unassuming, small but well-maintained motel with cable TV, restaurant, miniature golf adjacent. Handicap accessible rooms available.

Dodgeville

This city of 4,000 is the center of an outdoor recreation area. Most visitors come here on either Hwy 18/151, which runs east-west, or on Hwy 23, which runs north-south.

Things to Do

Governor Dodge State Park is one of the state's most popular. Encompassing more than 5,000 acres of hilly unglaciated topography, the park has two small man-made lakes for boating and swimming, hiking, off-road bike, and ski trails, horseback riding, picnicking, and camping. Boat and canoe rentals are available on Cox Hollow Lake. Naturalists give lectures and lead hikes during the summer. In addition to the off-road trails, bicyclists can ride the park roads or take the park's paved trail up to the Military Ridge State Trail.

On Hwy 23 three and one-half miles north of Dodgeville; mailing address 4175 Hwy 23, Dodgeville 53533; phone 608-935-2315. Handicap accessible picnic and camping facilities. Open daily year-round. $.

The **Military Ridge State Trail** runs from Dodgeville nearly 40 miles eastward to the Madison suburb of Verona. The trail follows an abandoned railroad right-of-way along the tops of ridges, then down into prairie and marsh areas. Communities and parks along the trail provide rest areas, lodging, bike rental, swimming, and food. The trail is used for biking, hiking, cross-country skiing, and snowmobiling.

Trailhead at north edge of Dodgeville off Hwy 23; mailing address 4175 Hwy 23, Dodgeville 53533; phone 608-935-5119. Open daily year-round. $ for bicycling.

The **Museum of Minerals and Crystals** displays more than 4,000 stones and crystals, including a 90-pound quartz crystal, a 315-pound Brazilian agate, fluorescing minerals, and much more. For rock hounds, this museum is a must.

Across from entrance to Governor Dodge State Park on Hwy 23; mailing address Rt. 1, Dodgeville; phone 608-935-5205. Open 9-5 daily April through mid-November. $.

Doby Stables provides one- and two-hour guided trail rides through Governor Dodge State Park. Rides leave every hour from the stable on Hwy 23 across from the park. Stable open 9-5 daily May through October. Phone 608-935-5205.

Winter Fun

Governor Dodge State Park has more than 18 miles of groomed cross-country ski trails for novice, intermediate, and expert skiers, plus 15 miles of snowmobile trails.

Where to Stay

The **Don Q Inn**, on Hwy 23 just north of Dodgeville; mailing address Box 199, Dodgeville 53533; phone 608-935-2321 or 800-666-7848. An unusual motel with a huge Boeing C-97 in the front yard and theme rooms throughout. The motel is well maintained, has an indoor/outdoor pool, whirlpool, cable TV with free movies, video games, suites, and a good restaurant. Kids will love such touches as the tunnel between the motel and the restaurant.

New Concord Inn, Hwy 23N; phone 608-935-3770 or 800-348-9310. A modern motel with indoor pool, whirlpool, cable TV, suites, and an adjoining restaurant.

Tourist Information

Dodgeville Chamber of Commerce
Tourist Information
1301 N. Bequette St.
Dodgeville, WI 53533
608-935-5993

Spring Green

This Wisconsin River village of 1,400 is famous as the home of architect Frank Lloyd Wright. The community is the center of a growing outdoor recreation area. Most visitors arrive on Hwy 23 (north-south) or Hwy 14 (east-west).

Things to Do

The House on the Rock is difficult to describe because it contains a little of everything—a huge carousel (no rides), doll houses, amazing music machines, a giant pump from a Madison city well, a miniature circus, a 250-foot sea monster locked in mortal combat with a giant squid, and literally thousands of other things. This seeming jumble is displayed in a mostly logical order that involves walking what seems like miles but is really a bit less than a mile. You can also tour the Alex Jordan Creative Center, named for the House's founder, where the machines, miniatures, and monsters are made and maintained. Overall, kids enjoy House on the Rock, but its sheer size may overwhelm smaller children. No strollers are allowed. There are snack bars and souvenir stands on the grounds, and, yes, there is a house on a rock, which used to be the center of attention, but is now about a tenth of the tour. Allow several hours for a House visit. Virtually everything is indoors, so rain need not deter you. One of America's great roadside attractions.

On Hwy 23 between Spring Green and Dodgeville; mailing address 5754 Hwy 23, Spring Green; phone 608-935-3639. Open 8 a.m.-dusk daily April through mid-November. Last tickets sold two and one-half hours before closing, verify last ticket time if you're arriving late in the day. From mid-November through early January the House opens for a special holiday season with decorations and a hugh collection of Santas on display. Open 10-4 daily for this event. $.

Tower Hill State Park features a restored wood and stone tower that was used to make lead shot in the 19th century. Molten lead was dropped down the tower, forming pellets before it landed in cold water at the tower's base. The tower is quite interesting, but your kids will drive you crazy leaning over the edge. The views from the tower are worth the uphill walk. Also in the riverside park are hiking trails, a picnic area, canoe landing and a rustic campground.

On County Hwy C, off Hwy 23 south of Spring Green; mailing address 5808 Hwy C, Spring Green; phone 608-588-2116. Handicap-accessible picnic facilities. Open daily mid-April through October. $.

Tower Hill is part of the **Lower Wisconsin State Riverway**, which protects the free-flowing Wisconsin River for 92 miles from Sauk City downstream to the Mississippi. Local outfitters provide services to help you get onto the river (see Rentals below).

For information, contact Riverway Coordinator, 3448 Hwy 23, Dodgeville 53533; phone 608-935-3368.

Older children will enjoy many of the performances by **American Players Theater**, an outstanding regional theater that specializes in classical productions, especially of Shakespeare, but also authors such as Moliere and Chekhov. Comedies are a staple of each season's repertory performances. The outdoor theater aims for informality and most patrons dress as they would for a baseball game. The theater has a large picnic area with lots of room to romp before the show. Food and beverages are sold before each performance.

Off County Hwy C on Golf Course Rd., Spring Green; mailing address Box 819, Spring Green 53588; phone 608-588-2361. Performances Tuesday-Sunday mid-June through early October. Children under 6 not allowed at the performances. $.

Older children may also enjoy a tour of **Frank Lloyd Wright's Hillside School**, which is part of Wright's Taliesin complex, his home and architectural school. The

45-minute guided tours provide insight into Wright's buildings and philosophy. A must for anyone with the least interest in art or architecture.

Tours begin at the Taliesin Visitor Center, at the intersection of Hwy 23 and Hwy C three miles south of Spring Green; phone 608-588-7900. Tours on the hour 10-4 daily May through October. $.

Winter Fun

The Springs Golf Club Resort has 20 miles of groomed cross-country trails designed for beginner through expert, from flat open fields to steep wooded hillsides. The touring center has rentals, lessons, snack bar, and ski shop. 400 Springs Dr., Spring Green. Phone 608-588-7000 or 800-822-7774.

Rentals

Bob's Riverside rents canoes and inner tubes for Wisconsin River trips and provides canoe and tube shuttle service. At S13220 Shifflet Rd., Spring Green; phone 608-588-2826.

Where to Stay

The Round Barn, Hwy 14, Spring Green; phone 608-588-2568. An excellent motel with both indoor and outdoor pools, whirlpool, game room, cable TV with free movies, available suites, and a very good restaurant.

The Springs Golf Club Resort, 400 Springs Dr., Spring Green 53588; phone 608-588-7000 or 800-822-7774. An all-suite luxury resort built into beautiful wooded hills overlooking a superb golf course. Amenities include indoor pool, whirlpool, sauna, fitness center, game room, cable TV, restaurants. In winter the golf course becomes a cross-country ski area.

Where to Eat

The Round Barn serves great food from a large menu that's heavy on traditional Wisconsin cafe and supper club items such as prime rib, fish, and chicken. Large salad bar, Sunday brunch buffet. Children's menu. On Hwy 14 on the east side of Spring Green; phone 608-588-2568. Open daily for breakfast, lunch, and dinner.

The **Post House and Dutch Kitchen** serves hearty meals of the stick-to-your-ribs variety. Good soups and sandwiches. Children's menu. 127 E. Jefferson, Spring Green; phone 608-588-2595. Open daily for lunch and dinner, except closed Monday and Tuesday November through March.

The **Spring Green Cafe & General Store** features informal dining adjacent to a well-stocked general store/antiques store/art gallery. Everything's homemade, including the bread, pastries, and desserts. Their soups are wonderful, sandwiches large and bountiful, and you can grab a locally-made beer out of the cooler. Lots of vegetarian items. Take-outs available. At 137 Albany St.; phone 608-588-7070. Open daily for breakfast and lunch.

Emergency

For fire, police, or ambulance, dial 911.

Tourist Information

Spring Green Area Chamber of Commerce
Box 3
Spring Green, WI 53588
608-588-2042
800-588-2042 (recorded message)

Monroe

This city of 10,500 was settled by Swiss dairy farmers. As a result, there are many cheese factories in the area. Monroe is at the junction of Hwy 69 (north-south) and Hwys 11 and 81 (east-west).

Events

SEPTEMBER. **Cheese Days** celebrates Monroe's Swiss dairy heritage with Swiss singing, yodeling, dancing, cheese factory tours, farm tours, a big parade, arts and crafts booths, and plenty of cheese and other dairy products. About the biggest homage to cheese in Wisconsin. Held throughout Monroe the third weekend in

September of even-numbered years. For information, contact the Monroe Area Chamber of Commerce, 1516 Eleventh St., Monroe 53566; phone 608-325-7648.

New Glarus

Swiss immigrants founded New Glarus in the 1840s, and today the community of 1,900 is one of the top destinations for Swiss tourists visiting the United States. You can visit by driving down Hwy 69.

Things to Do

The **Sugar River State Trail** is one of the most popular rails-to-trails conversions in Wisconsin. The 23-mile trail begins at the renovated rail depot in New Glarus and travels southeast through the communities of Monticello and Albany before ending in Brodhead. Bike rentals and shuttle service, food, picnic areas, and lodging are available along the trail. Bikers, hikers, snowmobilers, and cross-country skiers all use the trail throughout the year. For more ambitious bicyclists, Green County has a map of recommended bike routes on lightly traveled back roads throughout the county, some of which connect with the Sugar River Trail.

Trailhead at the old rail depot on Hwy 69 in New Glarus; mailing address Box 781, New Glarus; phone 608-527-2334 (summer) or 608-325-4844 (winter). Trail open daily. Depot open from late April through late October. $ for bicycling.

A visit to the **Swiss Village Museum** will show your kids how New Glarus' founders lived in the mid-19th century. An 1855 log cabin, an 1890 cheese factory, a blacksmith shop, and a turn-of-the-century fire station are among the displays, which also include household items and farm equipment from as early as 1829. Guided tours of this attractive museum are lively enough to keep older kids interested.

612 Seventh Ave., New Glarus; phone 608-527-2317. Open 9-5 daily May through October. $.

New Glarus Woods State Park occupies a lovely wooded hillside south of town. With hiking trails, picnic area, playground, and campground, it's a good

place for a relaxing afternoon or an evening by the camp-fire. Bike or hike to the park on an asphalt trail from downtown New Glarus.

On Hwy 69 two miles south of New Glarus; mailing address Box 256, Monroe 53566; phone 608-527-2335 (summer) or 608-325-4844 (winter). Open daily mid-April through October. $.

The village **swimming pool** is in the village park, 320 Second Street. It's open daily Memorial Day weekend through Labor Day, and you're welcome to drop by for a swim. $.

Swissland Miniature Golf offers 18 challenging holes plus a snack bar. At 700 Hwy 69; phone 608-527-5605. Open 10-10 daily May through October. $.

Events

JUNE. The **Heidi Festival** centers on a production of the play *Heidi,* with additional activities including folk danc-ing, Swiss flag throwing competition, a craft fair, and Swiss foods. Held the last full weekend in June at the high school and in the village park. For play tickets and other information, contact the Heidi Festival, Box 861, New Glarus 53574; phone 800-527-6838.

SEPTEMBER. The **Wilhelm Tell Festival** includes pro-ductions in both English and German of the Wilhelm Tell story. During the same weekend, there's Swiss entertain-ment that includes yodeling, alphorns, folk dancing, and Swiss music, plus an outdoor art fair. Held Labor Day weekend. For tickets and other information, contact Wil-helm Tell Community Guild, Box 456, New Glarus 53574.

Shopping

Kuchen Haus Gifts is a large shop that includes a major kids' section that sells locally made wooden toys, plus books and games, puzzles, toys, puppets, dolls, and other gifts for children. At 519 First St.; phone 608-527-2899. Open daily.

Treats

A stop at the **New Glarus Bakery** means the best doughnuts, cookies, pies, cakes, and Swiss pastries around. They have a tea room upstairs, so you can have a light lunch followed by terrific dessert. 534 First St.; phone 608-527-2916.

Where to Stay

Swiss-Aire Motel, Hwy 69, New Glarus; phone 608-527-2138 or 800-798-4391. Unpretentious but tidy motel with an outdoor pool, cable TV, adjacent to the Sugar River Trail.

Where to Eat

The **New Glarus Hotel** serves excellent Swiss meals, including fondue. The menu also includes sandwiches, soups, salads, and traditional Wisconsin favorites, or try Swiss pizza in the Ticino Pizzeria on the lower level. Save room for their wonderful desserts. 100 Sixth Ave.; phone 608-527-5244. Open daily for lunch and dinner.

Emergency

For fire, police or ambulance, dial 911.

Tourist Information

New Glarus Chamber of Commerce
Box 713
New Glarus, WI 53574
608-527-2095
800-527-6838

Car Games

The Deacon's Duck

Here's a game of adjectives. It's lots of fun, non-competitive, and guaranteed to produce gales of laughter from the kids in the back seat.

To begin the game, each player in turn says a word starting with the letter A to complete this sentence:

The deacon's duck is a (an) _____ duck.

For example,
The deacon's duck is an angry duck.
The deacon's duck is an aluminum duck.
The deacon's duck is an alarming duck.

Next round: Each player completes the sentence with a word starting with the letter B. And so on through the alphabet.

Who, What, When, and Where

This car game keeps all the participants in stitches, fully occupied until the next stop.

Four players, pencil and paper are required. The first player writes a list of ten "who" words. (Examples: John, Debbie, Mom, Michael Fox.) Players keep their lists to themselves.

The second player writes a list of ten "what" words or phrases. (Examples: flew to the moon, ate a bug, married Debbie, fell into a hole.)

The third player writes a list of ten "when" words or phrases. (Examples: last night, on Christmas Eve, after school, when dad came home.)

The fourth player writes a list of ten "where" words or phrases. (Examples: in the living room, at the circus, on Mars, in the snow.)

Then, the players read full sentences, each contributing his or her part. (Example: John ate a bug last night in the living room.)

Car Window Scavenger Hunt

See who can find these things before we stop for lunch (or dinner, or whatever). The player with the most points wins the game.

An American flag (4 pts.)
A blue silo (2 pts.)
A statue of a deer in a front yard (5 pts.)
An Illinois license plate (4 pts.)
A black-and-white cow (3 pts.)
A windmill (5 pts.)
A Green Bay Packers bumpersticker (4 pts.)
A barn mural (10 pts.)

I Packed My Grandmother's Trunk

Here's a memory game for any number of players. This game works best if players are of the same age group.

The first player says, "I packed my grandmother's trunk and in it I put "_____." (Example: "a banana.")

The second player says, "I packed my grandmother's trunk and in it I put a banana and "_____." (Example: "a banana and a cocker spaniel.")

Each additional player adds one more item to grand-mother's trunk, being sure to repeat all the previous items in order. Adding items to grandmother's trunk continues in a round among all players. When a player fails to recite the contents of grandmother's trunk in order, he or she drops out. The last player to remain is the winner.

Scrambled State Symbols

Here's a fun way to learn some of the Wisconsin state symbols. Just unscramble the letters and learn!

1. The state bird loves worms and appears early in the spring. It's the BRONI. ＿＿＿＿＿＿＿

2. The state farm animal isn't hard to find while driving in the country. It's the YRDIA WCO. ＿＿＿＿＿＿

3. Wisconsin even has a state insect. The NOYHE EBE.

4. The state flower is purple and can be found in woods everywhere. It's the OODW IETVOL. ＿＿＿＿＿＿

5. The state animal is a fierce and strong fighter. It's the GRBAED. ＿＿＿＿＿＿

6. Wisconsin also has another state animal. It's a big animal with antlers—the IHWET-LIAEDT REDE.

＿＿＿＿＿＿

7. Ever hear of a state rock? Wisconsin has one. It's a hard rock called NAITREG. ＿＿＿＿＿＿

8. The state tree is not only beautiful, it gives us sweet syrup, too. It's the RGSAU PAEML. ＿＿＿＿＿＿

9. The Wisconsin state drink comes right from the Wisconsin state farm animal. It's KIML. ＿＿＿＿＿＿

10. If you guessed all these symbols, then you must know that the Wisconsin state capital is INMDAOS. Congratulations! ＿＿＿＿＿＿

Wisconsin Kid Laws

AUTOMOBILES, MOTORCYCLES,
AND ALL-TERRAIN VEHICLES

1. All car and truck passengers must wear seat belts. Children under four must be in a child seat.

2. The driving age in Wisconsin is 16, if the individual has completed a driver safety course. Those who don't take driver education must wait until age 18 to obtain a drivers license.

3. Adult motorcycle operators need not wear helmets, but everyone under 18 must wear a helmet whether the person is operating the motorcycle or is just a passenger.

4. Children under 12 may not operate an all-terrain vehicle unless they are under adult supervision. Children ages 12-16 may operate an all-terrain vehicle if they have taken a safety course or if accompanied by an adult.

DRINKING AND GAMBLING

1. The drinking age in Wisconsin is 21. However, parents may bring their minor children into an establishment that serves alcoholic beverages.

2. Children under 18 are allowed at dog tracks and bingo parlors only when accompanied by an adult. No one under 18 is allowed to bet. Some gaming casinos do not allow children under any circumstances.

SNOWMOBILES

1. Children under 12 may not operate a snowmobile unless accompanied by an adult. Kids ages 12–16 may operate a snowmobile only if they've had a snowmobile safety course, or if accompanied by someone over 14 who has had the safety course, or by anyone over 18.

MOTORBOATS

1. Children under 10 may not operate a motorboat. Those 10 and older may operate a motorboat if accompanied by an adult, or, if the child is over 12 he or she may operate the boat alone if the child has completed a boating safety course.

2. Children under 12 may not operate a personal watercraft ("jet ski"). Children 12-16 may operate a personal watercraft only if they have completed a boating safety course.

HUNTING AND FISHING

1. Anyone born after January 1, 1973, must complete a hunter safety course in order to purchase a Wisconsin hunting license. The minimum age for purchasing a hunting license is 12.

2. Children under 16 do not need a fishing license.

For Further Information

Wisconsin Department of Tourism
Box 7976
Madison, WI 53707
608-266-2161
800-372-2737 (Wisconsin & neighboring states)
800-432-8747 (National)
Web site http://tourism.state.wi.us
Information about attractions, parks and forests, events, maps and local sources of tourist information throughout the state.

Wisconsin Innkeepers Association
509 W. Wisconsin Ave., Suite 729
Milwaukee, WI 53202
414-271-2851
Web site http://www.lodging-wi.com
Publishes a statewide listing of hotels, motels, and inns.

Wisconsin Department of Natural Resources
Bureau of Parks and Recreation
Box 7921
Madison, WI 53707
618-266-2181
e-mail wiparks@dnr.state.wi.us
Web site http://www.dnr.state.wi.us
Information about state parks, forests, and trails, including special guides to the bike trails, horseback riding trails, and handicap-accessible park facilities. Ask for the brochure showing which parks, forests, and trails have campgrounds, picnic areas, hiking and ski trails, and other facilities.

The Department of Natural Resources also has information about hunting and fishing. Contact the Bureau of Wildlife Management or the Bureau of Fisheries Management, both at
Box 7921
Madison, WI 53707
608-266-1877
or on the Internet at the same Web site as the Bureau of Parks and Recreation (above).

Wisconsin has six year-round tourist information centers at:
Beloit, rest area 22 on I-90
Hudson, rest area 25, I-94
Hurley, Highway 51
Kenosha, rest area 26, I-94
La Crosse, rest area 31, I-90
Madison, 123 W. Washington Ave.
Chicago, 342 N. Michigan Ave.

Amtrak provides daily rail service to Milwaukee, Columbus (near Madison), Portage, Wisconsin Dells, Tomah, and La Crosse. For information, contact Amtrak at 800-872-7245.

Index